Fruit for the Soul

Fruit for the Soul

Luther on the Lament Psalms

Dennis Ngien

Foreword by Robert Kolb

Fortress Press
Minneapolis

FRUIT FOR THE SOUL

Luther on the Lament Psalms

Cover Image: Käthe Kollwitz, The Parents (Die Ettern)

© 2015 Artists Rights Society (ARS), New York / VG Bild-Kunst, Bonn

Cover design: Tory Herman

Library of Congress Cataloging-in-Publication Data

Print ISBN: 978-1-4514-8521-9

eBook ISBN: 978-1-5064-0289-5

The paper used in this publication meets the minimum requirements of
American National Standard for Information Sciences — Permanence of
Paper for Printed Library Materials, ANSI Z329.48-1984.

Manufactured in the U.S.A.

This book was produced using Pressbooks.com, and PDF rendering was
done by PrinceXML.

To Alister E. McGrath,

in recognition of his

erudite Reformation scholarship

Contents

Acknowledgments

The genius of Luther is his commitment to the biblical text as a means of pastoral encouragement, and as such, his theology is essentially practical. His works diffuse the fragrance of Christ, and his knowledge is profitable for the care of souls. This volume on the psalms of lament shows just that.

I am immensely grateful to Robert Kolb, a renowned Luther scholar, not only for writing a stimulating foreword but also for reading the entire manuscript and providing helpful comments on it, which only makes this volume a better production. I am particularly indebted to the reformation scholarship of Alister E. McGrath, to whom this book is dedicated. I am also grateful for Michael Parsons, Ronald K. Rittgers, John Pless, and Neil R. Leroux, whose writings have aided in my understanding of Luther as a theologian in service of the church.

Special thanks must be extended to Janet Clark, the senior vice president academic and dean of the seminary, Tyndale University College and Seminary [Tyndale], for so generously granting me a research leave, without which this book would not have been completed; to Hugh Rendle and his library team at Tyndale, for assisting me in securing sources, without any hint of complaints; to John Kessler, an erudite Old Testament scholar, my senior colleague at Tyndale whose stellar publications spur me onto new heights; to Brett Potter, my teaching assistant in systematic theology at Tyndale, for typesetting and proofreading the manuscript, which helps rescue me from unnecessary lapses; to my centre leadership team, for supporting me spiritually and financially; and to countless pastors, leaders, and students, whom I have taught and mentored, for challenging me to amplify a close and causal linkage between theology and piety.

Last but not least, my deepest gratitude belongs to my wife, Ceceilia, for taking care of the family needs so that I could focus on being an author and for reminding me to be practically relevant while fulfilling the call of a theologian. I pray and trust that this volume will comfort the wounded, prick the smug, refresh the wearied, and sprinkle our hearts anew, as we daily learn to come under the causative nature of the Word of God, including the Psalter. To God be the glory!

Dennis Ngien
Professor of Systematic Theology
Tyndale University College and Seminary,
Toronto, Ontario, Canada

Foreword

All God's children really do have troubles. Martin Luther knew that from his own experience. He identified the origin of these troubles and the wickedness behind them in the doubt that broke the relationship between the Creator and his first human creatures. When Eve and Adam doubted the word the Lord had given them, they changed the orientation of their lives and brought disorder, dysfunctions of many kinds, and finally despair into daily human experience. Turning away from God as the first and last conversation partner of the day had introduced turmoil, tribulations of many kinds, and tragedies into the warp and woof of the reality human beings regularly face.

In the midst of such trials and troubles, believers often find it difficult to know whether Satan is the enemy or whether God has either become an active adversary or simply abandoned and forgotten them. The testing of tribulation can seem to invite God's faithful people to return to the doubt of Eden.

In such situations, which he often experienced, Martin

Luther defied the doubt that beset him with the words of 1 Corinthians 1 and 2 ringing through his thinking. God's ways are indeed not our ways, his thoughts quite different from ours. His wisdom and his power appear to be quite foolish and utterly impotent and his plan for restoring humanity through death on the cross absurd and ineffective. The word that delivers the benefits of Christ's dying and rising for his chosen people also seems foolish and impotent. But precisely in the death and resurrection of Jesus Luther found the exhibition and the experience of God's re-creative power as he puts sinners' identity to death and raises them up to walk as new creatures in Jesus' footsteps. He formulated his understanding of God's seemingly strange *modus operandi* as the "theology of the cross." This *theologia crucis* focuses on how Christians are to function as "theologians of the cross" rather than pursuing a theology of glory. Theologians of glory seek in one way or another to establish God's glory in "Gentile" terms (Mark 10:42–45), and they seek to establish human glory through reason's mastery of truth and the mastery of good works and godly performance over human destiny.

His new identity in Christ gave the Wittenberg professor and preacher a firm sense of who he really was by virtue of the almighty word of deliverance and absolution the gospel of Christ brought to him. Thus, in the midst of trial and testing, he could turn to God on the cross to find an anchor for life and a foundation for a sure hope.

Since Job or before, believers have wrestled with the problem of how evil could exist if God is almighty and good, as Scripture assures us he is. Since Gottfried Wilhelm Leibniz three hundred years ago, we have labeled the search for some justification for God in the face of evil "theodicy." Luther did not know the term, but he knew the human need. He refused to pursue that problem. In his *On Bound Choice* he conceded that the question of evil in the world created by the perfect and almighty God had often driven him to despair, and he counseled waiting for the "light of glory" since neither "the light of nature" nor "the light of grace" gave satisfying answers.[1] Luther believed Paul was correct when he wrote in Romans 3:25–26 that God has justified himself by justifying his chosen people through Christ's death and resurrection.

Luther identified the Evil One as the cause of all evils. He viewed all of human history as the battlefield on which God and Satan were locked in struggle, God's truth assured of ultimate victory but Satan's murderous deceit often seeming to win the battles of daily life (John 8:44). Luther labeled the attacks he experienced in several forms *Anfechtungen*, "assaults," for even when they came from God, he felt himself under siege. His confidence that God is almighty led him to recognize God's lordship even over the devil, so he firmly clung to assurance that God would remain his protecting Father.

In the midst of *Anfechtungen* of various kinds, Luther recognized that he had no answer that would give him

1. *Luther's Works* (Saint Louis/Philadelphia: Concordia/Fortress, 1958–1986), 33.190, 291–92; *D. Martin Luthers Werke* (Weimar: Böhlau, 1883–), 18:719, 9–12, 784, 35–785, 38; cf. Oswald Bayer, *Martin Luther's Theology, a Contemporary Interpretation*, translated by Thomas H. Trapp (Grand Rapids: Eerdmans, 2008), 211–13.

mastery over the question of the "why" of sin and evil. Therefore, Luther let God be master and simply turned to him in days of trouble, often with the cry of lament. As with so many elements of his theology, the psalmists gave him words to express what he found in his reading of all of Scripture. In sermons, lectures, and devotional works he turned to God with his plaintive cry for the presence of his loving Creator, Redeemer, and Sanctifier. He cried out to God, longing for the comfort that the Lord's presence gives, even when the foes—the devil, doubt, and disasters in many forms—assail. When no one else is listening, Luther was confident, God is.[2]

Dennis Ngien has spent years in the careful study of Luther's writings, exploring particularly the ways in which Luther's "theology of the cross" guided his exposition of Scripture and his proclamation of its message. Ngien has shown how Luther's theology developed between the poles of interpretation of the Scriptures and of pastoral care. In the former he experienced hearing God's voice addressing him and his contemporaries. In the latter he found arrogant sinners in need of the forthright evaluation of God's condemning law, and he found distressed sinners in need of the consolation of the gospel of Christ's death and resurrection that would give them confidence to cry out to God, also with lament.

In this volume Ngien recognizes the penitential nature

---

2. Cf. Oswald Bayer, "Toward a Theology of Lament," in *Caritas et Reformatio. Essays on Church and Society in Honor of Carter Lindberg*, edited by David Whitford (Saint Louis: Concordia, 2002), 211–20.

of many laments and builds upon the contrite approach to God of those who trust in Christ and in him recognize the Father's love. As the Holy Spirit moves the faithful from remorse to reliance on Christ's sacrifice and resurrection for the forgiveness of sins and the restoration of their relationship with their Creator, they gain a sense of sureness that permits them to lay their laments before their God. Ngien's conversation with Luther continues into Psalm texts that further illuminate the role of lament in the dialogue of human faith with the Faithful One as he explores further dimensions of lament in Luther's thought and exposition of God's word.

Ngien takes readers of this volume into his exchange with Luther and aids them in finding new and refreshing uses of these cries of agony and dismay from ancient believers and the early modern reformer. For times such as ours, being able to take our woes, weariness, and wailings to our Lord's lap and leave them there is a gift of his grace that does us immeasurable good. This book will help its readers and their conversation partners to grow in trust in the God who has shared our trials and triumphed over them so that they can cry out with Luther and the psalmists, in the common hope that is theirs through the resurrection of Jesus Christ.

Robert Kolb
Concordia Seminary, Saint Louis
Ash Wednesday 2015

Fruit for the Soul: Luther on the Lament Psalms

Aurelius rightly recognizes the significance the Psalms have played in the religious life of the church since its beginning. "No other book of prayers is used so diligently and is so highly Beloved as the Psalter."[1] Wallace claims that "throughout its life the Church has maintained two equally important traditions relating to the psalms. One has to do with the use of Psalms in prayer and song to God. The other concerns the use of the psalms for the instruction and guidance of the faithful."[2] Bayer avows that Luther's work

---

1. Carl Alex Aurelius, "Luther on the Psalter," in *Harvesting Martin Luther's Reflections in Theology, Ethics, and the Church*, ed. Timothy J. Wengert (Grand Rapids: Eerdmans, 2004), 226. The English translation of Luther's works, the American edition, will primarily be used in the presentation. References from *Weimar Ausgabe*, the original language version, will be cited where helpful. Abbreviations used in this book: LW, for *Luther's Works*, 55 volumes, American Editions, eds. Jaroslav Pelikan and Herbert T. Lehman (St. Louis: Concordia Publishing House; Philadelphia: Fortress Press), 1955–67. WA, for *D. Martin Luthers Werke: Kristische Gesamtausgabe*, 100 volumes (Weimar: Hermann Böhlau Nachfolger, 1883–); WA BR, for *D. Martin Luthers Werke: Kristische Gesamtausgabe. Briefwechsel*; WA TR, for *D. Martin Luthers Werke: Kristische Gesamtausgabe. Trischreden*.
2. Howard Wallace, *Words to God, Words from God* (Aldershot: Ashgate, 2005), 3.

was "embedded in the practice of praying the psalms daily," and that he devoted much of his scholarly energy "in particular to the psalms."[3] Pelikan wrote: "Throughout his career Luther paid very much attention to the Psalter.... His attention to it was personal, devotional, political, exegetical, polemical—all at the same time."[4] With Melanchthon, Luther considered Paul's epistle to Romans "truly the purest Gospel."[5] However, Luther adored the Psalms more than any other book in the Bible, regarding the Psalter as "a little Bible." This he wrote in his *Preface to the Psalter*:

> The Psalter ought to be a precious and beloved book. If for no other reason than this: it promises Christ's death and resurrection so clearly—and pictures his kingdom and the condition and nature of all Christendom—that it might well be called a little Bible. In it is comprehended most beautifully and briefly everything that is in the entire Bible. It is really a fine enchiridion or handbook. In fact, I have a notion that the Holy Spirit wanted to take the trouble himself to compile a short Bible and book of examples of all Christendom or all saints, so that anyone who could not read the whole Bible but have here anyway almost an entire summary of it, comprised in one little book.[6]

The Psalter was written in figurative and metaphorical

Robert Alter, *The Book of Psalms* (New York: Norton, 2007), xiii, says: "Through the ages, Psalms has been the most urgently, personally present of all the books of the Bible in the lives of many readers."

3. Bayer, *Martin Luther's Theology*, xv.
4. Pelikan, *Introduction to Volume* 14, ix.
5. See "Preface to the Epistle of St. Paul to the Romans," in LW 35.365. Also quoted by Timothy George, *Reading Scripture with the Reformers* (Downers Grove: IVP, 2011), 186, and Bernd Janowski, *Arguing with God: Theological Anthropology of the Psalm*, trans. Armin Siedlecki (Louisville: Westminster John Knox Press, 2013), 341–42.
6. See "Preface to the Psalter," in LW 35.254.

language, evincing an expansive and evocative style that invites people, as Luther said, to "find yourself in it [the Psalter], for it is the true *gnothi seauton* ('know thyself') and above all God himself and all his creatures."[7] It has furnished believers in every generation with an invaluable source of prayer and praise, and with models for their own response to God. Luther accentuated:

> Hence it is that the Psalter is the book of all saints; and everyone, in whatever situation he may be, finds in that situation psalms and words that fit his case, that suit him as if they were put there just for his sake, so that he could not put it better himself, or find or wish for anything better.[8]

The Psalms are God's address not only to the people of old but also to the saints in the present. The Psalter is timeless, as it bridges the gap between the past and the present. It is also timely, as it presents us with words that fit particular life situations. In the Psalter, human words that we speak to God, and God's word, that by which we speak, are woven in an inseparable unity. Luther shows keen interest in human personality of the past and in how their voices offer articulation for his deep-felt emotions. He found the Holy Spirit–given expressions in the Psalms that either resonate with his observations or are the source of his own experience in the course of daily life. His personality comes alive in his existential reading of the Psalms.

Unlike the legendary figures of *Legenda aurea*,[9] the

---

7. LW 35.257. Also quoted by George, *Reading Scripture with the Reformers*, 188.
8. LW 35.256 (WA DB 10.1.103, 22ff). Also quoted by Aurelius, "Luther on the Psalter," 226, and George, *Reading Scripture with the Reformers*, 188.

medieval collections of stories of the saints, who do not come into conversation with us, the saints of the Old Testament were not "silent saints," but "real, living, active saints" with whom we continue to have communion and from whom we continue to draw benefits.[10] In the psalms, Luther discovered not only the works of the saints but also their words—"how they spoke with God and prayed, and still speak and pray."[11] Compared with a speaking man, a silent one is the same as a half-dead man. Luther wrote: "There is no more mightier, no nobler work than speech."[12] Speech, more than any other faculty or capacity, is that which most distinguishes human beings from animals.[13]

In addition to words, Luther captured in the psalms "a view of the inner heart of the faithful."[14] "Just as I would rather hear what a saint says than see the deeds he does," Luther said of himself, "so I would far rather see his heart, and the treasure in his soul, than hear his words."[15] The Psalter presents to us "their very hearts and the inmost treasure of their souls," the very "foundation and source" of their deeds and words.[16] It

9. The most popular collection of such legends was probably that of Jacobus de Voragine (1230–1298). See LW 35.253, n. 50. The Latin *Legenda* simply means things that are to be read. In this context, it does not carry its modern meaning. Rather than referring to a story of doubtful historicity, the term simply designates a story designed to be read aloud for instruction.

10. LW 35.255.

11. LW 35.254.

12. LW 35.255 (WA DB 10.1.100). Quoted in H. G. Haile, *Luther: An Experiment in Biography* (Princeton: Princeton University Press, 1983), 61.

13. LW 35.254. See Birgit Stolt, "Luther's Faith of 'the heart'—Experience, Emotion and Reason," in *The Global Luther: The Theologian for Modern Times* (Minneapolis: Fortress Press, 2009), 134.

14. WA BR 10.1.98–105 as cited in Herman J. Selderhuis, *Calvin's Theology of the Psalms* (Grand Rapids: Baker Academic, 2007), 21.

15. LW 35.255.

enables us to look into the hearts of the faithful, to see what thoughts they possessed, how their hearts were disposed, and how they responded to all the occurrences, exigencies, and necessities of existence.[17] The legends and examples lay before us in the mighty deeds and miracles of the silent saints. They do not speak; we do not see their inner hearts. The Psalter leads us into the inner heart of the godly, from where their words spring with "double earnestness and life."[18] "And that they speak these [earnest] words to God and with God," Luther opined, "is the best thing of all," because "the depths of the heart" are open before God and us.[19] Luther vividly described this:

> A human heart is like a ship on a wild sea, driven by the storm winds from the four corners of the world. Here it is struck with fear and worry about impending disorder; there comes grief and sadness because of the present evil. Here breathes a breeze of hope and of anticipated happiness; there blows security and joy in present blessings. These storm winds teach us to speak with earnestness, to open the heart and pour out what lies at the bottom of it. He who is stuck in fear and need speaks of misfortune quite differently from him who floats on joy; and he who floats on joy speaks and sings of joy quite differently from him who is stuck in fear. When a sad man laughs or a glad man weeps, they say, he does not do so from the heart, that is, the depths of the heart are not open, and what is in them does not come out.[20]

16. LW 35.255.
17. See Emil G. Kraeling, *The Old Testament since the Reformation* (New York: Harper, 1955), 18.
18. LW 35.256.
19. LW 25.256.
20. LW 35.255–56 (WA DB 10.1.100ff). Also quoted by Timothy J. Wengert, *Reading the Bible with Martin Luther* (Grand Rapids: Baker Academic, 2013), 14–15.

Just as God's address in ancient times required a personal response, so it is with the contemporary believer, for the psalms are "not words to read, but to live."[21] The Psalter "creates in our minds good sturdy living saints," from whom we derive a proper discourse with God in the variety of life situations.[22] "[T]he greatest thing in the Psalter," Luther asserted,

> [is nothing but] this earnest speaking amid these storm winds of every kind[.] Where does one find finer words of joy than in the psalms of praise and thanksgiving? There you look into the hearts of all the saints, as into fair and pleasant gardens, yes, as into heaven itself. There you see what fine and pleasant flowers of the heart spring up from all sorts of fair and happy thoughts toward God, because of his blessings. On the other hand, where do you find deeper, more sorrowful, more pitiful words of sadness than in the psalms of lamentation? There again you look into the heart of all the saints, as into death, yes, as into hell itself. How gloomy and dark it is there, with all kinds of forebodings about the wrath of God![23]

Not only can the faithful, then and now, hear God addressing them in the Psalms, but their prayers in the Psalms done in faith also reach the throne of God. "The Psalter is a gem," for it gives us "the best of their language," with which we converse with God with great ardency and urgency, and on the most important matters, opening our hearts and pouring out what lies at the bottom of them.[24] So too, when speaking of fear and hope, the one praying is able to depict these

21. WA 31, I.63 as quoted in George, *Reading Scripture with the Reformers*, 188.
22. LW 35.255–56.
23. LW 35.255–56.
24. LW 35.254–55.

feelings in such earnest words that no painter could rival, portraying them in a manner that no Cicero or other orator could.[25]

We do not hear the words of the legendary saints or see their hearts. Instead their deeds are presented and extolled as worthy of imitation. However, imitation of the deeds does not necessarily bear godly fruits. Legendary figures and their examples present works that are beyond one's ability to imitate or accomplish, in which case despair or hypocrisy are the outcome. They mislead people to seek comfort in the wrong place, namely the works of the silent saints. In extreme cases, the imitation of their works produces dangerous fruits, as it leads to sectarianism and schism, thereby tearing people away from the communion of saints.[26] What is lacking in the legendary saints is the words by which people approach God in their diverse circumstances.

On the contrary, the Psalter functions as a well-tried and secure guide that the saints of all ages may follow without peril, for it offers us "most abundantly concerning the saints, so that we can be certain of how their hearts were toward God and of the words they spoke to God and every man."[27] So sweet a fragrance are the earnest words by which we call on God, for they emanate from a heart so inclined toward God. For prayers to be efficacious, they have to be done "in faith," as from the bottom of the heart. Whether we are in joy, fear, hope, or sorrow, we are to think and speak as all the

25. LW 35.256.
26. LW 35.256.
27. LW 35.256.

saints have done. So we are not to think we are praying alone, but the whole of Christendom, all devout saints, is standing there beside us, praying together with us in a common united petition, offering up a sweet fragrance of earnest words to God. This is indeed the fruit of the communion of saints that benefits the soul. Luther wrote:

> When these words please a man and fit his case, he becomes sure that he is in the communion of saints, and that it has gone with all the saints as it goes with him, since they all sing with him one little song. It is especially so if he can speak these words to God, as they have done; this can only done in faith, for the words [of the saints] have no flavour to a godless man.[28]

The Hermeneutic Principles of Luther's *Theologia Crucis*

The hermeneutical principles of Luther's theology of the cross (*theologia crucis*) laid down in *Heidelberg Disputation* in 1518 continue to govern his interpretation of the Psalms.[29] These features—the experience of temptation (*tentatio*), law and gospel, the paradoxical work of God under the appearance of contraries, the distinction between the hidden and the revealed God, Christ's atoning efficacy for sin, and faith in God's word rather than human experience or reason—shape his reading of the Psalms. For instance, in his introductory remarks on Psalm 143, Luther spells out the intent of Scripture: "Every psalm, all Scripture, calls to grace, searches for Christ, and praises only God's work, while

28. LW 35.256.
29. See Robert Kolb, "Luther's Theology of the Cross Fifteen years after Heidelberg: Lectures on the Psalms of Ascent," *Journal of Ecclesiastical History* 61, no. 1 (Jan., 2010): 69–85.

rejecting all the works of man."[30] Grace, Christ, and God's work also form the basic content of the gospel. They are the condition of possibility of hope, when the one under assault by faith lays hold of God's grace revealed in Christ and praises God's work. Ultimately these trials (*tentatio*) draw the psalmist (and us) back to God in meditation (*meditatio*) and prayer (*oratio*) so that he rests totally on God's provision. The triad—struggle, meditation, and prayer—when properly practiced, would lead the sufferers to a deeper apprehension of God's salvific ways with people in the gospel. The proper usage of God's Word, with the lament Psalms in view, as a method of comfort is integral to Luther's pastoral call. It is to this end that this book aims.

Lamentation as a Fitting Category for Discourse with God

In *Lament, Death and Destiny*, Richard A. Hughes argues that Luther, believing in divine providence, disdained lamentation, viewing it not only negative but actually blasphemous.[31] He has Luther saying that "humans should not complain when afflicted with evil, as in the plague, for example."[32] According to Hughes, "classical theology, from Augustine to Calvin, subordinated the idea of fate to the doctrine of providence, along with its rejection of lament."[33] This study is a corrective to Hughes's assumption that

---

30. LW 14.196 (WA 18.522).
31. Richard A. Hughes, *Lament, Death and Destiny* (New York: Peter Lang, 2004), 113–14.
32. Ibid., 161.
33. Ibid., 119.

lamentation, for Luther, is a sin of blasphemy. A more nuanced study of the Psalms proves that the reformer deemed godly lamentation appropriate in times of pain and desolation. Namely, there is a place in theology and liturgy for genuine lamentation that stems from a pure heart, disposed to repose in God's unfailing love, even at times of desolation and grief. However, one must exercise faith and moderation in the expression of lament, which not only protects the faithful from degenerating into sin and rebellion against God but also enables them to remain godly, "limping, but blessed," to borrow Moltmann's salient phrase.[34]

In Israel lamentation, according to Westermann, is "the chief component of prayers in the Old Testament."[35] Brueggemann speaks of the use of lament psalms as "an act of bold faith, albeit a transformed faith."[36] He mentions two major reasons of such use: first, "the world must be experienced as it really is and not in some pretended way," and second, because "all such experiences of disorder are a proper subject for discourse with God."[37] This is crucial in relation to Luther's response to the Psalms. The world in which the people of Wittenberg and the reformer lived was one that increasingly encountered life as disoriented,

34. As description of Jacob's wrestling with God, Moltmann coins the phrase, "limping but blessed." See Jürgen Moltmann, *The Source of Life. The Holy Spirit in the Theology of Life* (London: SCM, 1997), 1.
35. Claus Westermann, *Lamentations: Issues and Interpretations*, trans. C. Meunchow (Minneapolis: Fortress Press, 1994), 94.
36. Walter Brueggemann, *The Spirituality of the Psalms* (Minneapolis: Fortress Press, 2002), 27.
37. Brueggemann, *The Spirituality of the Psalms*, 27. On lamentation as a viable discourse with God, see David J. Cohen, *Why, O Lord? Praying Our Sorrows* (Milton Keynes: Paternoster, 2013).

no different from our world today.[38] Luther's usage of the Psalms is pastorally motivated and is in no way a theoretical undertaking,[39] as he sought to inculcate the word in congregants' lives. Luther's primary call as a pastor-theologian, deeply committed to the majesty of God's word and spiritual care of human souls, looms large in his exposition of the Psalter.

Lamentation belongs essentially to Luther's *Theologia Crucis*. It stands at the heart of Luther's theological hermeneutic, shaped as it is by a pastoral concern for the soul.[40] It is primal to the prayers and worship of the church, then and now. The lament Psalms, in particular, contain anecdotes of God's people calling God to account because their suffering defied not just rational explanation but also God's covenantal promises. There is no ready acceptance of their suffering, but protest against the workings of divine providence. Luther parted company with a tradition that readily submits suffering to the fate of divine providence without lamentation. Like the psalmist, Luther engaged with God and laid bare before him. Lamentation is the language of suffering and thus is a fitting category for a discourse with God.[41]

38. See Peter Matheson, *The Imaginative World of the Reformation* (Edinburgh: T. & T. Clark, 2000), 1–48.
39. See, for example, Lewis W. Spitz, "Luther *Ecclesiast*. A Historian's Angle," in *Seven-Headed Luther*, ed. Peter N. Brooks (Oxford: Clarendon, 1983), 117; H. Junghans, "Luther's Wittenberg," in *Cambridge Companion to Martin Luther*, ed. Donald K. McKim (Cambridge: Cambridge University Press, 2003), 25.
40. See Lester Meyer, "A Lack of Laments in the Church's Use of the Psalter," *Lutheran Quarterly* 7 (Spring 1993): 67–78.
41. Claus Westermann, "The Role of the Lament in the Theology of the Old Testament," *Interpretation* 28 (1974): 27.

Possessed of a general validity and a timely character, the Psalter penetrates into the innermost being of the one who prays, exposing the heart, thoughts, and emotions. The humanness or earthiness of the psalmist is revealed, characterized by a genuine disclosure of his painful situation, the problem and evangelical concern he has with his enemies, his struggle with God's providence, his confidence in God, and his earnest plea for God to act. Bold, sometimes vengeful, persistent, and forceful, lamentation reminds God of the promises he made to the faithful and challenges God to account for their afflictions. It also brings into view the paradoxical tension between protest and praise, doubt and trust, fear and hope. Abiding in this paradox is a potent resource for honest and audacious speech to God that tells it as it is. Commenting on Ps. 118:5, "Out of my distress I called on the Lord; the Lord answered me and set me free," Luther offered straightforward pastoral advice but with sensitivity and sensibility:

> Don't just sit there by yourself or lie on your belly with your head hanging down and let these thoughts bite into you, and don't get eaten up worrying over them. Get up, you lazy fellow, and then get down on your knees and hold up your hands to heaven and pray a psalm with the Lord's Prayer and bring your complaints to God.[42]

Part of what it means to be "a theologian of the cross" is to "call the thing what it actually is," wrote Luther in one of his famous theses for the Heidelberg Disputation.[43] So a

---

42. WA 31.I, 96 as quoted in George, *Reading Scripture with the Reformers*, 170.
43. See "Thesis 21, Heidelberg Disputation, 1518," in LW 31.53.

theologian of the cross voices the complaints as they actually are and speaks earnestly from the bottom of the heart to God with an unmitigated effrontery, devoid of pretense and avoidance. Above all, only a true theologian of the cross hears God speaking in his affliction, even contrary to his expectations and in God's apparent absence.

The Structure and Substances of a Lament: Movement from Grief to Relief

Generally lament Psalms have as many as five basic constituents: address to God in pain, complaint to God, confession of faith, prayer to God, and doxology.[44]

1. Address to God in affliction
2. Complaint to God about affliction

    a. Statement of trouble
    b. Description of enemies
    c. Complaint against God's indifference

3. Expression of faith in affliction

    a. Trust in God's grace
    b. Trust in God's help

---

44. Westermann, "The Role of the Lament in the Theology of the Old Testament," 26, where he wrote: "The structure of the psalm of lament is address (and introductory petition), lamentation, a turning to God (confession of trust), petition, vow of praise." See also L. William Countryman, *Conversations with Scripture: The Psalms* (New York: Morehouse Publishing, 2012), 67, where he mentions these five distinctive features in lament psalms; Richard P. Belcher, Jr., *The Messiah and the Psalms. Preaching Christ from all the Psalms* (Ross-shire: Mentor, 2006), 68.

4. Petition to God in affliction

    a. Imprecation against enemies
    b. Evangelical concern for his enemies
    c. Pleas for God's deliverance

5. Praise of God in affliction

    a. Pondering God's mighty works
    b. Promise of thanks offering or praise
    c. Gratitude for anticipated help

The structure is not meant to be a rigid formula to be followed. Not all of the features appear in every lament Psalm, and they do not occur in the same order. These elements are discernible in Luther's prayers of lament. Characteristically most lamentations move from frustrations with the actions of God and the psalmist's enemies toward a statement of confidence that God has heard the complaint and will respond. The assurance of being heard leads to doxology so that many laments culminate in the praise of God. Bayer elaborates:

> Although the full, uninterrupted praise of God's goodness, with which we praise God without affliction and temptation, will only happen at the end, the praise of God is nevertheless assumed in some way in every lament. If God could not be praised at all—be it even in tears—then humanity would not able to lament. At least there is no address for its cry of lament. The lament would be without direction or orientation; it would become an aimless and only self-related lamenting and sooner or later fall silent. Lament directed to God is always related to past and future praise.... The present distress is not made

insignificant or covered up, but it is taken seriously without becoming the ultimate reality or leading to resignation or cynicism.[45]

The unity or coincidence of opposites—sorrow and joy, lamentation and praise—embodies the life of the Christian who at various times is under afflictions, the cause of lamentation, and under divine comforts, the reason for praise. The coincidental opposites abide in the Christian life in tensions or as a mixture, sometimes in a confused order, thus making it difficult to discern where the afflicted is emotionally—that is, whether in joy or pain; at other times it is experienced as a distinct movement from one to another, without mixture or confusion. The mixture and movement of these coincidental opposites between sadness and joy, lamentation and praise, for Luther, is a real image of the Christian life:

> For those who are tempted must at various times be comforted so that they may endure. Therefore joyous Psalms and Psalms of lament are mixed with each other in different order, so that this mixture of various Psalms and this confused order, as one thinks, is an example and image of the Christian life, which is exercised under many afflictions of the world and comforts of God.[46]

The chief function of a lament is to provide a structure for crisis, pain, grief, or despair, which in turn facilitates a movement "out of the depths"[47] from hurt to joy, from

45. Bayer, "Toward a Theology of Lament," in *Caritas Et Reformatio*, 218.
46. WA 5.487ff as quoted by Aurelius, "Luther on the Psalter," 199.
47. Bernhard W. Anderson, *Out of the Depths: The Psalms Speak for Us Today* (Louisville: Westminster/John Knox, 2000). The phrase "out of the depths" is Anderson's.

darkness to light, from desperation to hope, from death to life. This movement is not solely psychological or liturgical, although it encompasses those experiences. It too is not a mere physical deliverance from the crisis, although that might be anticipated. The movement from hurt to joy, crisis to faith, grief to relief, is a profoundly spiritual one—a creative and salvific act of God. Luther trusts that God will intervene on his behalf in accordance with divine wisdom and is content when he does not because of his confidence in the loving character of God.

Proper Use of Lament Psalms

Speaking of the whole of Scripture, Luther said in his *Table Talk*, in a form of prayer: "God grant me grace to catch hold of its just use."[48] To read the Bible aright, Luther stressed in his lectures on Psalm 51, one must observe "the proper subject of theology"—"man guilty of sin and condemned and God the justifier and Saviour of man the sinner."[49] "Whoever follows this aim in reading Holy Scriptures will *read holy things fruitfully*."[50] The specific task of theology is to be preoccupied with the fruitful reading of the "holy things," namely the twofold theological knowledge—man guilty and God the justifier. Whoever reads holy things fruitfully must do so within this proper subject, lest "error and poison"

---

48. Luther, *Table Talk* (London: Harper Collins, 1995), 31, n. 62. The full sentence reads, "The Holy Scripture of itself is certain and true: God grant me grace to catch hold of its *just* use." The word *just* simply means proper. Cited in Michael Parsons, *Martin Luther's Interpretation of Royal Psalms* (New York: Edwin Mellen Press, 2009), 1.

49. LW 12.311.

50. LW 12.311. The italics are mine.

result.[51] So to read holy things fruitfully is to reap holy fruits for the care of the soul. This provides a cue for the title of the book, *Fruit for the Soul: Luther on the Lament Psalms*. It is this author's hope that his readers might reap from Luther's interpretation of the lament Psalms the richness of the holy things, which might constitute a fruitful source for public proclamation (preacher), church liturgy (worship leader), personal and corporate healing (pastors and spiritual directors), and personal growth in faith.

Accessible to the nonspecialist, more advanced theological students, pastors, and teachers in churches, the book is aimed to help the wider audience to experience the riches of the Psalms. In the Psalter we find manifold, unspeaking blessings or fruits which we could harvest, use diligently and properly, "exercising ourselves in them to the praise and honor of God, lest with ingratitude we earn something worse."[52] Luther counsels us not to loathe the Psalter as "worthless food" (Num. 21:5), as the Jews did in the wilderness, thereby incurring judgement and curses upon themselves.

Psalms 6, 51, 77, 90, 94, and 118 are the focus of discussion. As a whole, Luther's interpretation of the lament psalms has not been undertaken,[53] so this book fills the lacuna in Luther scholarship. In 2017, Christians around the world will celebrate the five hundredth anniversary of Luther's posting

51. LW 12.311.
52. LW 35.257.
53. In addition to Michael Parsons's *Martin Luther's Interpretation of the Royal Psalms*, for which I wrote a commendation, his *Luther and Calvin on Grief and Lament* (Lewiston: Edwin Mellen Press, 2013), discusses briefly the lament Psalms, with accurate reading of Luther's view. See chapter 4.

of the ninety-five theses on the door of the Castle Church in Wittenberg. There will be books revealing diverse pictures of the reformer. Whatever images of Luther one may have, one must bear in mind that Reformation itself, as George intimates, was "a movement of applied theology and lived Christianity."[54] Hence one should not overlook that Luther was fundamentally a pastor-theologian who sought to lead sinners to a saving knowledge of God's grace revealed in Jesus Christ.[55]

Readers will also discover that for Luther, the care of the soul is a theological task, focused on the proper usage of Holy Scripture. It is not so much about offering a solution psychologically or socially as it is about God addressing the people in law and gospel, wrath and mercy, condemnation and consolation.[56] Not worthless food, but the bread of heaven, the Psalter is given providentially, practically, and precisely for that noble purpose.

---

54. George, *Reading Scripture with the Reformers*, 228.
55. See Timothy J. Wengert, ed., *The Pastoral Luther. Essays on Martin Luther's Practical Theology* (Grand Rapids: William B. Eerdmans, 2009).
56. For a recent study of Luther as a pastor-theologian, see John T. Pless, *Martin Luther: Preacher of the Cross* (St. Louis: Concordia, 2013).

1

Psalm 6: Consolation Hidden in its Opposite: Profoundly Terrified but Profoundly Comforted

As early as 1517, Luther published the first edition of *The Seven Penitential Psalms*. Although the exposition was "good enough" at the time when nothing better existed, he later revised the work in 1525.[1] In the church, these Psalms were used after the hour of Lauds on Lenten Fridays, primarily as an expression of Christian repentance, despite Luther's break with the penitential system of the medieval church.[2] While

---

1. See "Preface," in LW 14.140.
2. See Introduction to LW 14, ix. See also Mark A. Throntveit, "The Penitential Psalms and Lenten Discipline," *Lutheran Quarterly* 1 (Winter 1987): 503.

retaining the element of repentance, Luther discerned the element of lamentation in some of these Psalms.

The analysis of Psalm 6, the first of the penitential Psalms, will be based primarily on his improved edition, with occasional reference to his earlier work. When expounding this Psalm, Luther dwelt on the prophet's complaint over his sorrowful plight rather than his sin and repentance, underscoring his desperate need for divine comfort. Far from rejecting lamentation as an unwitting sin of blasphemy or suppressing it as an irrational act,[3] Luther asserted that the whole of the believer's life is lamentation, genuine and godly. Commenting on verse 8, "For the Lord has heard the voice of my weeping," he wrote: "God is so disposed that He gladly hears those who cry and lament, but not those who feel smug and independent. Therefore the good life does not consist in outward works and appearances but in a lamenting and sorrowful spirit."[4] He sought support for this in the fourth of the penitential Psalms, Psalm 51: "The sacrifice acceptable to God is a broken spirit; a broken and contrite heart, O God, Thou wilt not despise" (51:17). "Therefore weeping is preferred to working," Luther concluded, "and suffering exceeds all doing."[5]

Luther's theology allows a discourse with God in which both praise and lamentation find their rightful place. Whilst one finds "finer words of joy... in the psalms of praise,"

---

3. See Hughes, *Lament, Death and Destiny*, 113–14, where he argued that Luther disdained lament, considering it not only negative but actually blasphemous.
4. LW 14.145 (WA 18.484).
5. LW 14.145 (WA 18.484).

Luther wrote in his *Preface to the Psalter*, one finds "deeper, more sorrowful, more pitiful words of sadness… in the psalms of lamentation."[6] As divine language, both praise and lamentation genuinely reveal the "very hearts and the inmost treasure" of the faithful.[7] Just as praise is the language of joy, so lamentation is the language of suffering and the language of faith, of the confidence that God continues to be God despite the contrary appearances, *sub contrario*.[8] As a fitting category of suffering, lamentation thus rightly belongs to what Luther called "theology of the cross" (*theologia crucis*), a phrase he announced in thesis 21 of his *Heidelberg Disputation* in 1518.[9] The cross of Christ and the cross of the Christian, for him, are distinguished, but not separated. Loewenich wrote:

> The meaning of the cross does not disclose itself in contemplative thought but only in suffering experience. The theologian of the cross does not confront the cross of Christ as a spectator, but is himself drawn into the event. He knows that God can be found only in cross and suffering…. For God himself is "hidden in suffering" and wants us to worship him as

6. LW 35.255ff (WA DB 10.1.103ff) as cited in Selderhuis, *Calvin's Theology of the Psalms*, 21.

7. LW 35.255 (WA BR 10.1.103ff).

8. I am indebted to Westermann, "The Role of Lament in the Theology of Old Testament," 27: "Just as lamentation is the language of suffering, so the praise of God is the language of joy. One is as much a part of man's being as the other. But it is an illusion to suppose or to postulate that there could be a relationship with God in which there were only praise and never lamentation. Just as joy and sorrow in alternation are a part of the finitude of human existence (Gen. 2-3), so praise and lamentation are a part of man's relationship to God. Hence, something is amiss if praise of God has a place in Christian worship but lamentation does not. Praise can retain its authenticity and naturalness only in polarity with lamentation."

9. LW 31.53; See also *Martin Luther's Basic Theological Writings*, ed. Timothy Lull (Minneapolis: Fortress Press, 1989), 43.

such…. If we are serious about the idea of God and the concept of faith in the theology of the cross, we are faced with the demand of a life under the cross.[10]

Proper Perspective

Luther stressed that to read Psalm 6 properly, we must bear in mind these things: First, in all trials and afflictions, we must hurry to God. Far from shying away from such experiences, we should accept that they are sent by God and are not without purpose. Suffering, though not soteriologically efficacious, might foster in us patience and a true fear of God. Those who run away from God and look for relief from creaturely beings become "impatient and a despiser of God."[11] Second, we must take note of the two ways in which God chastens us. "At times he does so in grace as a kind Father, temporally; at times he does so in wrath as a stern Judge, eternally."[12] People, by nature weak and fainthearted, and most manifestly so during trials, often fail to discern the correct way in which God seizes them. In verse 1, the psalmist, in fear of his wrath, cries out, "O Lord, rebuke me not in Thy anger, nor chasten me in Thy wrath." The psalmist was afraid that God might strike him "only in a punitive way," chastising him "without fruit while there is only wrath."[13] Knowing he is a sinner, the psalmist pleads that God might deal with him in mercy and gentleness. Not

---

10. Walther von Loewenich, *Luther's Theology of the Cross*, trans. Herbert Bouman (Minneapolis: Augsburg Publishing House, 1982), 113.
11. LW 14.140 (WA 18.480).
12. LW 14.140 (WA 18.480).
13. LW 10.81 (WA 3.72).

that the psalmist wished to be relieved of God's discipline, but that God's discipline be given him in grace as a child by his father. As proof, Luther quoted Augustine favorably: "O God, bear down there, strike here, beat here, but spare us in yonder life."[14] George explains beautifully: "For Luther God is a Father who shows his kindness through his wrath but once we have passed through the fire of his wrath we find Christ."[15] The law-gospel schema is Luther's hermeneutical key to reading holy things fruitfully.

a way of interpreting a concept

Weight of the Law, Alien Work and Proper Work

Basic to Luther's hermeneutical approach is the crucial distinction between law and gospel, a theme that already appears in his *Heidelberg Disputation*, in 1518.

> ...the law makes us aware of sin so that, having recognized our sin, we may seek and receive his grace.... The law humbles, grace exalts. The law effects fear and wrath, grace effects hope and mercy.... Thus an action which is alien to God's nature results in a deed belonging to his very nature: he makes a person a sinner so that he may make him righteous.[16]

A proper understanding of law and gospel was essential for the proper interpretation of the Scripture and the correct way of doing theology. Here in 1525, Luther continued with the same approach in reading Psalm 6. Commenting on verse 2,

14. St. Augustine, *Confessions, Book* IV as quoted in LW 14.141 (WA 18.481).

15. George, *Reading Scripture with the Reformers*, 97.

16. LW 31.50–51. See also Paul Althaus, *The Theology of Martin Luther*, trans. Robert C. Schultz (Philadelphia: Fortress Press, 1966), 254ff; Robert Kolb, *Martin Luther. Confessor of the Faith* (Oxford: Oxford University Press, 2009), 50–55.

"Be gracious to me, O Lord. O Lord, heal me. For my bones are troubled," Luther applied the theological use of the law to harvest holy fruits from it. Accordingly he read that the psalmist feels the weight of the law, through which he feels his own sins and is terrified by the awful judgement of God. This situation he knows can only be healed by clinging to the grace of God. Thus the psalmist prayed for grace, that by which he may be preserved from dissolution and sheer despair in fear and terror. At the threat of God's punishment, the psalmist lamented his helpless estate before God, "For my bones are troubled." This means all his strength and power pass away so that he expects nothing from himself but everything from God. Abiding here is a significant pastoral insight Luther offers to those who encounter disaster, as in death or at the last hour on earth. Luther commented:

> Blessed are they who experience this in life, for every man must finally meet his end. When man thus declines and becomes as nothing in all his power, words and being, until there is nothing but a lost, condemned and forsaken sinner, then divine help and strength appear as in Job 11:11-17: "When you think you are devoured, then you shall shine forth as the morning star."[17]

In verse 3: "My soul also is sorely troubled. But Thou, O Lord—how long?" the psalmist further laments his spiritual condition before God. Here Luther speaks of the gracious design of God's paradoxical work on his people under the appearance of contraries, a feature already appeared in his

17. LW 14.141 (WA 18.481).

Heidelberg Disputation (1518): in order that God might perform his proper work, he performs an alien work, a work that is not intrinsic but alien to his nature.[18] This he does by removing from the psalmist all creaturely consolations and making his soul deeply troubled in order that he might cry and long for God's consolation. Only he who has been "profoundly terrified and forsaken prays profoundly" from the bottom of his heart, thereby reaping the holy fruits—"God's strength and consolation."[19] With Luther, Melanchthon said the same thing in his *Apology of the Augsburg Confession* (1531): "But God terrifies ... in order to make room for consolation and vivification because hearts that do not feel the wrath of God loathe consolation in their smugness."[20]

Trials (*Anfechtungen*) are God's alien work, which is intended to break down people's self-confidence and reduce them to a state of doubt and despair in order that they might finally turn to God for aid. It is for this reason that Luther regards God's chastisements as "a blessed comfort."[21] Therefore it is folly for despairing hearts to remain secure in their own devices, repudiating God's gracious design aimed at them: "God hides and imparts his goodness under wrath and chastisement."[22] Hidden under God's wrath is his mercy;

[margin handwritten note: 1st & 2nd use of the law.]

---

18. LW 31.51.

19. LW 14.141 (WA 18.481).

20. See *The Book of Concord: The Confessions of the Evangelical Lutheran Church*, edited by Robert Kolb and Timothy J. Wengert (Minneapolis: Fortress, 2000), *Apology of the Augsburg Confession*, XII.51. Also quoted in Timothy J. Wengert, "'Peace, Peace ... Cross, Cross': Reflections on How Martin Luther Relates the Theology of the Cross to Suffering," *Theology Today* 59, no. 2 (July 2002), 200.

21. LW 14.142 (WA 18.481).

hidden under his chastisement is God's goodness. For Luther, the horror of human sin and the terror of God's wrath are real, not to be blunted or discounted.[23] It was from his experience of how real God's anger was that he gained deep insight into the underlying love God has for damnable, miserable sinners. The reality of a saving relationship is encountered in the paradoxical act of God, the one who works within the distinction between God's wrath and his mercy, law and gospel, God's alien work and his proper work.[24]

Suffering the Inner Hurt of the Soul and the Feeling of Being Forsaken

Verse 3, "But thou, O Lord—how long?" shows that lament is framed with the language of desperation and protest. In an exaggerated fashion, the psalmist paints his sorrowful plight in verse 6: "I am weary with my moaning. Every night I flood my bed with my weeping. I drench my couch with my weeping." In troubling times where tears are excessive, fear

22. LW 14.142 (WA 18.481).
23. See, for instance, Steven D. Paulson, "The Wrath of God," *Dialog* 33, no. 4 (1994): 245–51, where he argued that Luther saw the theological necessity for "the church's ministry of reconciliation to speak of God's wrath. For him, God does not have wrath among other anthropomorphic feelings. God is wrath, and becomes love in relation to particular persons only through the church's proclamation.... If the gospel is an eschatological reality, then God's wrath must also be real."
24. Vitor Westhelle, *The Scandalous God. The Use and Abuse of the Cross* (Minneapolis: Fortress Press, 2006), 55: "[The paradoxical distinction] is not a prescriptive statement but purely descriptive; it says that this is what our condition and our experience of it is. The rest is speculation. It seems as if God has abandoned us. Those who realize this are no longer resisting God's grace; nevertheless revolt and lament is not to be shunned." See also Wengert, "'Peace, Peace ... Cross, Cross': Reflections on How Martin Luther Relates the Theology of the Cross to Suffering," 200.

seems endless, and pain is unbearable, the psalmist protests against the working of divine providence. He complains against God for being indifferent and inactive immeasurably long. Alongside the wrath of God, Luther takes very seriously his indifference. The sense that God has forsaken or abandoned us is more intolerable than the sense of his wrath. Luther wrote: "Then a horrible terror and, as it were, the beginning of damnation is felt, as is written in Ps. 30:7: 'Thou didst hide Thy face, I was dismayed.'"[25] Couched in existential language and written in an evocative style, Luther conceived the psalmist's condition as "the inner hurt of the soul, the feeling of being forsaken and rejected by God."[26] This is "the severest and greatest illness of the soul, where it must perish eternally if it should remain in such a state."[27] God offers the psalmist an eschatological foretaste of the pain of God-forsakenness in hell in order that he might grasp God as the Savior of his life. "There is no greater pain than the gnawing pangs of conscience, which occur when God withholds truth, righteousness, wisdom, etc., and nothing remains but sin, darkness, pain, and woe."[28] This existential experience of God-forsakenness so pierces his soul that the psalmist is compelled to invoke God's return or intervention, or else he might perish eternally. In verse 4, he makes a plea for God's help: "Turn, O Lord, save my life." Whilst God's turning away from us implies "an inner rejecting and forsaking," for Luther, God's turning toward or returning

25. LW 14.142 (WA 18.481).
26. LW 14.142 (WA 18.481).
27. LW 14.142 (WA 18.481).
28. LW 14.142 (WA 18.481).

to us implies "inner consolation and a sustaining in joyous hope."[29] The psalmist's cries move God to turn away from his wrath and entreat him with his mercy, consolation, and hope.

Commenting on verse 5, "For in death there is no remembrance of Thee; in hell, who shall give Thee thanks?" Luther portrayed the psalmist's situation as that of death, not temporal but spiritual death, when the soul is dead. "For sin is the death of the soul, and pain is its hell. Both are felt by one who lies in this distress, namely, in sin and in punishment for sin."[30] The tribulation the psalmist undergoes is "a door and entrance into eternal sin and punishment, that is, into death and hell."[31] The psalmist was terrorized by the thought that he might consummate his life under divine wrath and descend to hell, forever excluded from the praise of God. Luther quoted Isa. 38:10, where King Hezekiah spoke of his experience of the horrible terror in hell: "I have said in great terror: I must enter the gates of hell in the midst of my days, that is, when I thought I was in the best years of my life."[32] The assailed came face-to-face with the most terrifying battle of all, the battle with death and hell, about which he cannot do anything. His soul is so severely burdened with affliction that he said in verse 7: "My body wastes away because of my grief." Luther borrowed a New Testament image to elucidate that the situation of the psalmist is likened unto that of "the poor and deformed Lazarus" (Lk. 16:19–20).[33] This graphic

29. LW 14.142 (WA 18.481).
30. LW 14.143 (WA 18.482).
31. LW 14.143 (WA 18. 482).
32. LW 14.142 (WA 18.481).
33. LW 14.144–45 (WA 18.483–84).

description conveys the effect that the psalmist's feeling of rejection brings: all his strength, merit, and worthiness are reduced to nothing; there is no comfort, except "only terror and wrath of God."[34] In the abyss of nothingness, the poor soul realizes that he has "nothing left but crying, imploring and praying."[35] Luther stressed: "This is what this temptation [*tentatio/anfechtung*] does."[36] The experience of nothingness is God's alien work, through which God crushes the claim of the believers to righteousness before him in order that they might cling to God alone as their redeemer.[37] This experience thus causes the psalmist to lament with profit, moving him from nothingness to blessedness, from wrath to mercy, from hurt to joy, from lamentation to praise. Ultimately God's grace is to be praised; all human works are reduced to naught. With relief, the psalmist acknowledged in verses 8b and 9, "For the Lord has heard the voice of my weeping. [He] has heard my supplication; the Lord accepts my prayer."[38]

Evangelical Concern for Enemies

Commenting on Ps. 6:8: "Depart from me, all you workers of evil," Luther quoted Matt. 7:22 to emphasize that Christ condemned the proud holy ones and wished that they might feel God's wrath or come to the knowledge of their sins and

---

34. LW 14.143 (WA 18.482).
35. LW 14.145 (WA 18.484).
36. LW 14.143 (WA 18.431–32).
37. See Ronald K. Rittgers, *The Reformation of Suffering: Pastoral Theology and Lay Piety in Late Medieval and Early Modern Germany* (Oxford: Oxford University Press, 2012), 112–13.
38. LW 14.145 (WA 18.434).

be terrified at themselves. This reflects what Luther has taught in thesis 24 of his Heidelberg Disputation, that a person is necessarily puffed up by his good works unless he has first been deflated and destroyed by suffering and evil; not until he learns that he is worthless and that his works are not his but God's would he ever seek God.[39] This, then, is directed against works-righteousness and human efforts to do what is morally good to merit justification, which only faith in Christ makes possible. This is borne out in thesis 25 of the same, where Luther asserted, "He is not righteous who does much, but he who, without work, believes much in Christ."[40]

The enemies or doers of injustice were clearly part of the psalmist's distress, although no action on their part was described. No explicit prayer for deliverance from the enemies was offered up. The psalmist manifested genuine concern for his enemies more than his genuine anger with them. Instead of imprecating his enemies, the psalmist intercedes for them in Ps. 6:10: "All his enemies shall be ashamed and sorely troubled. They shall turn back. And be put to shame in a moment." To glory in human achievements, for Luther, is "the greatest blindness on earth."[41] Pride has blinded and misled the enemies into thinking that all is well with them, when the truth is they are so devoid of blessing, despised, and dishonored before God. It is the psalmist's wish that his enemies' blindness be lifted so that they come to recognize how shameful and

39. LW 31.55.
40. LW 31.55.
41. LW 14.146 (WA 18.484).

poor they are before God and how very needy they are of God. This prayer reflects the psalmist's evangelical concern for the enemies, that they too might come under assault, feeling the same effect he had of God's alien work so that they might appropriate his proper work. Like the poor in spirit, they would have reaped manifold blessings had they returned to God, for God gladly dispenses his mercy, if only the unworthy flee to him in affliction. Precisely by their unworthiness and sinfulness, they prove themselves the very people whom God loves, for he finds above all the ungodly, not worthy in themselves to be loved.[42] God is kindly disposed toward those who claim nothingness, cry, and lament for him. Poverty of spirit, for Luther, constitutes the shape and substance of the Christian life.

> The life and behaviour of every Christian should be so constituted that he does not know or have anything but God, and in no other way than in faith. Therefore those who are not like this are not heard by God, for they do not call with the heart. They are not poor, nor are they in need of calling and praying: for they are sated and filled.[43]

Two Ways Forward in Lament: Unbelief and Faith

As previously discussed, Luther proposed two ways forward when dealing with lament in trials and afflictions. Either the lamenters fall into despair, become impatient, and despise

---

42. See Eric W. Gritsch and Robert W. Jenson, *Lutheranism: The Theological Movement and Its Confessional Writings* (Philadelphia: Fortress Press, 1976), 44, where Jenson speaks of being saved by unbelief: "Just by your very unbelief you prove yourselves the very man whom God loves. He chooses above all the ungodly."
43. LW 14.146 (WA 18.484).

God; or they allow the dreadful situation to move them toward God. The former is to lament in an impious or harmful way that drives them away from God, for it permits complaint or lament to so control their being and doings that they are deprived of any senses. This is tantamount to permitting the old Adam, who is "still fresh and green,"[44] to reign rather than God's word. This, to Luther, is unbelief. The latter is to lament in a pious and fruitful way that draws them toward God rather than away from him. This, for Luther, is faith.

Luther's pastoral sensitivity and psychological awareness come through when he insists on the discipline of moderation in godly lamentation. This is evident in the latter part of verse 5: "In hell who will give you thanks," where Luther spoke of the contemplation of praise and gratitude, even in the midst of the saint's afflictions:

> This is by far the noblest thought which the saints have in their crosses and by which they are also sustained. Otherwise they are in every way like the damned, as we read later in the last of these psalms: "Hide not Thy face from me, lest I be like those who go down to the pit" (Ps. 143.7). The difference is this, that the saints retain a good will toward God, and that they are more concerned about losing God's gracious will, praise, and honor than about being damned.[45]

Here we see in Luther the balance in his theological perspective he offers to the sufferer. It is not one-sided

---

44. LW 14.144 (WA 18.482).
45. LW 14.143 (WA 18.482). Also quoted in Parsons, *Luther and Calvin on Grief and Lament*, 118. Parsons recognizes the need of moderation in lament, lest the lamenter fall into unbelief.

emphasis on God's propitious favor and gracious love toward the sufferer who laments. No doubt it is God who bridles the sufferer in love and grants him a sincerely favorable disposition toward Him in the midst of trials (cf. Isa. 48:9). But Luther also puts the emphasis on the sufferer's responsibility to retain perpetually a "good will and love towards God" while lamenting. Unlike the condemned, the saints dread blasphemy of God more than hell, losing God's grace more than being condemned. Hell itself is not the cause of the psalmist's lamentation but the absence of the praise of God there is. In his earlier edition of Psalm 6, Luther wrote: "Not for this reason, that it is hell does [the psalmist] pray that he may not come to hell, but for the reason that there is no praise of God there."[46] This suggests a way of lament with constructive result. Those who lament must do so in faith and with moderation,[47] lest they fall into the trap of blaspheming God and losing his favor. Self-absorbing and excessive lamentation might beget sheer despair and hatred of God, and that is harmful. Godly and moderate lamentation is fruitful when the one who complains maintains his faith and reliance on the Lord in the midst of his crosses. Quoting Ps. 18:3: "I call upon the Lord, who is worthy to be praised, and I am saved from my enemies," Luther stressed again the lamenter's need to maintain his good will toward God, holding in check his inner attitude while complaining:

We must overcome afflictions, death, and hell. However, they

---

46. LW 10.51–52 (WA 3.73).
47. See Pless, *Martin Luther,* 112, where he speaks of moderation and grieving within faith.

will not be overcome by running away or by impatience, but with favour, good will, and love continuing toward God in their presence.[48]

Immediately following this indented sentence, Luther supplied a word of caution: "These are sharp words for the old Adam, especially if he is still fresh and green; but that does not matter."[49] This is noteworthy, for throughout his life as a spiritual adviser, Luther hardly ever lost sight of the prudence of the old Adam and the remainder of sin. He knows how eagerly the old Adam wants to gain the upper hand, especially in the context where complaint seems legitimate. The unruly flesh might incite the afflicted to become self-absorbed and rebellious in their grief, thereby stripping them of God's help. Even so, it can be subdued by the sufferer's perpetual reliance upon God, not upon his own strength.

Justification of Sinners *Ex Nihilo*

The psalmist's inner sorrow of the soul could be healed, and the feeling of being turned away by God could be conquered, both by the God who turns himself toward him with acceptance and consolation. God achieves this, not on account of any merit or worthiness in us but purely by his mercy. This too is in keeping with God's nature and work, the opposite of what humans are and do. God's justification of sinners by faith occurs *ex nihilo*, not on the basis of any preexistent salvific materials. Whereas humans make

48. LW 14.144 (WA 18.482–83).
49. LW 14.144 (WA 18.482–83).

something out of the preexistent materials, God makes something out of nothing (*ex nihilo*) so as to accomplish his saving purpose. God's aseity is such that he works independently or noncontingently. Only those who are reduced to naught become "God's material," out of which God makes something. This is borne out poignantly in Luther's exposition of Ps. 38:21: "Do not forsake me, O Lord! O my God, be not far from me!"

> It is God's nature to make something out of nothing; hence one who is not yet nothing, out of him God cannot make anything. Man, however, makes something else out of that which exists; but this has no value whatever. Therefore God accepts only the forsaken, cures only the sick, gives sight only to the blind, restores life only to the dead, sanctifies only the sinners, gives wisdom only to the unwise.... Therefore no proud saint, no wise or righteous person, can become God's material, and God's purpose cannot be fulfilled in him.[50]

Bielian Premise: Doing What Lies in Us

Gabriel Biel tried to balance God's grace and human performance by claiming that "out of purely natural powers" (*ex puris naturalibus*) sinners could "do what is in them" (*facere quod in se est*).[51] Fallen sinners still possess residual moral

---

50. LW 14.163 (WA 18.497).
51. See Gabriel Biel, *Collectorium circa quattuor libros sententiarum*, 4 volumes, ed. H. Rückert, M. Elze, R. Steiger, W. Werbeck, and U. Hofmann (Tübingen: J.C.B. Mohr, 1973–92), Lib. II. Dis. 27, art. 2. Also cited in Bengt Hägglund, "The Background of Luther's Doctrine of Justification in Late Medieval Theology," *Lutheran World* 8 (1961): 30. For a thorough study of Biel's theology of justification, see Heiko A. Oberman, *Harvest of Medieval Theology: Gabriel Biel and Late Medieval Nominalism* (Durham: Labyrinth, 1983), 57–89, 146–84; Brian Gerrish, *Grace and Reason: A Study in the Theology of Luther* (Oxford: Clarendon, 1962), 114–37;

capacities, which orient them toward God. "Confidence in the ineradicable goodness of creation," Steinmetz writes, "is the theological basis for Biel's cheery assessment of human prospects."[52] In the natural state, attempting their utmost, sinners are capable of performing meritorious deeds accepted by God as the basis for a reception of his grace.[53] What Luther taught in this Psalm was at odds with the Bielian premise, that we could obtain grace by "doing what lies in us," a widespread notion that he opposed not only in his *Heidelberg Disputation* but throughout his life and career as a theologian and pastor.[54] For him we obtain grace not by doing what is in us but by accepting what is done to us, even by God. Forde clarifies this issue: "[Grace] is acquired when we are completely humbled by God's alien work in law and wrath that we see how completely we are caught in the web of sin and turn to Christ as the only hope."[55] The gaining of humility is no way a human achievement but is given to us by God. Law so reduces us to a position where we claim absolutely nothing that we cling to Christ. We have no "active capacity" to humble ourselves but only a "passive capacity," that we are humbled.[56] Thus we obtain grace by

Alister E. McGrath, *Iustitia Dei. A History of the Christian Doctrine of Justification* (Cambridge: Cambridge University Press, 1986), 86–88, 99–102.

52. David C. Steinmetz, *Luther in Context* (Grand Rapids: Baker Academic, 2002), 61.
53. Kolb, *Martin Luther*, 32.
54. See "Heidelberg Disputation," in LW 31.50, and "Disputation against Scholastic Theology," in LW 31.10, footnote 5, where Luther repudiated the Bielian premise.
55. Gerhard O. Forde, *On Being a Theologian of the Cross: Reflections on Luther's Heidelberg Disputation, 1518* (Grand Rapids: William B. Eerdmans, 1997), 61.
56. Forde, *On Being a Theologian of the Cross*, 9. See John B. Webster, "The Grammar of Doing: Luther and Barth on Human Agency," in his *Barth's Moral Theology: Human Action in Barth's Thought* (Edinburgh: T & T Clark, 1998), 159, where he writes: "For

humbly accepting what is being done to us within the law-gospel distinction. All human works are dethroned and made ineffectual. It is not by our working that we are drawn near to God, so to speak, but by our not working that we are drawn near to God. Utter passivity is the basis of our justification.

The Movement from Lament to Praise

To a certain extent, this Psalm displays all of the elements of the genre of lament: address to God, complaint, petition for grace, confession of faith, and praise of God. The movement from lamentation to praise is meaningful, on which Luther remarked: "What a completely different emotion this is."[57] The shift creates order and stability in the midst of the disorder or disorientation of the psalmist under spiritual assault. The psalmist's tears move God to act with compassion; the troubled person is comforted; affliction and lament change into joy and gratitude. Prayer for grace under distress culminates in praise and hope grounded firmly in God's steadfast love, God's character.[58] The very reason for the psalmist's speaking of his distress to God is "for the sake of your [God's] steadfast love" (v. 4).

The transition from lament to praise, Aurelius comments, is an act of God's creation, which, like the first creation,

---

Luther, even in action one is utterly passive, that upon which another acts; for Barth, even in receiving one is a spontaneous doer, acting in correspondence to the action of the one whose act is received."

57. WA 5.387, 37 as cited in Carl axel Aurelius, "Luther on the Psalter," *Lutheran Quarterly* 14 (2000): 200.

58. See Ingvar Floysvik, *When God Becomes My Enemy. The Theology of the Complaint Psalms* (St. Louis: Concordia Publishing House, 1997), 42–43, 45.

occurs *ex nihilo* and through the word.[59] Creation and salvation are juxtaposed—both are God's work *ex nihilo* and through the word. The psalmist describes an existence from the point of view of the one assailed, a condition where no liberation or relief is to be found, unless God acts mercifully. As a result of God's salvific act, the person under assault was given a completely different view of reality about God and himself. For the one praying, God has changed, so that he now no longer appears as one who is against him but for him; he ceases to be a wrathful judge and instead appears as a merciful deity. God is no longer the problem, so to speak; he is the solution to those who seek him in distress. Consequently the one praying also changes his interpretation of the situation about himself, that though profoundly afflicted he is profoundly comforted by God. The one assailed experiences himself initially as the enemy of God, but now he experiences himself as an object of God's love. Transposition from pain to joy, lamentation to praise, has been made, and therefore he can again flee to God, from whom everything good proceeds. In the Psalter, Luther said, "you will have a fine, bright, pure mirror" that shows you the true knowledge of yourself and God himself.[60]

---

59. Aurelius, "Luther on the Psalter," 200.
60. See "Preface to the Psalter," in LW 35.257. See Franz Posset, *Pater Bernhardus: Martin Luther and Bernard of Clairvaux* (Kalamazoo: Cistercian Publications, 1999), 225–26, where he pointed out that Luther's twofold knowledge—self and God—has its root in Bernard of Clairvaux. In his exposition of Ps. 18:13, Luther quoted Bernard of Clairvaux favorably: "For just as, according to Bernard, knowledge of self without the knowledge of God leads to despair, so knowledge of God without the knowledge of self leads to presumption." See WA 5.508, 23–26, as cited in Posset, *Pater Bernhardus*, 226.

Final Words

The phrase "limping, but blessed,"[61] or profoundly afflicted but profoundly comforted truly characterizes the life of the psalmist. Though his life has become painful and restless, he is still at the grip of God's love, which is "as strong as death and as firm as hell, because it remains even in deathly and hellish pain."[62] God gladly communicates his grace to those who willingly submit to the paradoxical work of God, that those who have been profoundly terrified and forsaken under the alien work of the law will be profoundly comforted under the proper work of the gospel. One should neither despair of the paradoxical work of God nor resist it, for the God who works in him the opposite of justification also effects in him salvation. This working of God is completely hidden to the world; it is a scandal to the Jews and folly to the Gentiles. God's proper work is established and revealed through his alien work, and this is only perceived by the believer in faith. By way of summation of Luther's double way of God's operations, a dialectic between his alien work and proper work, Vercruysse wrote:

> It is an understanding of the two-fold way by which God operates with man. It is through the visible and apparent *opus alienum*, consisting of sorrow and tribulation, and also of judgement, wrath, death, and evil as summed up in the previous gloss, in brief, consisting of the cross, that God brings a man to his real, invisible, true work, the rejoicing and pacifying justification, yet not revealed but hidden *sub contrario*, within

61. Moltmann, *The Source of Life*, 1.
62. LW 14.144 (WA 18.482–83).

the storm of his *opus alienum*. This is, however, only understood by the believer ... (whose) whole life ... consists in faith, i. e., the cross and sufferings.[63]

Suffering reveals the futility of self-justification and the need of God's justification. As God's alien work, suffering strips believers of all intellectual and moral powers, reducing them to nothing so that they might become "Christ's action and instrument" (*Christi operatio seu instrumentum*), the end of human existence.[64] God creates for us the experience of suffering (*anfechtung*), through which God constitutes us as the beneficiaries of his salvific work.[65] Those who consent to God's gracious design, according to which God makes them sad before he makes them glad, really hear the gospel as God wishes them to. For hidden in a severe no is an assuring yes of God. Trials, for the reformer, are "a delicious despair,"[66] for

63. Joseph E. Vercruysse, "Luther's Theology of the Cross at the time of Heidelberg Disputation," *Gregorianum* 57 (1976): 530. Vercruysse's summary is based on Luther's exposition of Heb. 12:11.
64. LW 31.55 (WA 1.363.34); LW 31.56 (WA 1.364.15–16). Also quoted in Rittgers, *The Reformation of Suffering*, 113.
65. Alister E. McGrath, *Luther's Theology of the Cross* (Oxford: Blackwell, 1985), 151: "So far from regarding suffering and evil as a nonsensical intrusion into the world (which Luther regards as the opinion of a theologian of glory), the 'theologian of the cross regards such suffering as his most precious treasure, for revealed and yet hidden in precisely such sufferings is none other than the living God, working out the salvation of those whom he loves." See also John Strelan, "Theologia Crucis, Theologia Gloriae: A Study in Opposing Theologies," *Lutheran Theological Journal* 23 (Dec., 1989): 89–100.
66. See WA 5. 381, 18–19; 619.27 as cited in McGrath, *Luther's Theology of the Cross*, 171; Dennis Ngien, *Luther as a Spiritual Adviser* (Milton Keynes: Paternoster, 2007), 131.

hidden within is "God's embraces,"[67] the fruit of God's work within the law-gospel distinction.

67. WA 40, II.582, 5 (Psalm 45, 1532), quoted in Heinrich Bornkamm, *Luther's World of Thought*, translated by Martin H. Bertram (St. Louis: Concordia Publishing House, 1958), 73.

2

Psalm 51: No Other Theme but This: Wrapped in the Bosom of God Who Is Grace

Psalm 51, one of the seven penitential Psalms, was most widely used in church and daily prayers in Luther's day.[1] Luther offered three reflections on this text during the course of his career: during the period of his first lectures on the Psalms (*Dictata super Psalterium*) at Wittenberg, 1513–1515; in his separate work on *The Seven Penitential Psalms* in 1517, revised in 1525; and in eleven lectures given at Wittenberg during the summer of 1532. The question of unity and diversity, constancy and development, in Luther's exegetical procedure applied to this text,[2] is not in view here, but rather

---

1. LW 12.305.

the proper usage of it and the fruits one could reap from it for the care of the soul.

In Luther's introductory summary of his lecture in 1532, he discerned in David's prayer a shift from the description of the distress over his whole nature through the confession of trust in God's grace to the vow of praise as the outcome. Here Luther denounces the improper usage of this psalm in his own time. Some either chant or pray it daily in order to perform the works required by the church officials, and in so doing have applied it to the penance of works. Others have narrowed their definition of sin to simply "elicited acts," a famous Roman Catholic notion that undercuts the gravity of sin.[3] The proper usage of this Psalm is so that on the one hand, we must "look at sin more deeply and show more clearly the root of wickedness or sin," and on the other hand, we might "understand the nature of grace" accurately.[4] God loves those who acknowledge that they were lost, and turns toward them with grace and forgiveness. Of the doctrine of God, Luther writes:

> Here is a description or definition of God that is full of comfort: that in His true form God is a God who loves the afflicted, has mercy upon the humbled, forgives the fallen, and revives the drooping. How can any more pleasant picture be painted of God? Since God is truly this way, we have as much of Him as we believe.[5]

2. See C. Clifton Black II, "Unity and Diversity in Luther's Biblical Exegesis: Psalm 51 as a Test-case," *Scottish Journal of Theology* 38, no. 3 (August 1985): 325–45, where he analyzed the three different specimens of Luther's exegesis of a single text.
3. LW 12.304.
4. LW 12.304.
5. LW 12.406.

To Luther, a "holy man" is merely a fiction,[6] and moreover such a man is the one with whom God has nothing to do; an "exceedingly great sinner,"[7] though not worthy in himself to be loved, is the object of God's abundant mercies and steadfast love. Theology has no other theme than this: warped sinners but wrapped "in the bosom of God who is Grace."[8] "This is true theology," which Ps. 51:1 indicates, "According to Thy abundant mercy blot out my transgressions."[9] As Brecht writes of Luther, "If I could understand this [theology], I would be a theologian."[10]

The Proper Subject of Theology: Knowledge of Self and God

Based on this Psalm, the Reformer sought to explain what he found to be the heart of Scripture, that is "man guilty of sin and condemned, and God the justifier and savior of man the sinner" (*homo peccati reus ac perditus et deus justificans ac salvator hominis peccatoris*).[11] Accordingly any discussion of Luther's theology, in order to be faithful to the way he does theology, must take into account that the basis of his understanding is to be found in what he takes to be the character of the relationship between God the justifier and sinful humanity.

---

6. LW 12.325.

7. LW 12.319.

8. LW 12.323.

9. LW 12.323.

10. Martin Brecht, *Martin Luther. Shaping and Defining the Reformation 1521–1532*, trans. James L. Schaaf (Minneapolis: Fortress Press, 1990), 457.

11. LW 12.311. Also quoted in Bernhard Lohse, *Martin Luther's* Theology, trans. Roy Harrisville (Minneapolis: Fortress Press, 1999), 39–40.

This basis is borne out in his lecture on Psalm 51 (1532), where he asserts,

> The proper subject of theology is man guilty of sin and condemned, and God the justifier and savior of man the sinner. Whatever is asked or discussed in theology outside the subject is error and poison. All Scripture points to this, that God commends his kindness to us and in His Son restores to righteousness and life the nature that has fallen into sin and condemnation.[12]

A true theologian must adhere to "this aim of reading the Holy Scripture" so as to "read holy things fruitfully."[13] The twofold theological knowledge—man and God—is the twin fruits the theologian reaps from reading this Psalm aright: "A man should know himself, should know, feel, and experience that he is guilty of sin and subject to death, but he should also know the opposite, that God is the Justifier and Redeemer of a man who knows himself this way."[14] This has its root in Bernard of Clairvaux,[15] the only one Luther deemed worthy of the name "Father" in faith.[16] In his exposition of Ps. 18:13, Luther wrote in favor of Bernard: "For just as, according to Bernard, knowledge of self without the knowledge of God leads to despair, so knowledge of God without the knowledge of self leads to presumption."[17] Knowing our

---

12. LW 12.311. See my *The Suffering of God according to Martin Luther's 'Theologia Crucis* (New York: Peter Lang, 1995), 88.
13. LW 12.311.
14. LW 12.311–12.
15. See Posset, *Pater Bernhardus*, 225–26.
16. LW 22.52 (WA 46.580, 24–32); also cited in my *Gifted Response: The Triune God as the Causative Agency of our Responsive Worship* (Milton Keynes: Paternoster, 2008), 110.

sinfulness without knowing God as the justifier is likened unto someone knowing his ailment without knowing the cure for it, in which case it would certainly lead to utter despair. Conversely knowing God's mercy without knowing our misery is tantamount to knowing God without profit, in which case it would lead to pride. As in the content of the Psalm, the knowledge of self and knowledge of God are intrinsically connected with the doctrine of justification by faith. As the task of theology, this twofold knowledge, according to Lohse, is gained only in "mutual relation": "It is not true that for Luther knowledge of the self, say, would first be necessary in order from it to arrive at knowledge of God. Rather, knowledge of self is attained together with knowledge of God, just as knowledge of self is at the same time knowledge of God."[18]

Psalm 51 teaches us what sin is, where it originates, what damage it does, and where to find the remedy against it. Not by any creaturely means, including introspection, could sin be recognized in its radical depravity but only by God's revelation. And hence no creaturely works can alleviate sin; only God's grace and forgiveness can. Sin with its terror and despair will inevitably crush our bones, until God's grace comes to our aid. However no one could truly understand what sin, grace, and true repentance were had this not been given to him. In this, David was truly a student who needed the Holy Spirit as his schoolmaster. The papacy, Luther wrote, was not imbued with the gift of the Holy Spirit and

17. See WA 5:508, 23–26 as cited in Posset, *Pater Bernhardus*, 226.
18. Lohse, *Martin Luther's Theology*, 41.

therefore failed to truly understand the gravity of sin. Failing to apprehend "sin as an evil root and a sickness unto death," writes Brecht describing Luther's view, the papacy also failed to grasp the true meaning of grace.[19] Failure to apprehend the true meaning of grace "accounts for their ineptitude in comforting timid consciences and consoling hearts against death and divine judgment."[20] To speak theologically of sin and grace is to speak of the annihilating power of law and the life-giving power of gospel.[21] "Our true theology" is nothing but the juxtaposition of sin and grace, understood within the law-gospel distinction:

> But here comes our true theology and teaches that when minds are terrified this way, then one part of theology is finished, the part that uses the Law and its threats. Thus the sinner begins to know himself and casts out the smugness in which we all naturally live before this revelation of wrath. We must not stop here, but go on to the knowledge of the other part of theology, the part that fulfills the whole of theological knowledge: that God gives grace to the humble (I Pet. 5:5). Those threats and horrible examples apply to the hardened and smug sinners; to them God is jealous and a devouring fire (Deut. 4:24). The contrite and fearful are the people of grace, whose wounds the good shepherd wants to bind up and heal.[22]

19. Brecht, *Martin Luther*, 456.
20. LW 12.310.
21. Oswald Bayer, *Theology the Lutheran Way*, ed. and trans. Jeffrey G. Silcock and Mark C. Mattes (Grand Rapids: William B. Eerdmans, 2007), 17: "To speak theologically of sin and grace means to speak of God's promises (*promissio*) and of his law (*lex*), of the accusing and killing law (*Gesetz*) and the comforting and life-giving gospel (*Evangelium*)."
22. LW 12.316–17. See Bayer, *Theology the Lutheran Way*, 216, n. 4.

Justified by the Word: Law and Gospel

Human reason fails to judge the genuineness of the nature of sin. As such sin cannot be understood philosophically, by way of human rules, but theologically, by the word of God—both the law and the gospel or promise.

> Now since it is also part of sin that sin remains hidden in our nature and cannot be fully recognized, it had to be divinely revealed. This revelation of sin takes place through the Law and through the Gospel or promise. Both teachings denounce sins, which we would neither know nor feel nor believe to be sins unless we were admonished by the Word of God.[23]

The knowledge of sin does not come as a result of speculation, nor is it an idea arising out of rational deduction. While human reason may cover up the wickedness of sin or even decorate it, divine revelation peels off the masks of sin and proves clear and certain what sin is in essence. The basic rule Luther uses to determine the reality of who we are is: "By divine promises and laws, not by human rules, 'so that you are justified in your words'" (v. 4).[24] Here Luther appeals to Paul in Rom. 3:4: "But God is true, and every man is a liar, as it is written, 'That Thou mayest be justified in Thy words, and mayest overcome when Thou art judged.'"[25]

In his first Psalm lectures of 1513, Luther's concept of sin is more radical than in the marginal notes of 1509/1510. "This may be," Lohse contends, "due in part to the fact that he had

23. LW 12.340.
24. WA 40, II.369, 9f as cited in Bayer, *Theology the Lutheran Way*, 216, n. 6. I am using Bayer's rendering of the text.
25. LW 12.235.

31

to interpret texts that often contain confessions of sin. Indeed, Lombard's *Sentences* gave ample occasion to comment on the systematic treatment of the concept of sin."[26] In the first lectures, chiefly in the tradition of Paul and Augustine, Luther furnished four major theses on sin:

> First, all men are in sin before God and commit sin, that is, they are sinners in fact.
>
> Second, to this God Himself bore witness through the prophets and established the same at last by the suffering of Christ, for it is on account of the sins of men and He made Him suffer and die.
>
> Third, God is not justified in Himself, but in His words and in us.
>
> Fourth, we become sinners, then, when we acknowledge ourselves to be such, for such we are before God.[27]

By divine revelation, David comes to the realization that sin is fundamentally theological, defined in relation to God, thus David confessed: "Against Thee only have I sinned and done that which is evil in Thy sight, so that Thou art justified in Thy sentences" (v. 4). The "righteousness of God" is a Pauline phrase Luther uses to assert that the sinner, who acknowledges his sin, justifies God and his judgment. He develops this basic principle: "Hence these things conflict with each other: Denying that one has sin, or not confessing it—and justifying God. Justifying oneself before God—and glorifying God. Therefore God is not justified by anyone

---

26. Lohse, *Martin Luther's Theology*, 53.
27. LW 10.235 (WA 3.287–88) as quoted in Lohse, *Martin Luther's Theology*, 54.

except the one who accuses and condemns and judges himself."[28] Only when people humbly accept their true status before God (*coram Deo*) as sinners (*peccator*) do they really perceive who they are in God's sight. Only when they condemn and accuse themselves do their judgments concur with God's, and hence are in conformity to the will of God:

> He who justifies himself condemns God … He who judges himself and confesses his sin justifies God and affirms His truthfulness, because he is saying about himself what God is saying about him. And so he is now in agreement with God and truthful and righteous, like God, with whom he agrees. For they are saying the same thing.[29]

However radical his statements about sin are, Lohse argues, Luther's exposition of Psalm 51 has its roots in Occamism.[30] From it Luther appropriated the concepts of testament and covenant to speak of God's salvific ways with people. Both are closely connected with the distinction between God's absolute power (*potentia absoluta*) and ordained power (*potentia ordinata*), even though Luther did not mention these two powers.[31] It is a feature of the divine scheme that once God has established a covenant with us, which forms the basis of reality, he stays committed to that course of action.

Behold, I was conceived in iniquity (v. 6). "Therefore it is

---

28. LW 12.236.
29. LW 10.238 (WA 3.289). See Denis R. Janz, *Luther and Late Medieval Thomism. A Study in Theological Anthropology* (Waterloo: Wilfrid Laurier University, 1983), 12–18, where he discussed development of Luther's Theological Anthropology his *The Dictata Super Psalterium*, 113–16.
30. Lohse, *Martin Luther's Theology*, 54.
31. Ibid.

true that before Thee I am a sinner and have sinned, so that
Thou only mayest be glorious in righteousness and Thou alone
mayest be justified, when all of us are sinners." It is indeed true.
For we are still unrighteous and unworthy before God, so that
whatever we can do is nothing before Him. Yes, even faith
and grace, through which we are today justified, would not
of themselves justify us if God's covenant did not do it. It is
precisely for this reason that we are saved. He made a testament
and covenant with us that whoever believes and is baptised shall
be saved.[32]

Sinful Acts and Their Root: Symptomatic vs. Systemic

Luther makes full use of the story of King David—his
adultery, his wicked plan for Uriah's death, and his
subsequent confession under Nathan's rebuke—to speak not
only of individual actual sins of adultery and murder but also
of the whole of sin and its roots in all its radical universality.
Confession of sins heightens awareness of individuality
before God. It makes each person an individual, a unique
person who has sinned against God. "Otherwise," Bayer
remarks, "we would only be members of the general category
of 'humans,' not individuals."[33] The scholastic exegetes used
David as an example of actual sinful acts, which Luther did
not repudiate. But Luther goes beyond David's
acknowledgment of his "external sin," and leads us to "the
whole nature, and source and origin" of it.[34] Luther's own
experience counted against the mere quantitative, moralistic

---

32. LW 10.236–37 (WA 3.289).
33. See Bayer, *Theology the Lutheran Way*, 17, and his *Martin Luther's Theology. A Contemporary Interpretation*, trans. Thomas H. Trapp (Grand Rapids: Wm. B. Eerdmans, 2008), 38-39.
34. LW 12.305. See Kolb, *Luther and the Stories of God*, 104.

enumeration of specific sins.[35] For him, sin has a qualitative nature and is not simply a deficit, as if something good is wanting. Luther does not minimize the intensity of sin by relegating sin to merely a "disinclination" and "inhibition concerning the knowledge about God."[36] Rather than a moralistic enumeration of genuine sins, Luther understands sin as it really is, in the sense of its being the condition of fallen humanity at the root of each individual's being: "The psalm talks about the whole of sin, about the root of sin, not merely about the outward work, which springs like fruit from the root and tree of sin."[37] The meaning of David's complaint in verse 5, "Behold, I was conceived in sin, and in sin did my mother conceive me," includes not only adultery but his whole nature contaminated by sin. Sin is a systemic condition, an inheritance, born in us; it is not just a symptomatic manifestation; it is universal, not just individual; it is internal, not merely external. Luther regards David as an outstanding example of the close and causal linkage between individual sinful acts and their root, manner, and nature. "So we are not sinners because we commit this or that sin, but we commit them because we are sinners first."[38]

Though the structure of the image of God (*imago dei*) remains after the fall, its integrity is gone. The image of God is defaced, not effaced. It no longer functions now as it did in the paradise before the fall. This is confirmed in David's

---

35. For Luther's understanding of penitence, see his letter of May 30, 1518, to John von Staupitz, LW 48.64–70.
36. Bayer, *Martin Luther's Theology*, 180.
37. LW 12.305–06; cf. LW 12.339, 348, 390, 401.
38. LW 12.348.

own experience, in which he understood "sin as a corruption of all powers, inward and outward. No member performs its function now as it did in Paradise before sin. We have turned away from God, full of an evil conscience and subject to illness and death."[39] Thus Luther argues that it is "total ignorance of real theology" to take this verse, "And my sin is ever before me" (v. 3), to mean actual sin as Sadoletus did.[40] David saw in actual experience that his whole nature is so warped by sin that it cannot break free from calamity and death by its own power, unless God acts. To illustrate, Luther referred to Bernard of Clairvaux, who exemplified the holiest righteousness throughout his whole life, but at the end lamented the inefficacy of his monastic life. Bernard confessed as his last word, "I have lived my life shamefully."[41]

David's personal experience of sin mirrors the general truth applicable to the lives of his hearers:

> Therefore our sin is that we are born and conceived in sin. David learned from his own experience.... Therefore we believe that this psalm is a general instruction for all the people of God from the time it was composed until the present day. In it David, or rather the Holy Spirit in David, instructs us in the knowledge of God and of ourselves.[42]

David is speaking not merely in his own name but in the name of humanity as a whole. The particular knowledge of his sins indeed evokes a universal truth of the entire human

---

39. LW 12.310.
40. LW 12.335.
41. LW 12.335.
42. LW 12.310.

race. "The psalm teaches this knowledge of sin and of all human nature."[43] The anointed king moves from the knowledge of actual sin to universal sin and thus becomes paradigmatic of the human race. Luther wrote reflectively of David, as though he were to think out loud:

> Look at me, such a holy king! I have been so earnestly engaged in the holy service of the Law and of the worship of God. Now I have been so crushed by the inborn evil of the flesh and by sin that I have murdered an innocent man and adulterously taken his wife. Is not this an obvious proof that human nature is more seriously infected and corrupted by sin than I could ever have suspected? ... In this way it acquired this general feeling of all sin and concluded from this that neither the tree nor the fruit of human nature is good, but that everything that has been so deformed and destroyed by sin that there is nothing sound left in all of human nature.[44]

The Knowledge of Sin: A True Feeling of Divine Wrath

For Luther, sin is "a true feeling, a true experience, and a very serious struggle of the heart," as David testified of himself in verse 3, "I know my transgressions." However to know sin does not mean, as the Pope taught, a calling to mind what one has done or failed to do. In line with the Hebraic sense, Luther offers an affective definition of the knowledge of sin:

> ... it means to feel and to experience the intolerable burden of the wrath of the God. The knowledge of sin is itself the feeling of sin, and the sinful man is the one who is oppressed by his conscience and tossed to and fro, not knowing where to turn. Therefore we are not dealing with the philosophical knowledge

---

43. LW 12.310.
44. LW 12.337.

of man, which defines man as a rational animal and so forth. Such things are for science to discuss, not for theology. So a lawyer speaks of man as an owner and master of property, and a physician speaks of man as healthy or sick. But a theologian discusses man as a sinner.[45]

The theologian is concerned with a sinner who is aware of his nature, corrupted by sin. The sinner feels the weight of the law, by which "his whole nature has been crushed by sin and that there is nothing left on which he can rely."[46] The law condemns the sinner and reduces him to naught so that he expects nothing from himself but everything from Christ. On the one hand, the mind experiences despair under the law; on the other hand, it also feels joyful under the gospel. The law anticipates the gospel; the former leads to the latter. God corresponds to himself in both of these glorious activities, that the God who works in us the horror of sin is the same who works in us the remedy against it.

Luther distinguishes between the sinner who feels his sins, the "conscious" sinner, and the sinner who does not, the "unconscious" sinner.[47] The one who truly prays, "Have mercy on me, O God," must feel his sins and the uncleanness of his own heart, lest he rely on his own righteousness. Luther repudiates judging divine things according to nature, as it leads dangerously into trusting in its own merits against the merit of Christ. Nature tempts us with the "blasphemous presumption" that since we are born in sins, and that God hates sins, we should not pray unless we are pure of all sins.[48]

45. LW 12.310. Also quoted in Pless, *Martin Luther*, 15.
46. LW 12.310–11.
47. LW 12.327.

It causes the mind to look elsewhere, such as human counsels, sophistic consolations, good works, and the like, as legitimate means of expiation of sin. The mind can be so confused within itself by the consciousness of sin that it delays praying until it finds some worthiness within itself, which might form the basis of some confidence in calling on God. This, for Luther, is the improper usage of this psalm: "What does the word 'have mercy' accomplish if those who pray are pure and do not need mercy?"[49] David supplies Luther with the means to call on God, not because he is made worthy, but in the midst of his hideous sins, not because he has been made more fit, but simply because he is "an exceedingly great sinner" who to God is more than fit for a reception of his mercy.[50] It is precisely in the "very sea of our sins," in our unworthiness, that we prove to be the object of God's mercy, so that we do not put off praying. Luther added an autobiographical note that though he taught and commanded people to pray, he considered praying "most difficult of almost of all works," as he often recited the words ("have mercy") "very coldly," so vexed was he by his own unworthiness.[51] "Still the Holy Spirit won out by telling me: 'Whatever you may be, surely you must pray! God wants you to pray and to be heard because of His mercy, not because of your worthiness."[52] Nothing can conquer the mountain of our unworthiness, except his mercy. The more the self tries to overcome its unworthiness, the

48. LW 12.314.
49. LW 12.314.
50. LW 12.319.
51. LW 12.314–15.
52. LW 12.351.

more apparent is the weakness of faith, which drives prayer away, causing the fainted one to refrain from saying, "Having mercy on me, O God." However at the point where faith is weakest, we should be comforted that we are not alone, for the Holy Spirit, the Intercessor, prays the same thing with us in our hearts, "with sighs too deep for words" (Rom. 8:26).

Just as different sicknesses require different remedies, so those who are terrified should be comforted with words of grace, lest they plunge into sheer despair; those who are callous should be smashed with words of wrath, lest they perish in their permanent smugness. The sinners who feel their sins and divine wrath and are terrified in their consciences apply to themselves the threats of divine punishments set forth in the word of God. When the mind has thus been crushed by the hammer of the law, this is really "the place, time, and occasion" to console the terrified heart with the gospel, that God is wrathful only against those who are hard and impenitent, not to those who feel the burden of their sins.[53] Once the law has achieved its proper task of humbling, the contrite soul is made ready for a reception of God's grace. In Luther's words: "the lightning flashes of the wrathful God should stop, and in their place should shine the lights of mercy set forth in the Word of God: ... that God does not despise a contrite and humble heart (Ps. 51:7)."[54] Those who judge according to nature cannot perceive the rays of divine mercy beneath the clouds of divine wrath. However they who live by the word of God will know that

53. LW 12.316.
54. LW 12.316.

40

hidden in the clouds of divine wrath (law) are the rays of divine mercy (gospel).

The sinners who do not feel their sins are callous and impenitent. They are the enemies of the gospel because they look for forgiveness of sins through various acts of worship such as wicked masses, invocation, and the like. They reject God's word, remain stubborn, and make attempts at self-justification. Lay upon them, exhorts Luther, the burden of the law and before them set forth the sayings of divine wrath, in which God offers no mercy but eternal punishments, as in the First Commandment (Exod. 20:5): "I am a jealous God, visiting the iniquity of the fathers upon the children to the third and the fourth generation." Impress upon them that they are the ones of whom it is spoken, "God hates the sinners; God does not hear the sinners." Only when they are made aware of the judgment and wrath of God through the law and are brought low before God will they begin to plead for divine mercy.

True Repentance: Recognition of Sin and Grace

In addition to the true understanding of sin and grace, this Psalm also sets forth before us the doctrine of true repentance. Repentance consists not in the recollection of past transgressions, feeling sorrow over them, and expiating them by satisfaction, but in "recognition of sin and recognition of grace, or to use the more familiar terms, the fear of God and trust in mercy."[55] This is beautifully illustrated by David, who

---

55. LW 12.305.

at the outset of the Psalm was terrified in his conscience by
the knowledge of sin but at the end found consolation by
faith in the goodness of God.[56]

In confession, David is silent about his own righteousness
and merits. He wants God not to look at his sins but to close
his eyes in order that God might deal with him according
to his steadfast love and abundant mercy. The only picture
before his very eyes is that of "merciful, rejoicing, and
laughing God," who bestows life on him and banishes wrath
from him, as expressed in the pronoun "on me," and imputes
his righteousness on him in exchange for his sins, as expressed
in the phrase "blot out my sins."[57] Furthermore, we come
to God, not minimizing sin but freely acknowledging that
our sins are many and great. Just as we acknowledge the
magnitude and severity of sin, we too must believe in the
oceanic immensity of God's mercy. "As by its nature sin is
very great and serious, so we believe that grace or mercy
is immense and inexhaustible."[58] David taught us to confess
sin in such a manner that at the same time we confess his
abundant mercies, immensely greater than our transgression.
Likewise we too must confess his righteousness, by which
God has justified sinners, infinitely greater than sin, that
which we should despair over it. Luther concludes:
"Therefore it is completely of a divine power to be able to say
that I am a sinner and yet not to despair."[59]

Knowledge and confession of sin are merely two sides of

56. LW 12.316–17. See Bayer, *Theology the Lutheran Way*, 216, n. 4.
57. LW 12.324.
58. LW 12.325–26.
59. LW 12.326.

the one and same event. The former necessarily leads to the latter, or else knowledge of sin is merely a theoretical kind that does not benefit us. To confess our sin is not to earn God's mercy but rather to cast ourselves in the free mercy of God. "God does not want the prayer of a sinner who does not feel his sins, because he neither understands nor wants what he is praying for."[60] Such prayer, for Luther, is likened unto a beggar who cries out for alms but when offered begins to brag about his riches. In confession, the sinner ceases the futile attempt at self-justification but concurs with David in saying to God: "Against you, you only have I sinned and done what is evil in your sight, so that you might be justified in your words and blameless in your judgment" (Ps. 51:4). He acknowledges that God is right and agrees with God's verdict: guilty. "When sins are revealed by the Word, two different kinds of men manifest themselves. One kind justifies God and by a humble confession agrees to His denunciation of sin; the other kind condemns God and calls Him a liar when He denounces sin."[61] To confess, Elert writes,

> [is to] agree with the men of the Bible that God's Word concerning the question of guilt (Psalm 51:4; Romans 3:4) is decisive; and this means not only that His decree is infallible, but also that His whole course of action is blameless. The recognition of this fact, despite our inability to fathom all His motives, is expressed in the biblical idea of holiness (Isa. 6:3; Rev. 4:8). It means not merely that He can stand every moral test, but that His moral quality is an unsearchable mystery and superior to every human judgment.[62]

---

60. LW 12.315.
61. LW 12.341.

Luther broke with the penitential system of the medieval church, according to which the sacrament of penance is required to obtain forgiveness. To benefit from the sacramental character of the priest's absolution, the penitent begins with contrition of fear, followed by enumerating all sins committed since the last confession. This ensures him that the eternal guilt of sin was removed by the priestly absolution. But penance of works must be applied to satisfy the temporal punishment due to sin, or else they might suffer future punishment in purgatory. Logically, if the church has the power to impose the penalty, it should also have the power to remit it. This line of reasoning paved the way for the abuses associated with the granting and sale of indulgences, resulting in the theology of works righteousness. This theological understanding became the catalyst, on the one hand, for Luther's repudiation of the system, most evidently taught in the ninety-five theses in 1517, and on the other hand, for an ardent proclamation of the doctrine of justification by faith, the material principle of the Reformation.

Consequently Luther is adamant in his condemnation of the false teachers who require the penance of works:

> People were to collect the transgressions of the past year, sorrow over them, and expiate them by satisfaction, I ask you, does not a judge hang a thief if he confesses his theft and is sorry for it? Yet these people think God is satisfied if they pretend

62. Werner Elert, *An Outline of Christian Doctrine*, trans. Charles Michael Jacobs (Philadelphia: United Lutheran Publication House, 1927), 40–41.

to be sorry by dressing it differently, walking differently, and eating differently.[63]

The pope does it differently. First he urges contrition. Then from the contrition he wants to determine whether the Word is efficacious or not, as though the promise of God did not have the power in itself but needed the addition of our merits, contrition, or satisfactions.[64]

The heart is incapable of determining when it is contrite enough, and hence contrition offers no certainty of forgiveness. No one knows whether one's pious activities (vigils, studies, almsgiving, fasts, prayers, etc.) are found pleasing to God, in which case doubt remains in one's afflicted heart. Rather than recollecting specific sins, which leads to despair, Luther emphasized the proclamation of the forgiveness through the absolution, through which "you hear the sound and true manner of coming to righteousness, so that you can say in your hearts:"

If I have not prayed enough or done as much as I should, what is that to me? I do not build upon this sand (Matt. 7:27). If I have not been perfectly contrite, what is that to me either? But this does not pertain to me, and on this I do build, that God says to me through the brother: I absolve you in the name and merit of Christ. I believe this word is true, nor will my faith fail me. It is "built on the rock of the words of the Son of God" (Matt. 16:18), who cannot lie because He is the Truth (John 14:6). In this way your minds are filled with joy and the true gladness of the Holy Spirit, which consists wholly in the certainty of the Word or in hearing.[65]

---

63. LW 12.371. Also quoted in Mark A. Throntveit, "The Penitential Psalms and Lenten Discipline," *Lutheran Quarterly* 1 (Winter, 1987): 505.
64. LW 12.371.

FRUIT FOR THE SOUL

Confession is not to be done away with, but, as Grane has reminded us, "It is the absolution, however, that is decisive, being defined so that it becomes a proclamation of the gospel, emphasizing the comfort which it gives to the conscience. Thus, the absolution is the voice of God which promises the forgiveness of sins."[66] Contrition, even though it be the most perfect kind, still is minute in respect to righteousness. There is no merit in acknowledging sin or sorrowing over it. "So turn our eyes for away from your contrition, and with your whole heart pay attention to the voice of the brother absolving you. And do not doubt that this voice of the brother ... is divinely spoken by the Father, Son, and Holy Spirit, so that you completely depend on what you hear, not on what you do or think."[67] Unless contrition is followed by absolution, by what Nathan declared to David, "God has put away your sin" (2 Sam. 12:13), the bones remain broken. Confession itself is fruitless unless it is accompanied by the merciful promise of God. The wounded conscience finds no healing in anything but the word of divine promise, that our God is "the Father of mercies and of all comfort" (2 Cor. 1:3), and "the Lord takes pleasure in those who fear Him, in those who hope in His steadfast love" (Ps. 147:11).

However, God alone is responsible for both contrition, which God works in us through the Law, and absolution, which God works in us through his promise. This is already

65. LW 12.371–72.
66. Leif Grane, *The Augsburg Confession: A Commentary*, trans. John H. Rasmussen (Minneapolis: Augsburg, 1987), 128.
67. LW 12.370.

stressed in his *Discussion on How Confession Should Be Made* (1520–21), where Luther borrowed from Augustine this plea: "I do not have what I should have, and I cannot do it. Grant what you command and command what you will."[68] Not only does God promise, but he also fulfills it by creating faith in it. Faith's object is the promise, that of God. Our certainty rests not so much on good intention but ultimately on the promise of God, the object of faith. Faith is never vacuous, writes Paulson, "without a thing in which it trusts." God's promise is that thing to which faith clings. When faith obtains a promise, "it finally grasps the object it was made for and in so doing takes leave of itself and clings only to Christ."[69]

Order of Salvation: Forgiveness Is Prior to Repentance

Just as sinners takes no pride in their faith as the cause of their salvation, so also they claim no forgiveness on account of their repentance. Rather, faith, itself a gift, is the instrument through which the salvation wrought by Christ is appropriated. Repentance includes both sorrow over sin and faith that God has paid the price for it and resolved to be gracious to us on account of Christ. In the evangelical order of salvation, forgiveness is prior to repentance; the former causes the latter. If repentance is the cause of forgiveness,

68. LW 39.32 (WA 6.160), where Luther cited Augustine's *Confessions* 10.29. This is also quoted in Korey D. Maas, "The Place of Repentance in Luther's Theological Development," in *Theologia et Apologia. Essays in Reformation Theology and its Defense Presented to Rod Rosenbladt*, ed. Adam Francisco, Korey Maas and Steven P. Mueller (Eugene, OR: Wipf & Stock, 2007), 145.
69. Paulson, *Lutheran Theology*, 122.

then it is a form of works righteousness, according to which sinners who are blind, dead, and enemies of God by nature might add to the work of Christ. Commenting on verse 2, "For I know my iniquity, and my sin is ever before me," Luther writes that "the causative participle 'for'" does not regard recognition of sin as "the primary cause that merits the forgiveness of sins. For sin is sin, and by its nature it merits punishment, whether you acknowledge it or not."[70] However the acknowledgment of sin is "a sort of co-requisite" of forgiveness.[71] Does this mean that the sinner's confession contributes to his salvation, or causes divine forgiveness? At first glance, it seems so, but Luther clarifies that the promise that God wants to forgive those who repent is the "sole cause, the first, middle, and last cause; that is, it is everything in justification."[72] There is no merit in the acknowledgment of sin. "There is only one cause for justification, namely the merit of Christ, or the gracious mercy which hearts that are ignited by the Holy Spirit grasp by faith."[73] Luther thus conceives of repentance in relation to God's promise that he wishes to forgive the one who makes such a confession. The cause of forgiveness lies not in one's confession but totally in God's promise, the causative factor David recognizes when he says, "For I know my iniquity." Because of the causative character of God's promise to bestow grace upon those who do confess their sins, Luther insists that confession, the responsive factor, "a second cause or, as some learned say, *a*

70. LW 12.333.
71. LW 12.333.
72. LW 12.333.
73. LW 12.332.

causa sine qua non," is "necessary" for the forgiveness of sins.[74] The promise is infinitely effective, as it emanates from God, points us to God and finally draws us to God in repentance and faith. Luther had David saying: "I know that I am evil and a sinner, and that Thou art righteous. That I arise and dare to pray, all this I do with trust in Thy Word and promises."[75]

The Sure Way of Healing: The Hearing of Gladness in the Created Forms

This Psalm points to the efficacy of the word, the ground of our confidence, that which conquers death and all other evils, and the source of joy or gladness. The gospel of Jesus Christ is conveyed by the means that God has ordained as the vehicles of the economy of salvation. Luther extolled the power of the word of God as fundamental to an understanding of reality. To him, God's word is causative, determining the way things are. The gospel, Bayer writes, is "*promissio*" (promise), understood as "speech act that frees and gives confidence."[76] The promise of God is not "a constative utterance," which "simply establish(es), disclose(s), and confirm(s)" what already exists; it is a "performative utterance," which "actually brings it about."[77] The word bears a performative authority, by which God speaks reality into being. God's word acts and accomplishes his will. Of this, he wrote in his commentary on Psalm 90: "What happens to be more meaningless than a

---

74. LW 12.340. See William E. Hordern, *Living by Grace* (Philadelphia: Westminster, 1975), 70–82.
75. LW 12.319.
76. Bayer, *Martin Luther's Theology*, 50.
77. Bayer, *Theology the Lutheran Way*, 127.

word? And yet when God speaks a word, the thing expressed by the word immediately leaps into existence. God says to my mother: 'Conceive!' and she conceives. He says to me: 'Be born!' and I am born."[78] The word possesses its own efficacy and militancy, not to be borrowed from any extraneous factors such as human experience, philosophical reasoning or rationalistic apologetic, or human deeds. No preaching artistry or theological edifice adds efficacy to the word of God. God's word creates faith by the hearing of it. Human arguments might clear obstacles or objections to faith, although they do not create faith.

"The one and sure way of healing" the troubled conscience lies in what David calls "sprinkling" by which the word of God is heard and received.[79] This is God's ordained way of healing in which the heart finds joy and gladness. Troubled hearts may be tempted to disdain God's ordained means of healing and devise other means of relief, which only heap more dangers and useless works for themselves. To illustrate, Luther described the troubled hearts as like geese that when pursued by the hawks seek to escape by flying though they could do well by running, or when threatened by wolves, try to escape by running though they could have done it safely by flying.[80] The sprinkling of the law is imperfect and ineffectual for our justification. But the sprinkling by the word of grace and promise, which demands nothing from us,

---

78. LW 13.99.
79. LW 12.368.
80. LW 12.368.

offers plenary satisfaction through Christ, the perfect victim that annihilates the terrors of Moses and the entire law.

God's word is the instrument of divine power; it assumes created forms, through which God effects his salvific grace.[81] The absolution, as discussed before, is a separate instance of the word of God, which conveys to the church God's unwavering promises. In addition, Luther mentions four forms in which the word of God occurs: preaching, baptism, the Lord's Supper, and the power of the keys. There are at least five means of grace, through which God bestows the benefits of Christ's death to his people. All of these are the created instruments of divine power, through which God inculcates the blessings Christ won for us in the cross upon our hearts. The "hyssop" of verse 7 refers to the "mouth of a man who teaches the Gospel," the pastor as the sprinkling agent. The pastor (a) is the "sprinkler by which the teaching of the Gospel, colored and sealed with the blood of Christ, is sprinkled upon the church."[82] Pastors sprinkle their people with the blood of Christ not only when they preach the word, but also (b) when they baptize, and (c) when they distribute the body and blood of Christ in the Lord's Supper. Furthermore, the word of God occurs (d) in absolution and (e) the use of the keys where the word of forgiveness is declared. The ministry of the word in these forms is done in the stead and by the command of the Lord Jesus Christ. Everyone, whether a believer or an unbeliever, is sprinkled

---

81. For a study of the functions of the word of God, see Robert Kolb and Charles P. Arand, *The Genius of Luther's Theology* (Grand Rapids: Baker Academic, 2008), 129–223.
82. LW 12.363.

when he hears the word, is baptized, or receives the Lord's Supper. When the word is proclaimed and heard, the church is sprinkled anew only if she believes nothing but this: "Christ has made satisfaction for the sins of the world."[83] However the unbeliever does not receive the effects of the word, even when sprinkled by it. Instead "the blood of Christ and the Word of Christ will judge them, but their unbelief will prevent them from being cleansed."[84]

Luther's Reformation discovery of the effective character of the word of God, "that the verbal sign (*signum*) is itself the reality (*res*),"[85] so thrilled him that he was never tired of teaching on this subject. The justifying word God utters in these forms of the Word of God is indeed the action he performs through the created elements of bread and wine and the like. It is a word of address that ultimately transforms the reality of the addressee. Thus Luther called the hearing of God's word "the hearing of gladness."[86] These created forms in which the word of God comes bring confidence and joy, for they are revelatory of a God who delights in overwhelming us with these proofs of his mercy and love for us (*pro nobis*). All these means are indicative of Luther's optimism of grace, in which God endlessly and lavishly fills our hearts with his favor in many different ways. This is evident in his *A Short Order of Confession Before the Priest for the Common Man* (1529), where Luther, as part of the order of

---

83. LW 12.363.
84. LW 12.363.
85. Bayer, *Theology the Lutheran Way*, 129.
86. LW 12.369.

confession of believers to their pastors, had the pastor ask the parishioner why he desired to receive the sacrament after he had just received absolution. The parishioner was to answer that he desired to be strengthen his soul with God's word and sign. In reply, the pastors ask whether absolution has not already bestowed grace. To which, the parishioners retort, "So what! I want to add the sign of God to his word. *To receive God's word in many ways is so much better.*"[87] This is again stressed in his comment on verse 8, "For my hearing Thou wilt give joy and gladness, and the humbled bones will rejoice," Luther writes:

> Our whole certainty is placed in thy Word.... When the heart hears this voice, then the joy arises of which David speaks here. Why should the heart not rejoice when it hears that divine mercy is so great that He enjoys granting grace and does not look at our insufficient contrition, but considers only His mercy and our calamity? After hearing comes confidence, so that we say: "I am baptised. I have taken the body given for me on the cross. I have heard the voice of God from the minister or brother, by which the forgiveness of sins has been announced to me." This confidence conquers death and all other evils.[88]

No matter how impure we are, we are "purer than snow" (v. 7). This is not a reference to human nature, which is thoroughly wicked, but a new status, which is thoroughly pure, "not as he is in himself, but as he is in Christ."[89] Luther writes much about the wholly wicked nature of man, but his references to baptism are plenteous. Though remnants of

---

87. LW 53.118. Italics are mine.
88. LW 12.371.
89. LW 12.367.

sin cling to us, we cling to baptism, a created instrument of divine power. "Still we have obtained baptism, which is most pure; we have obtained the Word, which is most pure; and in this Word and Baptism we have by faith obtained the blood of Christ, which is surely most pure."[90] The remnants of sin are hidden and covered by the alien purity and blood of Christ, which we obtain by hearing the Word declared in baptism. Baptism is not primarily seen as a human response to God's action but as a vehicle through which the word of God acts, which anticipates our response. Just as God encounters us in the preached word, he also pledges himself unfailingly to us in the baptismal word. The promise that God acts in the baptismal word is so efficacious that Luther avers: "We should evaluate the Christian ... and look at him as he was brought out of Baptism, not as he was born of his parents. Regeneration is stronger than the first birth, because it is not from man but from God and His promise, which our faith grasps."[91] Baptism is a one-time event, but its salvific effect sustains the entire Christian life. It is "stronger than the first birth." We are regenerated and given new life in baptism, and to this condition we must return and be constantly assured that we are God's beloved, even when defilements abound. Baptism stands as a sturdy pledge of God's efficacious grace and abundant mercies, that by which a Christian life is to be measured and lived.

90. LW 12.366.
91. LW 12.367. See Kolb, *Martin Luther*, 135–41.

Faith as Gift: The Creative Function

In his *Large Catechism*, Luther writes: "Faith and God belong together."[92] In his commentary on Galatians, he asserts that "faith creates the deity."[93] This bold assertion has resulted in a Copernican revolution from theology to anthropology that makes of God the projection of human needs. The most famous theological assertion of the last two centuries came from Ludwig Feuerbach (1805–1872), according to whom the idea of God is anthropologically derived through one's objectification of one's own being.[94] This is far from Luther, according to whom the idea of God is independent of, and prior to, human experience of him. For when Luther says that "faith creates the deity," he immediately qualifies it with "not in [God's] person but in us."[95] Feuerbach failed to see the flow and whole of Luther's thinking, that the God who exists without us and before we believe is the same God who wants to be God "in us." But he is God "in us" only by faith. The heart and its faith indeed constitute reality, as Luther famously avers, "as you believe, so it will happen to you, because this faith is not taken from human judgement but drawn from the Word of God."[96] Faith does not constitute God's deity itself, but God's deity "in us."

---

92. WA 30, I.133; cf. *Book of Concord: The Confessions of Evangelical Lutheran Church*, ed. Theodore Tappert (Philadelphia: Fortress Press, 1966), 45.
93. LW 26.227 (WA 40, I.360).
94. See Althaus, *The Theology of Martin Luther*, 45. Also quoted in Paulson, *Lutheran Theology*, 105.
95. LW 26.227 (WA 40, I.360). Also quoted in Hans-Martin Barth, *The Theology of Martin Luther: A Critical Assessment* (Minneapolis: Fortress Press, 2013), 175.
96. LW 12.322.

Faith does not create the word; rather it hears and receives it. Faith is "drawn from the Word of God"[97] and does not follow the dictates of human reason and the senses. Once created, faith takes leave of itself and simply permits God to take the lead and reign over us. The grace offered in the word is of no use unless it is appropriated by faith. Our thinking about God, faith, or unbelief, Althaus wrote, "is not merely a subjective factor without meaning and significance for reality; it determines God's transcendental relationship to us."[98]

To be possessed of a true knowledge of God is, for Luther, a matter of life and death. Psalm 51 is the text Luther used to counsel people with the knowledge of a gracious God who moves toward them with acceptance and forgiveness, but this knowledge becomes real only when it is grasped by faith. Faith is creative and makes God's deity real for believers. Faith is the condition of the efficacy of prayer. It enables believers to grasp all reality in a new way. In faith, not only our view of God changes, that he is gracious to the humble, but also our view of ourselves changes, that we are wrapped in his mercy. God's very self is indeed ours, and we are his beloved.

---

97. LW 12.322.

98. Althaus, *The Theology of Martin Luther*, 46. Cf. Bayer, *Martin Luther's Theology*, 180: "Faith and unbelief are more than merely explanations about reality. In both cases, concerning both faith and unbelief, something actually *happens*; the judgment of God makes a determination about the existence of the human being; the judgment of the human being concerning God makes a determination as well—though admittedly not about the nature of God; it determines something about the human being instead. It is like what takes place in a relationship between those in love: what is affirmed by the other when I hear "I love you" affects my being. When I hear this and believe it, I really am the beloved one. But if instead I do not believe it, then I am not that beloved one. *Reality is constituted by one's assessment*." Italics are his.

To unbelief, God's being and divine blessing remain at a distance. In consolation, Luther warns against the contrary of faith, that the God we believe in is indeed the God we have: "[I]f you believe that God is wrathful, you will certainly have Him wrathful and hostile to you. But this will be a demonic, idolatrous, and perverse thought, because God is served if you fear Him and grasp Christ as the object of mercy."[99] The creative function of faith and the God of steadfast love as its object is a gift that liberates David, and us:

> The thought of God's wrath is false even of itself, because God promises mercy; yet this false thought becomes true because you believe it to be true. However, the other thought, that God is gracious to sinners who feel their sins, is simply true and remains so. You should not suppose that it will be this way because you believe this way. Rather be assured that a thing which is sure and true of itself becomes more sure and true when you believe.[100]

Forensic Justification: The Effective Declaration by the Word

Luther found in Psalm 51 strong support for his doctrine of justification, according to which faith must hold firmly to the promised mercy of God. Just as repentance has two elements, so also does justification.

> The first is grace revealed through Christ, that through Christ we have a gracious God, so that sin no longer accuse us, but our conscience has found peace through trust in the mercy of

---

99. LW 12.322.
100. LW 12.322. Frederick J. Gaiser, "The David of Psalm 51: Reading Psalm 51 in Light of Psalm 50," *Word & World* 23, no. 4 (Fall 2003): 393.

God. The second art is the conferring of the Holy Spirit with his gifts, who enlightens us against the defilements of spirit and flesh.[101]

A sinner is righteous by the mere imputation of righteousness, when sins are blotted out by grace. But grace, for Luther, is

> not something human; it is not some sort of disposition or quality in the heart. It is a divine blessing, given us through the true knowledge of the Gospel, when we know or believe that our sin has been forgiven us through the grace and merit of Christ and when we hope for steadfast love and abundant mercy for Christ's sake.... Is not this righteousness an alien righteousness? It consists completely in the indulgence of another and is a pure gift of God, who shows mercy and favor for Christ's sake.[102]

Justification means that we are accepted into grace on account of Christ's work. The conscious sinner knows that "in himself" he is not holy. He is called "holy," not by a holiness of his own, which is nonexistent, but by "an alien holiness, through Christ, by the holiness of free mercy."[103] "In Christ," the Christian is indeed righteous, yet not "formally righteous," according to "substance or quality."[104] He is righteous "in Christ," not "in himself."

> He is righteous according to his relation to something: namely, only in respect to divine grace and the free forgiveness of sins, which comes to those who acknowledge their sin and believe

101. LW 12.331.
102. LW 12.311.
103. LW 12.325.
104. LW 12.329.

that God is gracious and forgiving for Christ's sake, who was delivered for our sins (Rom. 4:25) and is believed in by us.[105]

Grace, this bosom, has appeared in Christ: "God sent His Son to reveal these abundant mercies to the world and to make known this teaching, which the human heart and reason do not know."[106] Take refuge in this bosom, lest we end up in despair. On account of grace, the dejected one cheers up and declares: "Though I am a sinner in myself, I am not a sinner in Christ, who has been made Righteousness (I Cor. 1:30). I am righteous and justified through Christ, the Righteous and the Justifier, who is and is called the Justifier because He belongs to sinners and was sent for sinners."[107]

Only by proclamation does the ear of the sinner "hear joy and gladness" and "the bones" that God has broken rejoice (v. 8). Luther says that both "the man of thought as well as the man of action" are in error.[108] Hearing or faith in the word puts an end to all justifying thinking and action.[109] Not in the worthiness of our work or by the mere performance of work (*ex opera operato*), but by the action of God's Word, or by the hearing of God's Word is the justifying reality established. He wrote:

> As far as we are concerned, the whole procedure in justification is passive. But when we are most holy, we want to be justified actively by our works. Here we ought to do nothing but this,

---

105. LW 12.329.
106. LW 12.325.
107. LW 12.311.
108. LW 12.369.
109. Oswald Bayer, *Living by Faith: Justification and Sanctification*, trans. H. Beveridge (Grand Rapids: Wm. B. Eerdmans, 2003), 25.

that we open our ears, as Psalm 45:10 tells us, and believe what is told us. Only this hearing is the hearing of gladness, and this is the only thing we do, through the Holy Spirit in the matter of justification.[110]

For the sixteenth-century reformer, justification is purely forensic, or declarative, that the word declared by God creates the identity of being God's children, a righteous people, as righteous as God's Son. This is at odds with many twentieth-century scholars, according to whom justification effects "a real change" in the sinner. Psalm 51 teaches that the effective declaration, not the effective transformation, is Luther's doctrine: we are justified only by the word and the hearing of it. Forde writes aptly: "The absolutely forensic character of justification renders it effective—justification actually kills and makes alive. It is, to be sure, 'not only' forensic but that is the case only because the more forensic it is, the more effective it is!"[111] God's word is "the death knell of the old and the harbinger of the absolutely new…. The unconditional word, the promise, the declaration of justification is that which makes new, that which puts the old to rest and grants newness of life."[112] Justification is no fiction. There is no "as if" in justification, but certainty: what the word says, it will surely occur.

The Remnants of Sin: the Holy Spirit and Human Agency

Though the power of sin is annihilated through free mercy,

---

110. LW 12.368.
111. Forde, *Justification by Faith*, 36. See also Bayer, *Living by Faith*, 42–57.
112. Ibid., 37–38.

there remains a true remnant of this poison. Therefore both assertions are true: "No Christian has sin"; and "Every Christian has sin."[113] Arising from this are two kinds of sin, one crushed by trust in mercy and the other that remains, which must still be destroyed or washed away. Justification is prior to sanctification; the former leads to the latter. "After we have attained this righteousness by faith," Luther writes, "then we need the bath or washing of which the psalm speaks."[114] Sin does not condemn us, for it has been swallowed up by an alien righteousness. "Yet because of this flesh, it still sprouts and struggles within our flesh to bring forth fruits like the old fruits, to make us smug, thankless, and ignorant of God, as we used to be. These are the efforts of the remnants of sin in us, which even the saints feel, but through the Holy Spirit they do not give in to them."[115] Conscience continues to accuse us. Neither can it pluck out the in-born "thorns": "I am a sinner, and God is righteous and angry at me the sinner"; nor can it lead us to the gracious and forgiving God.[116] "This is the gift of the Holy Spirit, not of our free will or strength."[117]

The saints feel and face constant battle with the remnants of sin, from which they want to be cleansed. When sin vexes us, we must wrap ourselves in this bosom: the free mercy of God that rules in us. By faith we cleave to "God the Promiser (who) turns the whole vision of our heart upon His mercy,"

113. LW 12.328.
114. LW 12.328.
115. LW 12.328.
116. LW 12.324.
117. LW 12.324.

as the remedy against the assault of sin.[118] It is smugness to think as though we are all spirit and without flesh. When mercy has freed us of guilt, there still is need of the gift of the Holy Spirit to wipe out the residual sins, or at least to enable us not to give in to sin and the lusts of the flesh. The justified saints must be aware of what the old creature of sin might do to us. They hinder us from loving God purely and trusting him fully, the way we could in spirit. By the Holy Spirit, we are, as Paul says in Romans 8:13, to "put to death the deeds of the body." Residual sins must be taken seriously; to minimize them is to "minimize Him who cleanses them and the gift of the cleansing—the Holy Spirit."[119] Without the Holy Spirit, whose task is to war against the flesh, the flesh that remains would naturally accomplish what it desires. This explains why David, after he has prayed for the forgiveness of sins and obtained God's mercy in which his heart rejoices, still pleads for what remains: "that he might be washed from his iniquities; that he might be granted the Holy Spirit, the power and gift that lives within the heart and cleanses the remnants of sin, which began to be buried through Baptism but have not been completely buried."[120]

Sanctification, a gift of the Holy Spirit, is that by which the old Adam is crucified with his passions and the new creature arises in new and holy obedience. New obedience, which necessarily follows justification, brings with it the daily growth of the new heart created by God. The Spirit sanctifies

118. LW 12.332.
119. LW 12.332.
120. LW 12.329.

us by battling against spiritual defilement, which includes the remnants of false opinions about God and against doubt; the Spirit also governs the actions of the body so that the flesh is mortified and the mind becomes accustomed to moral virtues. The church comprises those who proceed along their journey in the process of sanctification. The justified are not yet "unclothed" but are rather in the process of putting off the flesh. Luther wrote: "We are advancing and progressing in our sanctified life."[121] In this life, the church does not experience the fullness of the Spirit. Sin resides in the life of the justified but does not reign. Prayer in the Holy Spirit grants perseverance so that holiness may be produced in the justified saints.

Justification is no cause for passivity. Because of this new identity in Christ (Col. 3:1–3), we, on the one hand, seek the things that are above, as ones who are dead to the world; on the other hand, it is our labor to "cleanse ourselves from every defilement of body and spirit" (2 Cor. 7). In as much as we readily believe in Christ, we also belabor to keep this faith "fixed and sure and permanent" in our hearts.[122] Likewise, inasmuch as we believe in the sanctifying agency of the Holy Spirit, by which the remnants of sin are cleansed, we also assume daily cleansing as our own responsibility, a human work that is required of us in order that our newness in Christ might grow. Luther thus advises: "Let us take care to be washed daily; to become purer day by day, so that daily the new man may arise and the old man may be crushed,

121. LW 13.90.
122. LW 12.330.

not only for his death but also for our sanctification."[123] We are required to exercise our efforts to put to death the old creature, or else we indulge in sin. "It is as though all our members were working against the Law of God with their vices. Unless we oppose and fight this with great effort, there is danger that these vices will grow stronger and drag us back into our wickedness."[124] Sanctification, for Luther, is not understood in a way that excludes human agency. Luther elaborates:

> It also belongs to this exercise of Christians not only that God lets the church be oppressed by various troubles, but also He permits sects and heresies to arise so that the church might be exercised to keep the Word and faith and to clean out these remnants of sin. The Holy Spirit is given to believers in order to battle against the masks of wisdom in our hearts, which exalt themselves against the righteousness of God; and in order to arouse us to prayer and to the performance of the duties to humanity to all men, especially to the brethren, so that thus both mind and body might be exercised and we might become more holy day by day.[125]

The Christian continues to live in two realms, that of Christ and his righteousness and that of the old man of sin, which still clings to us. But these are not weighted equally, simply because God's grace reigns over us, not sin. Shepherd writes: "The old creature resides, but Christ alone presides."[126] Existing in grace is always greater than existing in the old

123. LW 12.330.
124. LW 12.329.
125. LW 12.330.
126. Victor Shepherd, *Interpreting Martin Luther. An Introduction to His Life and Thought* (Vancouver: Regent College, 2008), 149.

creature of sin. The remnants of sins continue to haunt us and work in us the opposite of justification, at which point we must cling to the new identity in Christ in accord with God's promise, by which the troubled hearts receive a firm and certain consolation. Though residual sins cling to us, they do not reign over us. Sin cannot condemn us or change God into a wrathful deity, and this is on account of the reign of God's grace and mercy over us. When sin assaults our conscience, Luther advises that we "simply turn our attention from sin and wrap ourselves in the bosom of God who is called Grace and Mercy, not doubting at all that He wants to show grace and mercy to miserable and afflicted sinners, just as He wants to show wrath and judgment to hardened sinners."[127]

The work we perform to crucify the old man does not merit or achieve justification, which is purely by grace. Even when there is a lack of evidence of our growth, or when our lives appear to contradict the truth we profess, we remain precisely the ones upon whom God wants to shower his mercy. Christ's alien righteousness is the sole ground of our standing before God, and no defilement of the old creature could nullify it. Our identity is forged in Christ, and nothing can undo it.

Satan and human reason work hard to have us do without the Word so that we trust in our own flesh or opinions, resulting in ungodliness. Due to residual sins, unbelief and smugness continue to abide in the believer's life, in which

127. LW 12.323.

case believers are never beyond law and gospel. They ought to be revealed and crushed by the law so that the true knowledge of God might increase. By "the bath of the Holy Spirit,"[128] not only are the indwelling sins of the old man driven out, but also newness in Christ, together with other gifts, like chastity, obedience, and patience, may grow daily. The bath or washing of sin is continual and thorough so that the new man might arise and become "stronger and surer against the terrors of the Law, till [he] finally become(s) master of the Law and of sin through *full confidence in Thy mercy*."[129] Having been crushed by the hammer of the law, his troubled conscience does not remain in or revert to the law but flees to the mercy of God. Thus Luther speaks of David's prayer for mercy "as though he were speaking against the whole Decalog."[130] Here Luther discovers in David "an art and a wisdom that is above the wisdom of the Decalog, a truly heavenly wisdom, which is neither taught by the Law nor imagined or understood by reason without the Holy Spirit."[131] In a situation when the sinner is tormented by the devil and driven by the law to despair of God's mercies, he must "completely set aside the whole Decalog" and apply to himself the heavenly wisdom of the gospel more abundantly so that "full confidence" in God's mercy might occur as the outcome. This is also borne out in Luther's letter to Jerome Weller where he writes: "When the devil attacks and

---

128. LW 12.331.
129. LW 12.331. Italics are mine.
130. LW 12.314.
131. LW 12.314.

torments us, we *must completely set aside the whole Decalogue.*"[132] However to set aside the whole Decalogue is not to deny it but to "make the most of the Gospel"[133] so that the afflicted heart might not be overcome by the terrors of the Law. In turmoils and trials, we must apply to ourselves mostly the free mercy of God against his wrath, for the former triumphs over the latter:

> Thus mercy is our whole life even until death; yet Christians yield obedience to the Law, but imperfect obedience because of the sin dwelling in us. For this reason let us learn to extend the word 'Have mercy' not only to our actual sins but to all the blessings of God as well: that we are righteous by the merit of another; that we have God as our Father; that God the Father loves sinners who feel their sins—in short, that all our life is by mercy because all our life is sin and cannot be set against the judgment and wrath of God.[134]

Reconciliation with God: Flee from the Hidden God to the Revealed God

Throughout his career until he died in 1546, the year he wrote his lectures on Genesis, Luther warned against any speculative incursion into the majesty of the naked God and led us to God as he hides himself in the incarnate Son. There Luther observes "this general rule: to avoid as much as

---

132. Theodore Tappert, ed., *Luther's Letters of Spiritual Counsels* (Philadelphia: Westminster Press, 1955), 86. Italics are mine.
133. See Lutheran Church—Missouri Synod, *Lutheran Service Book. Pastoral Care Companion* (St. Louis: Concordia Publishing House, 2007), 307. Note the section, "Guilt and Shame," where it is stated: "For the Christian who is driven by the Law to despair of the mercies of God in Christ Jesus, the pastor 'must set aside the whole Decalogue aside' (Luther's) and make the most of the Gospel."
134. LW 12.321.

possible any questions that carry us to the throne of the Supreme Majesty. It is better and safer to stay at the manger of Christ the man. For there is a great danger in involving oneself in the mazes of the Divine Being."[135] This understanding was already furnished in Luther's christological interpretation of Ps. 51:1: "Have mercy on me, O God, according to Thy steadfast love; according to Thy abundant mercy blot out my transgressions," where he declares that the "absolute God" (or "naked God") and the human creatures are "the bitterest of enemies."

> From this absolute God everyone should flee who does not want to perish. ... Human weakness cannot help being crushed by such majesty.... We must take hold of this God, not naked but clothed and revealed in His Word; otherwise despair crushes us. ... The absolute God ... is like an iron wall, against which we cannot bump without destroying ourselves. Therefore Satan is busy day and night, making us run to the naked God, so that we forget His promises and blessings, shown in Christ and think about God and the judgment of God. When this happens, we perish utterly and fall into despair.[136]

The distinction between the hidden God and the revealed God does not entail two deities but one, for the hidden God is the revealed God. This is borne out in his lectures on

135. LW 2.45 (WA 42.194–95).
136. LW 12.312. For a study of hiddenness as a predicate of God, see Marc Lienhard, Luther: *Witness to Jesus Christ*, trans. Edwin H. Robertson (Minneapolis: Augsburg Publishing House, 1982), 255–58; Brian A. Gerrish, "'To the Unknown God': Luther and Calvin on the Hiddenness of God," *Journal of Religion* 53 (1973): 263–92; David C. Steinmetz, "Luther and the Hidden God," in *Luther in Context*, 2nd edition (Grand Rapids: Baker Academic, 2002), 23–31; Hans-Martin Barth, "Breakthrough: From the Hidden to the Revealed God," in *The Theology of Martin Luther. A Critical Assessment*, 101–34; Steven Paulson, "Luther on the Hidden God," *Word & World* X1X: 4 (Fall 1999): 363–37.

Genesis, where Luther has God say: "From an unrevealed God I will become a revealed God. Nevertheless I will remain the same God."[137] Immediately after affirming the identity of the hidden God and the revealed God, Luther continues by having God say:

> "I will be made flesh, or send my Son. He shall die for your sins and shall rise again from the dead.... Behold, this is My Son; listen to Him (cf. Matt. 17:5). Look at Him as He lies in the manger and on the lap of His mother, as He hangs on the cross. Observe what He does and what He says. Therefore you surely take hold of Me."[138]

Luther expressly affirms that in His Word, the one God has lifted his veil, taking a step out of his absolute concealment. He insists that God, who is hidden in his naked majesty and nature, does not concern us because God has come in the person of Jesus Christ and therefore has been revealed. The naked God does not concern us because clothed in his word, he is offered, worshiped, and proclaimed and therefore is accessible. God's essence is accessible insofar as God defines his hiddenness precisely in his self-revelation in Jesus' crucifixion and resurrection. The undefined God—the hidden God—has defined himself freely in his Word as the revealed God. God in his own life corresponds to Christ come and crucified. God really is what he claims to be, according to which the absolute hiddenness of God cannot be spoken of as a hiddenness that possibly contradicts the revelation of God. Jüngel writes: "Briefly, the differentiation between

137. LW 5.45 (WA 43.459).
138. LW 5.45 (WA 43.459).

God and God cannot be understood as a contradiction in God."[139] Henceforth Luther summons theology to stay with God's self-revelation in the incarnate and crucified Christ, with God's precise hiddenness in the humanity of Christ.

Although the Reformer's emphasis is on God as revealed, he never abandoned the doctrine of God as hidden and the paradoxical doctrine of God who smites in order to enliven.[140] Integral to Luther's theology is the revelation of anything but salvation—that is, God's impassible and inscrutable wrath, before which we are terrified. Yet reflection on this God must not be done apart from Christ, the revealed God. For Luther, the negative aspects of the hidden God and the law are not identical. The hidden God truly condemns the sinner to hell as the sinner's ultimate end, whereas the Law sends the sinner to hell as its alien work in order that he might be raised up as the proper work of the gospel. The distinction between God as hidden and as revealed parallels the distinction between the law and the gospel, however, only insofar that the hidden God condemns so that we might cleave to God as he is revealed in mercy. The annihilating knowledge of the hidden God is causally useful if it causes the sinner to flee from its inscrutable terror into the immeasurable grace of God as revealed in Christ. Like the Law, the hiddenness of God functions as an alien work by which God keeps us from self-justification through thought and action.[141] Not until we

139. Eberhard Jüngel, *God as the Mystery of the World. On the Foundation of the Theology of the Crucified God in between Theism and Atheism*, translated by Darrell L. Gruder (Grand Rapids: Wm. B. Eerdmans, 1983), 346.
140. See my discussion on God as Hidden and Revealed in *Luther as a Spiritual Adviser*, 79–80.

reach the point of utter despair under the hidden God are we prepared to receive God's grace under the revealed God.

David is not speaking with God as he is in his naked majesty, "the absolute God," but "God as He is dressed and clothed in His Word and promises, so that from the name 'God' we cannot exclude Christ, whom God promised to Adam and the other patriarchs."[142] The distinction between the hidden and revealed God evinces for Luther a paradox in virtue of which, even in God's human hiddenness, God remains the divinely unsearchable and unapproachable majesty in whose presence David would be annihilated if he does not take refuge in the love of God that has appeared in Christ. As said earlier, the distinction between God hidden and God revealed does not mean two deities or contradiction in God. Both as the hidden deity and as the revealed deity, the one God directs us away from God as he is in himself when we seek to grasp him above his human life, cross, and resurrection, toward God as he defines himself in the incarnate Word.

Luther's distinction between the hidden and revealed God constitutes a "battle" between them: "God not preached devours sinners without regret, but the preached God battles to snatch us away from sin and death." Based on his analysis

---

141. William C. Placher, *The Domestication of Transcendence. How Modern Theology about God Went Wrong* (Louisville: Westminster John Knox Press, 1996), 49, where he qualifies his analysis with a verb "seems": "Here the hiddenness of God seems to function … as an alien work by which God keeps us from trying to justifying ourselves through reason and work."

142. LW 12.312.

of *Luther's Bondage of the Will*, Forde writes of this veritable battle:

> It is God against God. The abstract God cannot be removed but must be dethroned, overcome, "for you" in concrete actuality. The clothed God must conquer the naked God for you in the living present. Faith is precisely the ever-renewed flight from God to God: from naked God to the God-clothed and revealed. Luther insists that we cling to the God at his mother's breasts, and the God who hung on the cross and was raised from the tomb in the face of the dangerous attack launched from the side of the hidden God.... There is just no other way. The question at stake is whether one can believe God in the face of God.[143]

What to do with the terror of the naked or hidden God? Nothing, except by fleeing to the revealed God, as David did in this Psalm: "From this absolute God everyone should flee who does not want to perish." By "flight," it is, says Gerrish, "not repose, but movement."[144] The forbidden image of the hidden God "determines (in some measure) the content of faith, which has the character of turning away from the hidden God"[145] to the revealed God. We are invited, in Luther's words, "to flee from and find refuge in God against God" (*ad deum contra deum confungere*).[146] Under the experience of temptation (*Anfechtung*) before the hidden God,

143. Gerhard O. Forde, *Theology is for Proclamation* (Minneapolis: Fortress Press, 1988), 22. See also his "Reconciliation with God," in *Christian Dogmatics*, 2 volumes, ed. Carl E. Braaten and Robert Jenson (Minneapolis: Fortress Press, 1984), vol. 2: 22. Forde's analysis is based on Luther's *Bondage of the Will*, where Luther discussed the distinction between God hidden and God revealed, between God not preached and God preached.

144. Gerrish, "'To an Unknown God'," 291.

145. Ibid.

146. WA 5.204, 26ff as quoted in Westhelle, *The Scandalous God*, 56–57.

the believer moves from the hidden God to the revealed God, which underlies hope against hope. This movement coincides with God's activity in his opposite, that God reaches us not in his naked God but in his opposite, the clothed God, not in his majestic power but in abject weakness, not in glory but in humility. In that movement, enmity with God is abolished, that God ceases to be against us, but reconciliation with God occurs, that God begins to be for us. The haunting specter of the terrifying hidden God is revealed but more crucially conquered in the gospel for those who believe. As Forde puts it, "The fact that the terror of the absolute God reigns until the proclamation that creates faith announces its end and liberates believers from it."[147] He puts it differently: "The only solution to the problem of the absolute is absolution."[148] It is God who in hiding himself in Christ absolves his absolute hiddenness. It is only in Christ where God is revealed, that an enormous antinomy between God hidden and God revealed occurs and is finally resolved for those who believe. That which overcomes the absolute hiddenness of God is not faith itself but the revealed God, to whom faith clings. The incarnate/crucified Christ fights against the naked/hidden God to conquer the terror and inscrutability of the absolute God, and this is revealed to faith. Divine mercy has triumphed over divine wrath, but only for those who believe.

David's prayer enables him to live fruitfully, yet paradoxically, between on the one hand the radical hiddenness of God about whom he has nothing to do and on

147. Forde, *Theology is for Proclamation*, 29–30.
148. Forde, "Absolution: Systematic Considerations," in *The Preached God*, 152.

the other hand the specific hiddenness of God in Christ where the certainty of God's love is found. Having been crushed by the law, his terrorized conscience flees not to the naked God, before whom he perishes utterly, but to the mercy of God as revealed in Christ. David clings to the revealed Word painstakingly, where God hides himself as a witness of his steadfast love. The precise hiddenness of God in Christ, this "God as he is clothed and revealed in his promises and Word," is thus for Luther a predicate of the revelation of God's steadfast love. In Jenson's words: "(God) defines his hiddenness, and thus he makes it speakable, and speaks it, as the hiddenness of love."[149] When facing the terrifying and death-causing naked deity, we are to grasp "this God, not naked but clothed and revealed in His Word, otherwise certain despair will crush us."[150] For faith, the absolute hiddenness of wrath is truly absolved by the precise hiddenness of love, as Luther asserts: "As you believe, so it will happen." Faith lays hold of the crucified God who has conquered the absolute God for us in concrete actuality; unbelief, on the contrary, encounters the naked God before whom it faces total annihilation and damnation if it does not cleave to the clothed God of mercy. When one trusts God, as David did, the divine wrath is placated, "according to Christ's saying (Matt. 18:13), 'As you have believed, so be it done for you'."[151]

The theologian of glory and unbelievers tend to devise

149. Robert Jenson, *The Triune Identity* (Philadelphia: Fortress Press, 1992), 28.
150. LW 12.312.
151. LW 12.322.

their own ladders to God "outside His Word and promises,"[152] thereby bypassing the revealed God. To grasp the God beyond us (the hidden God) is to make oneself God's bitterest enemy. But to grasp God beyond or outside the revealed God is to elevate oneself above the revealed God, and in so doing, to make oneself God's enemy too, even of the revealed God. He who refuses to have the clothed God not only does not have the God of mercy in Christ but also encounters the inscrutable and impassible naked God who devours sinners without regret. Not only does the revealed God direct our gaze away from the hidden God of wrath but also directs us to his self-revelation in the man Jesus, where he awaits us as a friendly God.

The promises of God, though definitive in Christ, are not beyond dispute here on earth. The disputing of promise is more acute when confronted with the agony of life's harsh realities of pain and evil, in which one seriously doubts if a loving, merciful God is presiding over things. Luther writes in his lectures on Genesis: "Even after the promises which have been given, even after the covenant which has been most certainly concluded with us, [God] nevertheless allows us to perish as if he has forgotten his promises."[153] Luther admittedly was cognizant of the incompatibility between God's inscrutable hiddenness and his tangible promise but did not see the need to reconcile them. The dispute of promise is part of Luther's experience of temptation (*anfechtung*). It occupies a significant place in the Christian life on this side

152. LW 12.312.
153. LW 6.360.

of the grave, which makes better theologians out of us. "Theology does not gloss over the painful discrepancies between the promise of life ... and our daily experiences that contradict the promise. Rather, it resonates with the passion of the complaint, which echoes this discrepancy. Thus, theology is a theology of *Anfechtung*: it involves trial, testing, and spiritual attack."[154] The discrepancy between God's promise and its dispute is the cause of lamentation and complaint, the legitimate forms of human response to divine speech. Despite this discrepancy, Luther still believes in the goodness of God against the contrary appearances. The certainty of his faith lies with the incarnate God: "This God, clothed in such a kind appearance and, so to speak, in such a pleasant mask, that is to say, dressed in His promises—this God we can grasp and look at with joy and trust."[155] In the face of the utterly dark God, Luther can speak very confidently of who God is in light of his having spoken definitively in the clothed God. While the depth of God's immanent being remains hidden in himself, the depth of God's mercy is hidden in Christ. Rather than trying to comprehend God's hiddenness rationally, faith recognizes that it will always remain an ineffable mystery until the end.

The God to whom the afflicted David flees is not the absolute God, or "vague" God of the Turks, but "a sure God or a Promiser" of the prophets.[156] "He is a God *revealed*

154. Bayer, *Theology the Lutheran Way*, 95–96. For further discussion of the motif of promise in Bayer, see Matt Jenson, "Suffering the Promise of God: Engaging Oswald Bayer," *International Journal of Systematic Theology* 13, no. 2 (April, 2011): 134–53.
155. LW 12.312.
156. LW 12.352.

and, so to speak, *sealed*."[157] God has circumscribed "a certain place, Word, and signs" where we may seek him.[158] Whoever wants to find God must shun the majestic God and stay with the revealed God, not move beyond or outside him. The true theologian must grasp God in the way Scripture teaches us: starting therefore at the point where God himself starts, namely, in the Virgin's womb, in the manger, at his mother's breasts. Any attempt to execute the opposite movement, according to Luther, will either end in sheer despair or dash us against the terror of the true God's majesty. Not human accretions, but the revealed God, Christ and the merit he won for us on the cross, is the very ground of consolation of the wounded hearts and the basis of healing of despair. As long as we pry into the forbidden area of the absolute God, it leaves us with absolutely nothing, no joy but despair, no liberty but bondage, no consolation but terror, nowhere to go except hell. However, as long as we cling to the incarnate God where he is sealed, it leads us into joy, freedom, comfort, and confidence, as we soon find ourselves wrapped in his grace against the wrath of the absolute God. This is indeed David's experience, which culminates in the vow of praise.

Confession: Proclamation of God's Praise

Luther described the three gifts of the Holy Spirit in this sequence, beginning with justification through sanctification to confession. We have discussed the first two, so this section

---

157. LW 12.352. Italics are mine.
158. LW 12.352.

will focus on the third. The first gift is justification, in which we are already righteous, as confirmed in the word of grace, which guarantees the forgiveness of sins. The second is sanctification, by which the old Adam is mortified with his passions and the new creature is vivified with new and holy obedience.

The third is free and fearless confession, in which the justified person is emboldened to speak of his God not privately but publicly, despising the dangers that confront him. Not of free will but God's creation, our lips are opened and mouths loosed for the proclamation of the praise of God. The Holy Spirit is the causative agency of our confession. Here Luther also speaks of a sequence that begins with the conviction of the truth through the confession of it to cross-bearing as the outcome. The knowledge of the truth, fused with the Holy Spirit, brings with it an inward compulsion to dare to speak of what one has experienced. Those who are justified are compelled to say with David: "I believe, therefore have I spoken" (Ps. 116:10). Not only does the confession of the truth about God originate with an inward compulsion to undertake so great a thing as confession of the name of the Lord, but it also precipitates an outward cruciform life as the outcome of the faithful proclamation of the praise of God. Public confession is "the highest work," "the virtue of virtues," for there is no greater thing than confessing the name of the Lord. And yet it is "the hardest work," for there is no greater danger than this public undertaking.[159]

159. LW 12.394–95.

Whoever proclaims arduously the praise of God not only draws bitterest hatred but also open dangers. For no one confesses his name without having first accused and condemned the world with all its righteousness. To "announce the praise of the Lord" (v. 15) is to engage in a battle against these enemies—the devil, the world, the flesh, and all vices. Thus there is a humiliation that is basic to the task of public confession.

While the knowledge of God will quicken our speech, the world will quench it. There are various factors that hinder this confession. People close their lips, sometimes for fear of danger, sometimes for gain of security, and often due to the ill advice of friends. In these situations, David prays and sighs that he might not hear the suggestions of the Satan, or gratify the lust of the flesh, and that he might be confirmed by the Holy Spirit. Not that he does not have the Holy Spirit, or else he would not have prayed, "Take not Thy Holy Spirit from me" (v. 11), but rather he does not have the Spirit "perfectly or totally."[160] Thus he pleads that the Spirit might enable him to persevere when humiliated and preserve him for all dangers. By the Holy Spirit, whose princely presence in his life is his sustaining power and supporting consolation, he would not defect from what he boldly confesses. He will keep proclaiming and leave the outcome to God. He vows not only to announce the praise of God but also to instruct sinners in God's salvific ways so they might be converted to partake of the same benefits of the gospel (v. 13). As in the gospel

160. LW 12.387.

of Mark 7:36, those who are healed, though forbidden by Christ, could not help proclaiming God's blessings, praising his righteousness and persuading others of the same hope. The righteousness of God is a "pleasant" kind, for it is not a condemning but forgiving kind. It makes of God not an angry judge but a forgiving Father, who desires to use his righteousness not to judge but to justify and forgive sinners.[161] Neither past sins nor recollection of them could rob us of the joy of God's salvation. There is nothing left to do except to praise and give thanks to him. This we do not as though God is deficient, in need of completion, but purely out of sheer gratitude for God, acknowledging that all we have or can achieve we possess by God's blessings. We attribute praise and glory, which are rightly due to God, whose very being consists in nothing other than giving.

Pastoral Counsel on Pride and Despair

The sacrifice of a humbled and contrite heart is most pleasing to God (v. 17). "This theology," Luther insists, "must be learned in experience," without which the afflicted would not know that God is most favorably disposed to them when they feel most forsaken and distressed.[162] Luther was keenly aware that our frailties might cause us to swerve either to pride or despair. He advises that we aim at the middle between the two extremes, lest we turn the most pleasing sacrifice into "the highest abominations."[163] When we are carried away by

161. LW 12.392.
162. LW 12.406.
163. LW 12.407.

success that leads to pride, we moderate our smugness with the terrifying reality that God is most fearful to the arrogant unless they cast themselves beneath God's mercy amid the feeling of God's wrath and judgment. However, when we are crushed by failure, which results in despair, we moderate it with the assurance that God is most consoling to humbled and broken spirits. Both pride about our righteousness and despair about our unworthiness are equally grievous sins. However the latter, for Luther, is "the highest wickedness,"[164] for it robs God of his divinity, who is pure grace. It ultimately ends in total destruction, as it puts one outside the orbit of God's comfort. Luther's pastoral sensitivity comes through as he advises us not to add despair to "a dimly burning wick," nor permit Satan to bruise further a "bruised reed" (Isa. 42:3), but to cling to Jesus Christ, the physician of the wounded and friend of people, especially of crushed spirits. In tribulations, we must know that we are in grace, which enables us to bear our sorrows in faith without being smashed by them and lapsing into sheer despair.

When we feel smugness or despair, it pleases God that we battle against them, not give in to them. Even when we hardly manifest the first fruits of holiness, we become acceptable tithes and are regarded as holy through Jesus Christ, our mediator. This encourages the weak to press on, not deserting the sacrifice but completing it, as the Holy Spirit commends it. Walk in the fear of God when tempted

---

164. LW 12.407.

by presumption; stand firm in our trust in God's mercy when assaulted by despair.

Final Words

While "true theology" consists of nothing but God's promise that he is gracious toward those who acknowledge their sins, "false theology" claims that God is wrathful to miserable and afflicted sinners.[165] Sin, "a heavy, grievous and terrifying burden," cannot be lifted unless God intervenes.[166] Thus the whole of the Christian life is "to accept grace," to be grasped by "a God of favor and blessing, to be in the lap of God's mercy, and to have confidence in the sure promises that have been given us about the grace of God."[167] By the God who manifests his mercy Luther means none other than Christ, the revealed God whose promise faith lays hold of and whose mercy hearts that are ignited by the Holy Spirit turn upon. The only salvation lies in fleeing to the abundant and endless mercy of the God who hides in the incarnate Son, through whom the sinner is made partaker of the benefits of the gospel. Theology must leave the naked God alone and can only speak of the God who has spoken finally in the history of Christ. The mystery of the naked God calls for a cessation of speculation, but the mystery that is *revealed and sealed* in Christ calls for ceaseless contemplation, through which the terror of the inscrutable hiddenness is banished.

With respect to the justified life, the sinner is in agreement

165. LW 12.322.
166. LW 14.171.
167. LW 12.327.

with God's verdict and thus has justified God and accused himself. In Trinitarian terms, he has discovered himself, warped in his whole life or nature but wrapped in God's abundant mercies, all for the praise of the solely good God, whose promises of forgiveness find their yes in Christ, and in the testimony that the Spirit of God confirms in the Word and cements in his heart. That indeed is the victory of the gospel, which forms the condition of the possibility of doxology.

3

Psalm 77: Meditation on All God's Works: Reaping Justification by Faith as the Fruit

Commenting on the opening verses of Psalm 77, "With my voice I cried to the Lord; in the day of my trouble I sought the Lord; my soul refused to be comforted" (vv. 1–2), Luther interpreted "the day of my trouble" (v. 2) as a condition of remorse and total wretchedness like that of David (Ps. 51). The whole of the believer's life is likewise affliction toward sin in which lamentation is not baptized with praise so that its remorse is covered. While tormented by the knowledge of systemic wretchedness, the psalmist refused to be comforted by external and earthly consolations; instead he meditated at night, when he could think more clearly, because trouble caused him to "cry to God," the only help.

As is borne out in his commentary on Psalm 51, the project subject of theology is humanity guilty of sin and God the justifier and savior of sinners. Repentance comprises two elements: recognition of sin and fear of God, and recognition of grace and trust in God's mercy. To those who feel the intolerable wrath of God, God appears as merciful, not wrathful. Not to feel one's sin and God's wrath is a sign of arrogance and self-justification. The sacrifice that is pleasing to God is a lamenting and broken spirit. Psalms 6 and 51 show that Luther subordinates lament to penitential experience. He develops the penitential insights further in his exposition of this psalm, where he describes vividly "the characteristics, actions and reflections"[1] of a remorseful person. Meditation places him in the rhythm of repentance and faith that becomes the distinction of law and gospel. While meditating in remorse, he obtained the revelation of his sin and God's wrath under Law, which leads him to the revelation of God's fervor and mercy under Gospel. As a result of this revelation, the shift from lament to doxology occurs, causing the psalmist to move from inside himself to outside himself, or in Luther's words, "leaping out of wretchedness into the status of salvation."[2] The uniqueness of Luther's study of this psalm lies in how he craftily wove the Exodus account into the psalm interpretation to yield justification by faith as its proper fruit. To achieve this, he

1. LW 11.19 (WA 3.536).
2. LW 11.36 (WA 3.548).

applies the tropological sense of interpretation, focusing on God's power and not ours, on God's saving actions in us and faith as the actual manner in which we respond to Christ.

Introductory Comments on Psalm 77

Psalm 77 constituted one of the first series of lectures on the psalms Luther wrote during the period of 1513–15. An extended introductory section[3] to Psalm 77 was added only after the commentary on Psalm 77 had been completed and while he was already working on the exposition of Psalm 78. It includes the threefold works of God we are to meditate on, a systematic method of meditation, and the medieval fourfold hermeneutic (*Quadriga*): literal, tropological, allegorical, and anagogical, which Luther used as an exegetical aid to Scripture.[4]

Based on verse 12: "All Thy works," Luther sums up the threefold works of God:[5] first, the works of creation shown to all so that they might remember them, give thanks, and serve their Creator; second, providential care of God's people, namely, the Jews, so that they might remember the

3. LW 11.10 (WA 3.531).
4. Whether Luther defended the value of the *Quadriga* as the hermeneutic device throughout his career is beyond the scope of this chapter. For further discussions, see Marc Lienhard, *Luther: Witness to Jesus Christ*, trans. Edwin H. Robertson (Minneapolis: Augsburg Publishing House, 1982), 39–42; Alister E. McGrath, *The Intellectual Origins of the European Reformation* (Oxford: Basil Blackwell Inc., 1987), 153–54; 160–65; Lohse, *Martin Luther*, 101–2, where he argues that after the beginning of his lectures on the Psalms in 1518, Luther abandoned the medieval *quadriga* in favour of "an integrated philological and theological interpretation.... The reason of this change lay in the interrelationship between the letter and spirit. This new form of commentary eventually was universally applied—simply because it is more appropriate to the subject matter."
5. LW 11.10 (WA 3.531). See n. 1.

wonderful works and give thanks to God "because of the figure of things to come";[6] and third, the manifold works of Christ, "most particularly"[7] the spiritual works of redemption and justification, which are "the most wonderful"[8] works to be remembered only in Christ. In all three, we must remember not only the bountiful blessings God bestowed but also the curses he brought to the evil, so that we may obtain hope and love from the good things and fear and hatred of sin from the evils. All of these works are ordained for salvation; they are equally weighted as stimuli to serve God, and to shun evil. Luther fostered his position by a corollary:

> It is the mark of a perfect Christian to remember God in connection with any creature and its use. So the apostle exhorts that we should "give thanks in all circumstances" (I Thess. 5:18). Thus every Christian should certainly fear, hope, love, and hate in connection with every use of creature, for he should recognize that these are the works of God, who does good to him and admonishes him.[9]

Unlike the animals that relate to things by means of senses such as feeling, seeing, and hearing, the "thinking and spiritual person"[10] relates to the works of God by meditating. "Musing in the heart"[11] will bear fruit, if only it is rooted in "delight"[12] in that which the mind fixes. The efficacy of

---

6. LW 11.10 (WA 3.531).
7. LW 11.10 (WA 3.531).
8. LW 11.10 (WA 3.531).
9. LW 11.11 (WA 3.531).
10. LW 11.15 (WA 3.533).
11. LW 10.17 (WA 3.19).
12. LW 10.17 (WA 3.19).

meditation flows from reflecting on things he loves, in which his delight takes root.

"All Thy works" form not only the content but also the extent of the psalmist's meditation. In this, Luther captured the psalmist's intent: "so that there is nothing left of my righteousness, but I may be perfectly under Thee and obey Thee,"[13] Constant meditation on "all Thy works" and constant exercise (speaking, proclaiming, or doing) in them yields the gospel of justification by faith as the right fruit. In us there is nothing but feebleness and wretchedness; in God, there is nothing but strength and grace. The knowledge of the former under Law leads to the knowledge of the latter under Gospel. God corresponds to himself precisely in this mutually contradictory state of affairs: he brings low in order that he might lift up; he strips of all resources within us so that we cling to God alone. By faith, the godly can see the greater wonder of the truths and realities signified in God's mighty works of old and in the present.

Of the fourfold sense of traditional medieval hermeneutic, the literal christological sense is primary, on which the others are largely dependent. The tropological sense, which Luther used to interpret this psalm, evinces the knowledge of God as the only justifier of believers and by the same token causes believers to renounce their own justification and to confess their sins, trusting God's works rather than their own. Hence the contact between the self and God is not by means of any preexistent soteriological materials such as human resources

13. LW 11.27 (WA 3.542).

and outward righteousness, which are naught before God, but purely by God's grace, that is, by "the right hand of the Most High." It is noteworthy that Luther cited the formal, scholastic idea of *synteresis* (residual goodness) only once in Psalm 77.[14] The material principle of *synteresis*, that which disposes us to grace, does not permeate or govern Luther's exposition of this psalm.

Thinking vs. Meditating

Luther drew a distinction between thinking and meditating. Commenting on Psalm 1:2, "And on His law he meditates day and night," he wrote:

> Meditating is an exclusive trait of human beings, for even beasts appear to fancy and to think. Therefore the ability to meditate belongs to reason. There is a difference between meditating and thinking. To meditate is to think carefully, deeply, and diligently, and properly it means to muse in the heart. Hence to meditate is, as it were, to stir up in the inside, or to be moved in the innermost self. Therefore one who thinks inwardly and diligently asks, discusses, etc. Such a person meditates.[15]

Meditating is careful, deep, and diligent thinking, that musing in the heart that moves our innermost being into actions. That which separates us from the animals is the capacity to think and muse in the heart the things of God.

---

14. LW 11.15 (WA 3.533). Concerning the idea of *synteresis*, see also chapter one of this book.
15. LW 10.17 (WA 3.19). Cited in Curtis L. Thompson, "Interpreting God's Translucent World. Imagination, Possibility, and Eternity," in *Translucence. Religion, the Arts, and Imagination*, edited by Carol Gilbertson and Gregg Muilenburg (Minneapolis: Fortress Press, 2004), 12.

The "irrational creatures" (for example, mules or horses) perceive God through the senses and cannot understand the works of God; the "thinking and spiritual" persons remember and meditate on God's works and are capable of relating to them properly.[16] Luther wrote:

> Therefore the Holy Spirit exhorts us in Ps. 32:9 not to become like the horse and the mule, which have no understanding. For to make use of creatures only according to the body, and not through them to direct the heart and the mind toward God, is to perceive them only with the senses, like the horse and the mule. They can see them only as long as they are present. Thus these, too, forget the works of the Lord and do not remember them. To indicate this, the psalmist does not say "I will see," "I will hear," or "I will feel" God's works, which all irrational creatures do, but "I will remember and meditate," which only the thinking and spiritual person does.[17]

Delight: The Root of Meditation

Meditation, however, is rooted in delight in that upon which our gaze is fixed. It is efficacious only in so far as it works in conjunction with delight. Luther elaborates:

> But one does not meditate on the law of the Lord unless his delight was first fixed in it. For what we want and love, on that we reflect inwardly and diligently. But what we hate or despise we pass over lightly and do not desire deeply, diligently, or for long. Therefore let delight be first sent into the heart as the root, and then meditation will come of its own accord.[18]

The meditation of the ungodly does not take root, for they

16. LW 11.15 (WA 3.533).
17. LW 11.15 (WA 3.533).
18. LW 10.17 (WA 3.19).

do not incline their hearts to "the testimonies of the Lord" (Ps. 119:36). Instead they reflect on things they love, in which their delight takes root, such as gold or honor, vanities, and false or frenzied ideas about the Scriptures. "All of the following do not meditate on the Law, but outside the Law: the greedy, the carnal, and the arrogant. Or they meditate on glosses of the Law, or dross and hulls."[19]

Memory vs. Recollection

With Aristotle,[20] Luther also distinguishes between memory and recollection, referring the former to "the persistence of any power [to a memory in reality and one with love][21] in praise of God," and the latter to a temporary or momentary recollection of something, "this only once and with one stroke," without being moved in the heart.[22] To remember the works of God is not a bare contemplation of them with no impact; it is to engage with God's works with our whole being: "the intellect remembers when it keeps busy meditating on these things; the will remembers when it keeps on loving and praying; the hand remembers when it is constantly active."[23] Luther expanded:

> To remember … means always to thank Him in them, and
> thus through them to place one's hope in God, fear Him, love

19. LW 10.17 (WA 3.19–20).
20. Aristotle, *On Memory and Recollection* as cited in LW 11.11 (WA 3.531), n. 3.
21. LW 11.11 (WA 3.531). See n. 4, where it speaks of the parenthesis as a marginal addition. The parenthesis sharpens the distinction between the irrational creatures, devoid of understanding, and the rational beings, endowed with the power to retain the memory of the things that seize the hearts.
22. LW 11.11 (WA 3.531).
23. LW 11.11 (WA 3.531).

Him, seek Him, and to hate evil and flee sin. He who acts thus shows that he is truly remembering the works of God and not forgetting them. But he who does otherwise certainly shows that he has forgotten.[24]

Spiritual Discernment: Fourfold Systematic Procedure

Luther lamented that many souls, "melancholic, thick-skinned, of a very bad constitution, stolid and dull in their feelings,"[25] are not skilled in the art of meditating or remembering or speaking or being exercised but are capable of only feeling and seeing, like the irrational creatures. To teach us how to meditate, he draws on 11–12: "I remembered the works of the Lord, for I will be mindful of Thy wonders from the beginning. And I will meditate on all Thy works, and I will be employed in Thy inventions."[26] Here Luther prefers the Vulgate version, which has "I will be employed," to the Hebrew,[27] which has "I will speak." Luther underscores the important "four verbs, 'I remembered,' 'I will be mindful,' 'I will meditate,' 'I will be exercised.'"[28] He also counsels the reader to "observe the order": "Again, 'the works of the Lord.' 'Thy wonders,' 'all Thy works,' 'Thy inventions,' whether there is not something more in them than what has appeared and was said."[29] The four verbs constitute a four-step

---

24. LW 11.11–12 (WA 3.531).
25. LW 11.15 (WA 3.534.)
26. LW 11.11 (WA 3.531).
27. LW 11.11 (WA 3.531). See note 7, where it stated that Luther probably was not referring to the Hebrew text, but to Jerome's *Psalterium iuxta Hebraeos*, where *loquar* ["I will speak"] was used in lieu of the Vulgate's *exercedor* ["I will be employed"].
28. LW 11.15 (WA 3.534).
29. LW 11.15 (WA 3.534). Cited in Thompson, "Interpreting God's Translucent World. Imagination, Possibility, and Eternity," 12.

meditative disposition, or a systematic procedure for a proper discernment of one's apprehension of God. "Step by step devotion and instruction, understanding and love increase. Therefore these four parts can be applied one by one to any work of the Lord, whatever it might be."[30]

The first step is remembering, by which one sees the works, recalling the way in which the works of the Lord become transparent before the mind. "First, the heart remembers, acknowledges, and confesses His work to the Lord. And thus it appears that it is the work of the Lord, for the heart does not remember what the mind does not show. But when it does, the heart is touched and it remembers."[31]

The second step is to be mindful, to be so seized in the present by the wonders of God that "a greater flame of love"[32] emerges as the outcome. This knowledge is not open to the irrational; they cannot understand but can only feel it. Only the spiritual person may understand and remember the works of the Lord with profit, and say, "I will be mindful of Thy wonders from the beginning."

> Then the works will be regarded as amazing and wonderful, because their knowledge and clearer grasp increases. Indeed, the more profoundly a created thing is recognized, the more wonders are seen in it, namely, how full it is of God's wisdom. Hence the spiritual man sees in the same matter many things and the wonderful wisdom of God. The irrational, however, as the psalm points out, did not understand the works of the Lord; they only felt them. But from this knowledge there arises

30. LW 11.15–16 (WA 3.534).
31. LW 11.15–16 (WA 3.534).
32. LW 11.16 (WA 3.534).

a greater flame of love, so that the person wishes always to remember in this way and says, "I will be mindful of Thy wonders from the beginning."[33]

Step three is meditating, where the spiritual person moves beyond God's wonders in God's acts in the temporal realm to the conclusion that all works are wonderful. Given the correspondence between God's being and God's act, the spiritual person then "sees all things," on which he wishes to meditate diligently and wisely.

> From there he now turns the word toward the Lord, which he at first speaks only of "the works of the Lord" as in the third person, and then "of Thy [wonders]." For from the works the mind is lifted to a higher level toward God, so that now it may see God more than the works, as on the first step it had seen the works more than God. Then, on the third step, he has advanced still more and draws the conclusion that thus all works are wonderful, and he wishes to meditate on them in like manner, that is, remember them thoughtfully and wisely. But here the end has been achieved, since it is perfection. The first step begins, the second advances, and the third brings to perfection. For the first sees only the works of the Lord, the second sees that they are wonderful, and the third sees all things; for nothing remains beyond these. And to have been mindful is less, to be mindful is more, but to meditate is most.[34]

Luther's three steps of interpretation—remembering, being mindful, and meditating—are transcended by a fourth step, in which a person moves outside of himself to share with others so that they too might participate in his "translucent experience,"[35] that is, the experience of God's glory. Without

---

33. LW 11.16 (WA 3.534).
34. LW 11.16 (WA 3.535).

the fourth step, the discerning process is incomplete. "But the perfect man [Christian] is like this: Behold, he wants to be of benefit also to others, not have the talent just for himself. He says, 'I will be employed in Thy inventions,' that is, 'I will relate, I will speak to others in word and deed about Thy wonders, so that they, too, may know the works of the Lord.'"[36] There abides in discernment a movement from the works of God to the wonders of God to being inwardly moved or caught up with the experienced reality, which culminates in communal sharing of it.[37]

Fourfold Method: The Priority of the Tropological Sense

Luther also included in his introduction to Psalm 77 a fourfold interpretation of Scripture, which he inherited from traditional medieval exegesis:[38] first, literally, as done personally in Christ; second, tropologically, the same works in the soul against the flesh; third, allegorically, in the world

---

35. The term *translucent* was coined by Curtis Thompson. See his "Interpreting God's Translucent World. Imagination, Possibility, and Eternity," 15.

36. LW 11.16 (WA 3.535).

37. Thompson, "Interpreting God's Translucent World. Imagination, Possibility, and Eternity," 15: "Having remembered that a particular reality is part of God's creation, then wondering over God's presence within it, and then seeing it in relation to the whole endeavor of eternal freedom that interpenetrates the world of temporal realities, one indeed experiences God's glory shining through creation and is moved to communicate the results of one's meditation to others."

38. LW 11.12 (WA 3.531). Nicholas of Lyra taught four senses, but with an emphasis on the "literal" sense. The four senses is traceable to Clement of Alexandria, the Greek theologian of the second century as the origin. See Irena Backus, "Bible: Biblical Hermeneutics and Exegesis, in *The Oxford Encyclopedia of the Reformation*, 4 volumes, ed. Hans J. Hillerbrand (Oxford: Oxford University Press, 1996), I.153. For a historical study of traditional medieval exegesis, see Henri de Lubac, *Medieval Exegesis: Four Senses of Scripture*, 4 volumes (Grand Rapids: William B. Eerdmans, 1998–2000).

by saving some and condemning others; and fourth, anagogically, in heaven and hell.[39] Luther gave priority to the tropological interpretation of this Psalm: "[T]he tropological (moral) is the primary sense of Scripture, and, when this has been expressed, the allegorical (figurative) and anagogical (eschatological) and particular applications of contingent events follow easily and of their own accord."[40] "If Luther insists on the tropological sense," Lienhard rightly observes, "it is only in relation to the two others."[41] The tropological interpretation brings in the allegorical and anagogical sense, when the prophet speaks especially of the work of redemption and God's power. Accordingly "God's work and His strength is faith,"[42] that which makes people righteous and produces all virtues. Not by our own work or strength but solely by God's power and strength are we saved and strengthened. Faith crucifies and weakens the flesh, so that it cannot claim anything except cling to divine agency alone. "And when this happens, then all who do this become God's work and God's strength allegorically."[43] Just as the allegorical evil [the body of the devil] arises from the tropological evil [sin and unbelief], which leads to the anagogical evil [eternal judgment], so also the allegorical good [body of Christ] arises from the tropological good [faith and its works], which leads to the anagogical good [eternal life]. Luther elaborated:

---

39. LW 11.10–11 (WA 3.530–31). McGrath, *The Intellectual Origins of the European Reformation*, 152–54.
40. LW 11.12 (WA 3.532).
41. Lienhard, *Luther*, 41.
42. LW 11.12 (WA 3.532).
43. LW 11.12 (WA 3.532).

And so the church is God's work and strength. The world, however, is weak and worthless, and, as in the flesh, so also in the world there is no work of God, for the reason that it is separated from the church and the faithful people. But if they (the world) persevere in this, they will finally arrive at the final destiny of the evil and the eternal judgment, while the believers will arrive at the final destiny of the good. Thus the tropological evil is first, and from it arises the allegorical evil, which is the Babylonian body of the devil, born from the body of sin, because evil men cling to sin and unbelief. On the contrary, the tropological good is faith and its works, and from this by itself arises the allegorical good, that is, the body of Christ, namely those who cling to the Lord until the coming glory, the anagogical good.[44]

Luther also considers various ways in which the works of the Lord may be distinguished, each understood in its proper sense. The first division refers to all the visible works of creation, understood in the literal sense; the second comprises the works that Christ has done for us, and the whole new creation, the church, understood allegorically; the third refers to the moral works and the works of faith, understood tropologically; the fourth represents the works of the coming resurrection, understood anagogically. Here the first category takes precedence, for in the literal, the spiritual person can comprehend all the other three. Luther wrote: "And perhaps it is because of these four that this psalm says it four times: 'I remembered the works of the Lord, for I will be mindful of Thy wonders from the beginning. And I will meditate on all Thy works, and I will be employed in Thy inventions'" (vv. 11–12).[45] The first refers to the anagogical works of the

44. LW 11.13 (WA 3.532).

Lord; the second, to the literal; the third, to the allegorical; and the fourth, to the tropological. "In all these one must be employed, and they are the inventions and counsels of God for the purpose of providing our salvation."[46] "But if this is not acceptable,"[47] Luther granted, the entire verse 11 may be understood literally as referring to the work of creation and the miracles in Egypt, for both are worth remembering. Verse 12, however, speaks of the works Christ did in person, including those he taught us to do, for on these one must meditate constantly. Thus here Luther approves of still another fourfold division:[48] in the first, the psalmist calls the works of creation not miracles but simply "works," in which we cannot be employed; we can only remember them, since they are beyond our capacity. In the second, he understood the miracles done of old "miracles," not just works. Because they, too, are not in our power, they could be only remembered. The third refers to "all" the works of Christ, by which He has redeemed and regenerated us and built up our church. These are many works Christ did in person, which, likewise, are not yet in our power; therefore the psalmist says, "I will meditate on all Thy work." But in the fourth, "I will speak in Thy inventions," the psalmist refers to the works we are to tell and do, since they are in our power. Whereas the ungodly "will walk in their own inventions," as Ps. 81:2 tells us, the godly "will speak in Thy inventions." No matter how many divisions one may come up with, Luther said he had no

45. LW 11.14 (WA 3.533).
46. LW 11.14 (WA 3.533).
47. LW 11.14 (WA 3.533).
48. LW 11.14 (WA 3.533).

objection, so long as "the rule of faith [i.e., the Scripture] does not object."[49]

The Work of Creation: The Lord's Prayer and the Creed

In the introductory remarks on the first works, namely, the works of creation, Luther wrote: "All things were created as an aid to the mind and the heart of men."[50] Such understanding runs contrary to the Western culture, which, under the grip of the influence of ancient Greece, tends to differentiate the spiritual from the material and elevate the former above the latter. In contrast, Luther, thinking Hebraically, rejects this so-called platonic spiritualism. He teaches us how to meditate on God's creation or nature in a way that does not lead to the pantheistic collapse of the temporal-eternal distinction as the outcome. He affirms that differentiation occurs between God the Creator and his created order, not between the spiritual and material, since both belong to the created order, which is intrinsically good. God's creatures are instruments of divine power, through which God ministers to us, if only we allow God's wisdom or glory to "shine forth in them." Luther elaborates:

> Thus the great Creator has created all things in wisdom, so that they may minister in such countless functions and services not only to the body, which nevertheless, cannot grasp the wisdom in which they were created and which shines forth in them, but also to the soul, which can grasp the wisdom, as far as the mind and the heart are concerned.[51]

49. LW 11.14 (WA 3.533).
50. LW 11.15 (WA 3.533).
51. LW 11.15 (WA 3.533).

Luther links the first work of creation to the first part of the Lord's Prayer, "Our Father, who art in Heaven," and to the first article of faith: "I believe in God the Father Almighty, Creator of heaven and earth."[52] He lamented that we have not perfectly prayed the first part of the Lord's Prayer and the Creed, and as a result, few believe. For in every creature and its function, we failed to acknowledge, praise, fear, and love Him and receive instruction from Him, as our Father who bestows these gifts to us and the Creator from whom all these proceed. We are to make use of these creatures not only according to the body, which is what the irrational creatures do, but also through them to direct the heart and the mind toward God. Luther warned against relating to the works of God only with the senses, for it might lead to unbelief. Only a soul that engages confidently with God, like the audacious youths in the furnace (cf. Dan. 3:19f), triumphs over the contrary appearances and perceives God as their sole rescue, even when thrown into life's dreadful and painful crises. Here is an early hint of the development of Luther's theology of the cross, in which God is discernible under the appearance of the opposite. Luther elaborated:

> It must be especially noted that few believe them (the works of creation) to be the works of God. Indeed, if they believed it, they would act differently. Therefore no doubt the soul that is truly delicate and of a good constitution, altogether blood-red and of the most lively feeling, is the one that from everything and its function, through whatever sense it may be experienced, perceives God, elicits fear of God and reverence for Him; also

---

52. LW 11.16 (WA 3.535).

love and hope and devotion and affection toward God, as well as hatred of evil and sin. [Such were the souls of the three youths in the furnace, Dan.3:19f.][53]

God is to be experienced, not only with the senses but with meditative disposition toward Him, an exclusive trait of being God's creation. To reduce the experience of God to the senses only is to reduce us to the status of the animals. The irrational creature can see the works of God only as they are present; they forget and do not remember them, thus depriving the thing that is perceived of any saving efficacy. However the thinking and spiritual person (which we are as human beings) not only remembers the acts of God as they are present but also allows their wonders to become so effective in him that it causes a flame of love to rise for God, even amid the physical flame, which should have consumed Daniel and his three friends but did not. Not physical eyes but meditative faith can perceive God's wonder and wisdom hidden in places least expected (e.g., in a physical furnace). And the heart and mind, having been seized by the wonders in "all Thy works," are animated to love and fear God and to tell others so that they too might participate in the same.

The Rule of Righteousness: Confessing His Wonderful Works

It is "the rule of righteousness"[54] to confess to the Lord His wonderful works which he did in one's conversion. The

---

53. LW 11.14–15 (WA 3.533).
54. LW 11.37 (WA 3.548).

works of the Lord also include those acts God did in the prophets and in those praying this Psalm in conversion. Those whose lives have been changed cannot help but proclaim that this change in them has been effected by "the right hand of the Most High" (v. 10). Like the blessed Augustine did in his *Confessions*,[55] they constantly confess his works in thanksgiving. God commanded the children of Israel freed from Egyptian bondage always to remember the exodus account and the misery in which they had been so that they could speak of the efficacious works of the Most High. The same procedure also occurs in the gospel account where the Lord commanded the person liberated from the demon to go and proclaim what great things God had done for him (Lk. 8:39). Thus Luther claimed: "This psalm can be interpreted as first referring to the whole church and to the individual man tropologically."[56] Using the medieval fourfold senses, Luther substantiated his proposition in his comment of Ps. 77:1: "I cry aloud to God":

> So when this psalm is spoken in the person of the faithful synagog[57] [*sic*] or the primitive church, the church confesses

---

55. Saint Augustine, *Confessions,* ed. and trans. Henry Chadwick (Oxford: Oxford University Press, 1991). Luther quoted Book 8 of the *Confessions* as an example of meditation in remorse. See LW 11.17 (WA 3.536).

56. LW 11.37 (WA 3.548).

57. For Luther's use of medieval Old Testament exegesis as an elucidation of "the faithful synagogue," see James H. Preus, *From Shadow to Promise: Old Testament Interpretation from Augustine to Luther* (Cambridge, MA: Harvard University Press, 1974), 212–14; Scott Hendrix, *Ecclesia in Via: Ecclesiological Developments in the Medieval Psalms Exegesis and the Dictata Super Psalterium (1513–1515) of Martin* Luther (Leiden: E.J. Brill, 1974), 267–78; 278. Preus argued against the medieval "elitist" position of the faithful minority of the Old Testament. However for Hendrix, the faithful synagogue remains a small group that included the prophets and few who heeded the proclamation of the promise of Christ. See also Lee-Chen A. Tsai, "The

the works of the Lord Christ, by means of which He led it out of the spiritual Egypt, out of the rule of sin and world and devil. Hence the spiritual crucifixion and the plagues of Egypt in a moral sense are here beautifully depicted. First the moral Egypt must be stung and humbled and destroyed, and then, finally, follows the change of the right hand of the Most High. But if you seek abundance, behold, the whole psalm has what the book of Exodus has from the beginning [the liberation from the yoke of self-righteousness].[58] Therefore, the latter, like the former, can be explained in a fourfold way, literally, tropologically, allegorically, and anagogically.[59]

Just as the children of Israel in Egypt, oppressed by the yoke of hard slavery, lamented to the Lord for liberation, so also the sinner, oppressed by sins, suffering the assault of the devil and the world, cries inwardly with a voice of a burdened conscience to God for liberation. Such cries will never go unnoticed, as the Lord says in Matthew 11:28, "Come to Me, all who labor and are heavy-laden, and I will give you rest." So this psalm begins with an earnest lament for divine intervention: "With my voice I cried to the Lord" (v. 1).

God does his wonders in a person, by first humbling and afflicting him in order to effect remorse in him, in a rhythm

Development of Luther's Hermeneutics in His Commentaries on the Psalms," PhD dissertation (Aberdeen: University of Aberdeen, 1989), 178–84. Based on Ps. 119:84, Luther argued that the faithful synagogue includes godly people like Simeon and Anna who were waiting for the kingdom of God and the redemption of Israel at the time of Christ's birth. These faithful were the remnant of Israel, endowed with spiritual insights into the coming of Christ. They could be identified with the primitive church of the New Testament which was ready to become "the bride of Christ." See LW 11.474 (WA 4.357–48).

58. See Eric W. Gritsch, *Martin Luther's Anti-Semitism* (Grand Rapids: William B. Eerdmans, 2012), 49. The parenthesis [the liberation from the yoke of self-righteousness] is Gritsch's.

59. LW 11.17 (WA 3.535). Also quoted in Gritsch, *Martin Luther's Anti-Semitism*, 49.

of repentance and faith that becomes the distinction of law and gospel. Without remorse, meditation on the wonderful works of God on us does not bear fruit. "No one can worthily speak or hear any Scripture, unless he is touched in conformity with it, so that he feels inwardly what he hears and says outwardly and says, 'Ah, this is true'."[60] Luther resonated with the conversion of Augustine, who was so disturbed at the revelation of his sins that he did not utter a word. Luther made mention of Book 8 of *Confession*, where Augustine related his lament:

> From a hidden depth a profound self-examination had dredged up a heap of all my misery and set it 'in the sight of my heart' (Ps. 18:15). That precipitated a vast storm bearing a massive downpour of tears. To pour it all out with the accompanying groans, I got up from Alypius (solitude seemed to me more appropriate for the business of weeping), and I moved further away to ensure that even his presence put no inhibition upon me. He sensed that this was my condition at that moment.... So I stood up while in profound astonishment he remained where we were sitting. I threw myself down somehow under a certain fig tree, and let my tears flow freely. Rivers streamed from my eyes, a sacrifice acceptable to you (Ps. 50:19), and (though not in these words, yet in this sense) I repeatedly said to you: 'How long, O Lord? How long, Lord, will you to the uttermost? Do not be mindful of our old iniquities' (Ps. 6:4). For I felt my past to have a grip on me. It uttered wretched cries: 'How long, how long is it to be?' 'Tomorrow, tomorrow.' 'Why not now? Why not an end to my impure life in this very hour?'[61]

---

60. LW 11.37 (WA 3.549).
61. Augustine, *Confessions,* edited by Chadwick, Book 8.12, 28. Luther mentioned book 8, but he did not quote the above paragraph. See LW 11.37 (WA 3.549).

Meditation in Remorse

Using the ten plagues of Exodus as background, Luther suggested that verses 2 through 6 of this Psalm display the characteristic condition of the one "meditating in remorse."[62] He offered ten steps as follows:

Step 1: Crying to God in Silence

"[My] trouble" in verse 2: "In the day of my trouble I sought the Lord," expresses knowledge of the remorse and the total wretchedness of this life that the psalmist gained for himself in his meditation. This knowledge is wonderfully "salutary,"[63] causing him to forsake the earthly things and turn to God. Luther has the Hebrew rendering: "My hands is stretched forth in the night and is not silent."[64] As convenient as the night is for evil deeds to be done, so beneficial it is also for praying in remorse to occur; the former carnally, the latter spiritually.

Step 2: Relinquish All External Consolations

Verse 2 reads: "My soul refused to be comforted," which expresses the futility of all external consolations. Because the psalmist "remembered God and was delighted," he repudiated the prompting of the flesh. He is so disturbed and angry at the emptiness of the external consolations that he would rather find comfort in God. He forfeited all earthly consolations

---

62. LW 11.19 (WA 3.536).
63. LW 11.19 (WA 3.537).
64. LW 11.19 (WA 3.537).

and kept silence about the good things of the flesh but kept confessing God's wondrous deeds in him. Having tasted the spirit, all else becomes truly empty, bitter, and tasteless. This is illustrated by the water of pleasure in Exodus 7:17ff, which no one should taste, for it has been changed into blood and death for the soul.

Step 3: Inner Conflict (Anfechtung)

Verse 3: "I was exercised and my spirit swooned away" points to the inner conflict of the heart aroused by the memories and remnant of past sins, making the soul sick of pleasures. Sin is like the frogs (Exod. 8: 12ff) that gnaw the soul with their harsh croaking; like the gnats (Exod. 8:18) that sting and bite sharply without noise, prodding the conscience in remorse. A remorseful person truly feels the inner combat with the flesh and its lusts.

Step 4: Thoroughly Humbled

Verse 4: "My eyes awaited the night watches" means the putting out of "the evil light"[65] so that the gaze is no longer on the things that are of the world, or things that are in conformity with the devil. It is like the flies (Exod. 8:21ff) that prevent us from seeing the external things.[66] However Luther preferred the Hebrew version: "I prohibited the upward look of my eyes," that is, "I did not dare lift them up to heaven because of the knowledge of my vileness and

---

65. LW 11.18 (WA 3.536). The "evil light" refers to the devil's lure and eyes of the flesh.
66. LW 11.18 (WA 3.536).

unworthiness."[67] Having been thoroughly humbled, he also casts down the eyes of the flesh and moves about as a quiet person. The sign of the "most genuine remorse" is that he inclines his eyes in the spirit, unlike "the unprincipled and vagrant man (who) scatters his most shifty eyes in every direction."[68] The remorseful one becomes so insensitive toward the things of the world that he is no longer moved by them. For "God has given them the spirit of insensitivity, eyes that they should not see" (Rom. 11:8). He who is remorseful is also moved into action; he is thoroughly prepared for the works of the Lord and in this way anticipates the watches so that he might do them.

Step 5: Silence in Remorse Preferred

Verse 5: "I was troubled and I did not speak" describes an action of a remorseful person who loathes seeing, hearing, speaking, public spectacles, music, stories, or jokes; rather he cherishes silence, quiet, and praying because he is disturbed and enraged within himself by the revelation of his wretchedness. Luther qualified his silence with a gloss: "'I was loath to speak because of the bitterness of a remorseful heart,' in Hebrew, 'I was dumbfounded and did not speak,' that is, I would not let my own inclinations exalt themselves but kept thinking along humble lines."[69] One must observe the proper timing for speech or silence. In this instance, speaking in remorse might "permit concupiscence to offer suggestions

67. LW 11.20 (WA 3.537).
68. LW 11.20 (WA 3.537).
69. LW 11.21 (WA 3.538). See note 19 for the gloss and the explanation.

and intrude (reign) itself," thereby kindling divine wrath against the wordy, idle and the slothful.[70] Luther quoted Job 22:29, "He who lowers his eyes will be saved,"[71] to indicate that humility, sorrow, and lament are sacrifices found acceptable to God. Luther interpreted "I have been troubled" as, according to the Hebrew, "I was stunned."[72] Here the remorseful person becomes confounded and insensitive, when the old Adam is killed like cattle (Exod. 9:3ff), the tempting of the desire and its cravings ceases its power over him. Furthermore corresponding to "I did not speak" is the sixth plague, the boils and ulcers (Exod. 9:9ff), which inflict severe pain so that they "impose silence on all sins."[73] Just as the prompting of desire and its lust are annihilated, so also all desire to speak or think of sins is annihilated.

Step 6: Reflection on Death

Verse 5: "I thought upon the days of old," refers to meditation on death. Only a Jeduthun, "one who passes quickly over"[74] the river of earthly goods and the flow of this world can properly say these things: "I saw how everything that was has passed away, how time and everything (including the many deeds of the ancients) in it is nothing."[75] Since he has overcome the world, by means of despising the world and all

---

70. LW 11.21 (WA 3.538).
71. LW 11.21 (WA 3.538).
72. LW 11.21 (WA 3.538).
73. LW 11.18 (WA 3.536).
74. LW 11.21 (WA 3.538). Cf. LW 10.183 (WA 3.321). The term *Jeduthun* is a predicate of the one who has overcome the world.
75. LW 11.21 (WA 3.538).

that is in it, and by loving heavenly things, he is entitled to be a Jeduthun. Such meditation on the hard and tough reality of death and its impending judgment crushes everything that sprouts from the flesh, as the hail (Exod. 9:18ff) destroys everything green, or fresh from the ground.

Step 7: Terrified by Meditation as in Law

Verse 5: "I had in my mind the eternal years" refers to eternity with regard to the good as well as the evil. Above all, he urges us to contemplate the punishments of the wicked as lasting without end and the joys of the righteous equally without end. Reflection on them ought to cause the soul to be horrified and stunned, or else it is not genuine meditation. Thus the psalmist insisted: "I had in my mind," which means, "I kept" in my mind.[76] "He who is not horrified does not really think nor carefully ponder, but passes through them superficially and carelessly."[77] Unless his reflection is done carefully and scrupulously, it does not touch the heart. If he fixes his mind on it, he will feel the effects of the law, that he is terrified. He will feel this if he thoughtfully reflects on the fate of the wicked, the condemnation that they truly deserve. He does not keep it in mind, if his thought disappears with the sound of the words, as Ps. 9:6 says, "Their memory [actively and passively][78] has perished with the sound." He merely passes over the surface of the carnal heart, like a froth upon the face of the water (Hos. 10:7). Contrary to

---

76. LW 11.22 (WA 3.538).
77. LW 11.22 (WA 3.538).
78. LW 11.22 (WA 3.538). Parenthesis is Luther's.

this, the one who truly meditates will keep in mind the things that were heard and thought about and allow them to move him into actions, either to serve God or shun evil. This is borne out in his preceding psalm (Ps. 76:10): "The remainders of the thoughts will keep holiday for Thee." The word *remainders* means that which quickly disappears from the heart disappears altogether so that there is no memory of it.[79] But how will there be remainders, if they perish with the sound? Luther wrote:

> Consequently, since they caused the memory of the truth and of Christ to perish with the sound, also their memory justly perishes with the sound, and so it is true, both actively and passively, that their memory perishes with the sound. For as quickly as they forget Christ, He also forgets them. Indeed, to forget Him means that He allows them to forget the truth, just as to remember Him is to cause them to be mindful. For He remembers us, that is, He causes us to remember Him.[80]

"This, then, is the rule, that when we forget Him, He has forgotten us, since it is one and the same forgetting."[81] To forget God and his benefits is to break our trust in God, and thus is another form of doubt. The remorseful person trusts God and says in this psalm: "I remembered God" (v. 3), and latter: "I remembered the works of the Lord," and "I will be mindful" (v. 11). Luther held that our fathers did not understand because "they were not mindful of the multitudes of Thy mercies" (Ps. 106:7). That is, they neither reflect on

79. LW 11.22 (WA 3.538).
80. LW 11.22 (WA 3.538).
81. LW 11.22 (WA 3.539).

nor fix it in their hearts, and consequently they could not understand and be instructed. "Meditation is, indeed," Luther averred, "the supreme, most effective, and most succinct form of instruction."[82] It yields fruits, like water gushing out of the rock (Num. 20:11), and like the oil sucked out of the hardest stone (Deut. 20:11).

Step 8: Meditation in the Night

In verse 6: "I meditated in the night with my own heart," Luther further elaborated on how to meditate aright. Meditation does not bear fruit unless a person first fixes in his mind what he will do. Luther offered two examples to prove his point:

> When a smith or carpenter wants to function, he first gets a firm grip on the material on which he will work. He cannot work on something that is elusive, unstable, and mobile. The tools of the workman are the acts of the mind and heart, which cannot be put to work unless they have something fixed before them. To offer a clearer comparison: Behold, the builder cannot inwardly in his heart plan the shape of the house to be built, unless there be a firm decision about its shape.[83]

No one can build a stable house unless he first fixes his mind or sets his heart on which he will work. Luther warned against those possessed of a slippery heart, who in one instance speak endlessly on one thing and then another, hopping from one subject to another aimlessly. Such is the action of the delirious and those wounded in their heads, who

82. LW 11.23 (WA 3.539).
83. LW 11.23 (WA 3.540).

contemplate such things "with neither order nor agreement nor coherence."[84] Fruitful meditation occurs most fittingly in the night, both literally and spiritually. For it is at night, understood spiritually, that we forget everything external and are seized inwardly, that we do not consider nor see the visible things but set our mind on God. It is like being in darkness for three days (Exod. 10:21ff), where "nothing can be seen or done, so that, instead of the lust of the flesh and of the eyes and the pride of life, faith, hope, and charity, which those three would darken, might shine."[85] However the foolish soul or the carnal soul, at which the locusts (Ex. 10:4ff) gnaw, incessantly devouring its vigorous flesh, does the opposite, and thus says, "What do I have to do with the Bible and the Gospel? I know those things."[86] Against such presumption, Luther advised that we meditate on them by which the ticking of the flesh will cease. Meditation adorns the soul, like the blossomed valley in the garden of nuts (Song of Sol. 6:11).

Step 9: A Soliloquy of the Soul

Verse 6: "With my own heart I was exercised [I spoke],"[87] refers to a soliloquy of the soul, speaking to himself about that which seizes him (God's mercy)—as Psalm 4:4 says, "the things you say in your heart." The psalmist argued within himself about his identity: past ["who he was"], present ["who

84. LW 11.23 (WA 3.540).
85. LW 11.18 (WA 3.536).
86. LW 11.18 (WA 3.536).
87. LW 11.24 (WA 3.540). See note 24 where the Hebrew has "I spoke."

he is"] and future ["who he will be"],[88] in light of God's mercy that has seized him. The soliloquy is just efficacious as public preaching, although they are not weighted equally. As Luther put it: "It is a soliloquy of a soul, where it exercises itself with hierarchical acts, which happen very abundantly and wonderfully. For whatever the office of preaching does for people (creating faith in the hearer) this speaking with the heart does for the soul (effecting repentance)."[89]

Step 10: Cleansing the Spirit

Verse 6, "And I swept my spirit," refers to the act of cleansing by sweeping, as in Luke 11:25. This occurs as a result of chastisement, reproof, and remorse, as the next statement in Psalm 4:4 shows: "And be sorry upon your beds." This is something the carnal soul cannot do, except the faithful Asaph.

As divine judgment, God struck down Pharaoh with the tenth plague, the death of the firstborn (Exod. 12:29ff). This terrifying act of God causes the psalmist to say, "And I searched my spirit" (v. 6), and to consider what might happen to him, if he were completely beyond the merciful act of God. The next section will bear this out.

Meditation via Negativa: The Opposite of Justification

Verse 7, "Will God cast off forever?" speaks of the ways in which the psalmist meditated with his own heart in a negative

88. LW 11.24 (WA 3:540).
89. LW 11.24 (WA 3.540).

way (*via negativa*). It may be interpreted in more than one way. First, meditation on the opposite of justification, namely, on the seriousness of his wretchedness, worthy of wrath and judgment. The psalmist places himself under the law, through which he came to the knowledge of his sinfulness. Such revelation terrorizes the conscience in the remorseful person, causing him to lament to God for help. To indicate this, Luther quoted Isaiah: "From thy fear we have conceived the spirit of salvation" (cf. Isa. 26:16–18). This is a word of one, who upon experiencing the negatives (despair and hell), cries, "Will God cast off forever?" Will I be found worthy of wrath and damnation, as in the plagues? Or will I be found in the grip of the right hand of God, though there are many sins in me that deserve nothing but damnation?

Second, this could be a word of amazement expressed negatively by the one to whom something grand is done. When that occurs, he is so struck with wonder as if it were incredible, and thus he bursts out, "Is that so?" This interpretation seems to coincide with the preceding.

Third, verse 7 could be taken as the psalmist's plea on behalf of his people who are about to perish eternally. The psalmist indulged in his heart the dreadful outcome of the opposite—that is, being found outside the realm of God's grace. Meditation on the incalculable wrath and eternal and impending judgment of God upon his people stuns him: "Alas, for God will truly cast off forever, and yet that seems an unbelievable punishment!"[90] The aforementioned

90. LW 11.24 (WA 3.540).

115

interpretations are the meditations and statements of the one filled with remorse:

> He reflects on these things and ponders this eternal wretchedness in his own mind. And he said in his heart, "Will God cast off forever?" Because of the greatest[91] [sic] of the issue he seems, as it were, to doubt, which happens to those who think about this matter profoundly, so that they almost doubt whether it will be thus, because of the exceeding seriousness of the matter.... But when they attend to the fact that God has so ordered, they are violently terrified and horrified, and so they are filled with remorse.[92]

New Life as God's Work: Conversion by Grace and Fervor

Verse 10, "And I said: Now I have begun; this change is of the right hand of the Most High," speaks of the psalmist's remorse and conversion, the effects of a consideration of the exceeding seriousness of the matter: the terror of eternal wretchedness and God's wrath against sin, as taught in verse 7. He has begun new life, not by his own powers but because this change is of the grace and fervor of God.[93] Not to be moved by meditating on such things is to be foolish and senseless. "Yet if he is moved, he is changed not of himself, but of God."[94] As a contrast to "the right hand of the Most High," Luther referred to the Hebrew text which has "And I said: 'It is my feebleness'."[95] The psalmist confesses himself to be weak and powerless to effect transformation into a

91. LW 11.24 (WA 3.540). The word *greatest* means importance.
92. LW 11.24 (WA 3.540).
93. LW 11.25 (WA 3.540).
94. LW 11.25 (WA 3.540).
95. LW 11.25 (WA 3.540).

different life. "This change, by which I have changed myself,"
Luther had the psalmist say, "is not mine, for out of remorse,
it is my understanding that feebleness is mine. That is, see that
nothing is mine except my wretchedness and weaknesses."[96]
The one who has begun new life does nothing but proclaims
that this has been done in him. Hence salvation is not of his
own but of God alone. Luther quoted Hosea 13:9, "Therefore
destruction is yours, O Israel. From Me only is your help."

This Psalm teaches us how to think of ourselves aright
in order to be seized by the right hand of the Most High.
Through meditation, the psalmist arrived at a true knowledge
of himself, that he owned nothing except feebleness and
wretchedness. Consequently he incurred nothing except
God's wrath and damnation, his just deserts. His growing
recognition of the horror of his sinfulness and terror of God's
wrath would have enabled Luther to break with the scholastic
idea of *synteresis* (residual goodness) as the condition for the
effectiveness of grace, although at this point of his career,
he did not formally dismiss it. However what is obviously
taught in this Psalm is not the material principle of *synteresis*,
that which disposes us to grace, but the material principle of
justification: it is all God's works, in which the psalmist says
he would meditate, and nothing of himself. Regeneration is
grounded solely in God's grace. "No one can begin the new
life, unless he repents of the old, unless he has burned in this
remorse."[97] Even the remorse is not of himself but wrought
by God. A proper consideration of this Psalm thus results in

96. LW 11.25 (WA 3.540).
97. LW 11.25 (WA 3.541).

confession: "Now I have begun," yet not of his own, but of God alone, his grace and fervor. Meditation acquaints us with a knowledge of who we are before God—feeble and wretched, by which we are terrorized as in law, in order that it might lead us to the knowledge of who God is towards us—his power and grace, by which we are comforted as in gospel.

The Theology of Humility: Content, Extent, and Intent of Meditation

Verse 12, "I will meditate on all Thy works," elucidates the content, extent, and intent of the psalmist's meditation. Not our works, but "Thy works" forms the content; "all" indicates the extent. Furthermore by "all Thy works," Luther described the psalmist's intent: "I will be at pains that all the works I meditate are Thine, so that there is nothing left of my righteousness, but I may be perfectly under Thee and obey Thee."[98] The work of God is so thoroughly efficacious and his righteousness is so complete in itself that nothing needs to be added unto it. The recognition that there is nothing worthy of merit in the psalmist works in him humility, so that he might be "perfectly under God," and obedience, so that he might willingly "obey Him" as a sign of humility. The proper meditation on "all Thy works" results in the radical annihilation of any human quality of holiness or virtues and thus harvests the gospel of justification as the outcome. It is by meditating on "all Thy works" that the psalmist comes

98. LW 11.27 (WA 3,542).

to see that he possesses "nothing," no righteousness of his own except God's, no works of his own but God's, and no resources of his own, including a natural inclination toward moral good, but the eternal wretchedness within himself, which renders him the very object of the opposite of justification unless he cries to God for aid. The knowledge of "the oppressive nearness of God's wrath" the psalmist reaps from meditation is salutary, as it leads him to the knowledge of "the healing nearness of God's grace."[99] This psalm illustrates that Luther was operating fundamentally with the theology of humility, which he inherited from the mystical tradition of Tauler.[100] Luther's reading of Tauler's sermons in early 1516[101] made a significant impact on him, directing him away from inside himself to outside himself, from self-righteousness to self-deprivation, from action to suffering as the proper preparation for the reception of God's mercy.

Humility is in no way a human achievement but a gift of God. We possess no "active capacity" to humble ourselves but only a "passive capacity," that we are humbled.[102] Thus we obtain grace by humbly accepting what is being done to us

---

99. Bernd Hamm, *The Early Luther: Stages in a Reformation Reorientation,* trans. Martin J. Lohrmann (Grand Rapids: William B. Eerdmans, 2014), 46. It is Hamm's conviction that justification by faith was already the harvest of Luther's first lectures on the Psalms (1513–15).

100. Steven Ozment, *Homo Spiritualis: A Comparative Study of the Anthropology of Johannes Tauler, Jean Gerson and Martin Luther (1509-1516) in the Context of Their Theological Thought* (Leiden: E. J. Brill, 1969), 27–34. See also Loewenich, *Luther's Theology of the Cross,* 152ff; Hamm, *The Early Luther,* 224ff, where he speaks of the structural affinities between Tauler and Luther.

101. See WA BR I:160, 8–14, no. 66, and WA 9.95–104 as cited in Hamm, *The Early Luther,* 225.

102. Forde, *On Being a Theologian of the Cross,* 9.

within the law-gospel distinction. Meditation thus performs both works, which he will later call the alien work of the law and the proper work of the gospel: both belong to the one God who kills in order to bring life. It takes us down so we might despair of our own righteousness before God and cling to the power of God.

To meditate on "all Thy works" is to abandon all our works and abase ourselves before God so that we expect nothing from ourselves but everything from God. This is in opposition to the proud and the self-righteous, who meditate on how they may establish their own works and edifice, teach their so-called wisdom, and proclaim their own inventions or ideas. "The proud and the heretics meditate on all their own works. Everything they handle and do is their own."[103] In so doing, they prate about the efficacy of their own works, and repudiate the efficacy of God's salvific works. They become puffed up; they have allowed the Old Adam to reign and are thus "snatched to despair and hell,"[104] from which there is no remedy except by God's aid. Unlike the proud, the saints relinquish their own works but "seek the inventions of God, that is, wisdom which He finds, according to Baruch (Baruch 3:26). These are the inventions of God, the wonderful counsels by which He has overcome the devil and captured the world, as He prefigured in the invention and plan by which He drowned Pharaoh."[105]

103. LW 11.27 (WA 3.542).
104. LW 11.24 (WA 3.540).
105. LW 11.27 (WA 3.542). Luther wrote: "because he recounts the ancient miracles in order to prophesy the new ones in them." What Luther meant is that both the old and new deeds are solely of God, monergistically rather than synergistically.

Verse 15, "Thou didst with Thy arm redeem Thy people, the sons of Jacob and Joseph," can be interpreted in both senses: literal and spiritual. Just as the wonderful works of God in ancient times occurred apart from human agency, so also all the wonderful works of God by which he redeems his people occur apart from it.[106] With this, the psalmist came to a deeper realization: "If the symbolic things were done by God, how much more the real and spiritual?"[107] Hence Luther not only spoke against the fools who exhibit indifference in the midst of God's wonders but also against the skeptics who wonder if believers are really in the midst of so many holy things in the present day. Since the nature of these miracles is spiritual, they are not heeded. Luther decried that few think of the works of the Lord, meditate on His wonders, and exercise themselves in all His works. Instead they are active in the works of the flesh, the world, and the devil. On the contrary, "the church promises in this psalm"[108] to exercise herself in "all Thy works," so that she might abstain from boasting and humbly confess to God. "Not to us, O Lord, and not to us, but to Thy name give glory, for They mercy and Thy truth's sake" (Ps. 115:1). Recounting the deeds of the Lord elicits in us thanksgiving for his works; it causes us through them to place our hope in God, fear him, love him, seek him, and to hate evil and flee sin.

Here Luther interjects his thoughts with the "remembrance"[109] of God's wonders in the Mass, a salvific

106. LW 11.29 (WA 3.544).
107. LW 11.30 (WA 3.544).
108. LW 11.29 (WA 3.544).
109. LW 11.29 (WA 3.544).

work of God that is of inestimable value to believers. In this Psalm Luther puts the emphasis on remembrance, not yet the words of promise. In the Mass, the believers see the wonders of God in a hidden way: the Most High has accommodated himself in his incarnate Son and become "most common"[110] like us, to meet us efficaciously in the visible elements. There "the right hand of God leads the saints wonderfully," as it enables them (the partakers) to receive "the invisible things" (forgiveness) or God's grace that has already appeared in Christ, and come under God's alien work of mortification:

> If only this one work of the Lord, the Mass, were performed, that would be exceedingly much, because it is the remembrance of God's wonders. Therefore conquering pride, restraining riotous living, crucifying the flesh, these are great beyond all the power of men. And they are wonderful indeed, because they take place for the sake of invisible things. And by what reason? Men do not know. The right hand of God leads the saints wonderfully (cf. Ps. 45:4). Therefore speaking about these things and meditating on them, these are the works of the Lord, as apostle says to Titus (Titus 2:11): "The grace of God has appeared, ... training us to renounce irreligion and worldly passions and to live sober, upright and godly lives in this world." Then follows (Titus 2:15): "Speak and exhort these things" in Christ.[111]

Luther was cautious of the order: the work of God is prior to our works; the righteousness of faith is prior to the works of faith; the former leads to the latter. We do not seek justification through works of our own but seek God and all

110. LW 10.346 (WA 3.407). This is taken from his commentary on Psalm 68:35, "God is wonderful in His Saints."
111. LW 11.29 (WA 3.544).

his ["Thy"] inventions. For it is not by the performance of good works that we are justified before God; precisely the opposite, it is by faith that God's works become wonderfully effective in us. Faith in God orients a meditative soul toward God and conquers the world, the devil, and the flesh. Our works contribute nothing to justification; they proceed from faith in Christ. "The right hand of God leads the saints wonderfully," by clearing the way for piety and good works. God does this by performing an alien work of crucifying the Old Adam and his worldly passions in order to achieve his proper work: the new person rises, to live a sober, upright, and godly life in this evil world. Put it in another way, meditative faith in God crushes the Old Adam and its evil passions and creates in a new person godliness and rectitude. Therefore the good works we do are not inherently ours but God's.

Be Employed in Thy Inventions: Do the Works of the Lord

The section regarding verse 11 reads: "I remembered the works of the Lord," the Hebrew has "the thoughts of the Lord," instead of "the works of the Lord" (v. 11). For Luther, they are basically the same. "For 'work' is taken instead of 'works that are thought'."[112] The works God performs openly are a manifestation of his thought. To show that "work reveals the thought," Luther quoted Psalm 40:5: "In Thy thoughts there is no one who is like Thee."[113] What God does corresponds to what he has in mind, his thought.

112. LW 11.26 (WA 3.541).
113. LW 11.26 (WA 3.541).

123

In meditation, the psalmist firmly fixes God's works before himself in his heart, that he might do them. The one who has been terrorized and changed by God is now drawn in the works of God, which he purposes to do. "As for the remorseful man and one who has now been changed because of the terror of eternal wretchedness, what should he do except purpose to do the works of God?"[114] Luther stressed that the works here are best taken in a moral sense (tropological), namely, the works done "prophetically (spiritually) or in spirit" are those we should do in accordance with God's will, such as "the righteousness of God"[115] or "the way of God."[116] Quoting favorably Isaiah 5:12, "The harp and the lyre are in your hands, and you do not regard the works of the Lord, nor do you consider the works of the His hands," Luther divided the works of the Lord in a slightly different way than the regular threefold works of God in the introductory section:

> The works of God are the moral works of faith.
> But in particular the work of God is Christ in His entire life.
> The work of His hands are the saints and the church of Christ.[117]

114. LW 11.26 (WA 3.541).
115. Based specifically on Psalm 72, in LW 10.408 (WA 3.466-67), McGrath points out that some scholars including Erich Vogelsang, have argued that Luther's evangelical breakthrough came as a result of his recognition of the tropological meaning of the phrase "the righteousness of God" (*iustitia Dei*), which is interpreted as "faith in Christ" (*fides Christi*)." See Erich Vogelsang, *Die anfänge von Luthers Christologie: nach der ersten Psalmenvorlesung, insbesondere in ihren exegetischen und systematischen zusammenhängen mit Augustin und der scholastik dargestellt* (Berlin: W. de. Gruyter, 1929). For McGrath's critique of this view, see McGrath, *Luther's Theology of the Cross*, 119–28. McGrath argues that Luther, at this point, "merely clarifies [rather than alters] his existing views."
116. LW 11.26 (WA 3.541).

The tropological good Luther defines as faith. He interprets the concept as God's works rather our works. Thus he treats phrases such as "the righteousness of God" (*iustitia Dei*) or "the judgment of God" (*iudicium Dei)* tropologically not in terms of what God demands of us but what God does for us. He identified three arenas in which God's works occur: in Christ, in the church, and in the individual believer. There abides in this Psalm a close and causal connection between the frequently repeated assertion that power lies with God and the central message of Scripture as God's act.

Tropologically, we ought to do the works of God in accordance with God's will, by having regard for the works of God; we should consider the works of His hands, namely, the virtues of the pious ones and the examples of the fathers. We are to exercise ourselves in them, thereby manifesting the mark of a perfect Christian. However to constantly meditate on these works, in which we must continually exercise ourselves, is to acknowledge and proclaim God as the efficient cause of them. Of the saying, "For I will be mindful of Thy wonders from the beginning" (v. 11), Luther paraphrased: "of Thy works from the ancient past, which Thou didst perform in the ancient fathers."[118] It is all God's work, not theirs, that accomplished these things, as Psalm 44:1–3 wrote: "Our fathers have declared the work Thou hast wrought in their days." And then immediately it says: "And they did not get possession of the land by their own sword."

Verse 13, "Thy way, O God, is in the holy place," further

117. LW 11.27 (WA 3.542).
118. LW 11.26 (WA 3.541).

accentuates how one should be mindful of the ways or works of the Lord. The meaning of this verse consists in this: since all is God's causality, we ought to abandon our own labor, but learn to do [proclaim, teach, or be active] the works of the Lord. Neither can we work with "our own resources" nor "our own righteousness," for they are naught in His sight.[119] The prophet perceives in all the works of the fathers that God indeed was working with them, not they themselves. Unless God performs these works in them, they are not the works of God. The repeated emphasis on "Thy work" means we are the passive recipients of God's work he performs in us rather than the causative agency of his works.

Letter-Spirit Model: Law and Gospel Distinction

For the reformer, the antithesis between the inefficacious works of outward righteousness and the effectual works of God, between our works and God's, is the antithesis between "the letter that kills and the spirit that makes alive" (2 Cor. 3:6).[120] In the *Preface to the Glosses* to his first lectures on Psalms, Luther formulated the principle of interpretation: "In the holy scriptures it is best to distinguish between the spirit and the letter; for it is this that makes a true theologian."[121]

---

119. LW 11.26 (WA 3.541).
120. LW 11.26 (WA 3.542); See Gerhard Ebeling, *Luther: An Introduction to His Thoughts*, translated by R. A. Wilson (Philadelphia: Fortress Press, 1970), 93–109, for a discussion of the between the letter and the Spirit in Luther.
121. LW 11.4 (WA 3.11). Lohse, *Martin Luther's Theology*, 52–53. Luther's distinction between "letter" and "spirit," Lohse argues, paves the way for a differentiation between our relation to the world (*coram mundo*) and to God (*coram deo*). This is contrary to Luther's dialectical understanding of the gospel: law that kills and the gospel that makes alive, the former serves the latter.

For Augustine, "the letter of the law which teaches us not to commit sin, kills, if the life-giving spirit be absent, forasmuch as it causes sin to be known rather than avoided, and therefore to be increased rather than diminished, because to an evil concupiscence there is now added to the transgression of the law."[122] Luther tied the distinction between the letter and the spirit to the distinction of law as God's demanding plan for human life and performance and gospel as God's salvific activity in Christ. This is evident as early as his commentary on Psalm 45:1:

> Again, "to utter" can also signify by another mystery that it declares the spirit from the letter. The spirit is concealed in the letter, which is a word that is not good, because it is a law of wrath. But the spirit is a good word, because it is a word of grace. Therefore to draw this out of the letter is to utter the spirit itself.[123]

One and the same word can be "letter," thus God's judgment; however when spiritually understood, it can also be a word of grace, since the spirit is hidden in the letter. Following Nicholas of Lyra,[124] each element of the traditional fourfold device could be either the killing letter or life-giving spirit.[125]

---

122. Saint Augustin, "A Treatise on the Spirit and the Letter," in *Nicene and Post-Nicene Fathers Volume 5: Augustin: Anti-Pelagian Writings*, ed. Philip Schaff, trans. Peter Holmes and Robert Ernest Wallis (Grand Rapids: William B. Eerdmans, 1956), v. 8, 86. See McGrath, *The Intellectual Origins of the European Reformation*, 157; See also Randall C. Gleason, "The 'Spirit' and 'Letter' in Luther's Hermeneutics," *Bibliotheca Sacra* 157, n. 628 (Oct.,–Dec., 2000): 478.

123. LW 10.212–13 (WA 3.256) as cited in Mark D. Thompson, "Biblical Interpretation in the Works of Martin Luther," in *A History of Biblical Interpretation.*, vol. 2. *The Medieval through the Reformation Periods*, edited by Alan J. Hauser and Duane F. Watson (Grand Rapids: William B. Eerdmans, 2003), 309.

124. Thompson, "Biblical Interpretation in the Works of Martin Luther," 307.

With this, Luther applied the letter-spirit model to the tropological hermeneutic: it compels the psalmist to face his own nothingness before God except wretchedness and wrath, as in law; it causes him to hear the gospel, that he is at the grip of God's grace and fervor, the opposite of wrath and damnation.

The Cross as God's Revelation: More Wonderful than Theological Virtues

The doubling causes in verse 16, "The waters saw Thee, O God, the waters saw Thee," furnishes a spiritual sense signified by the waters. Luther supported this understanding by several factors: first, by a marginal addition: "[For he says "they saw." Ps. 68:24 reads: "They saw the processions of my God."]"[126] Second, by the fact that he says "and they were afraid." "In the proper sense," Luther explained, "fear does not harmonize with majesty, unless it behaves in the manner of a most far-fetched metaphor, in the manner of one who is afraid, namely, by fleeing and giving around."[127] Fear is more often understood by Luther as that sense of awe before the almighty Creator; but here it is understood in the sense of being terrified by God's majesty. Third, followed by the phrase "and the deeps were troubled." The "deeps" means "deep waters." Drawing on Ps. 33:7, "He puts the deeps in storehouses," Luther understood "the deeps" as a metaphor

---

125. LW 10.4 (WA 3.11). Listed in the diagram, Luther indicated that every sense of the fourfold method could be interpreted via the letter-spirit distinction, or law and gospel distinction.
126. LW 11.30 (WA 3.544).
127. LW 11.29-30 (WA 3.544).

for people of a deep and hidden heart. Some "deeps" live inwardly in spirit, a godly life that is hidden to physical eyes; others live in the flesh, under the judgment of God, as is borne out in Isa. 29:15: "Woe to you who are deep of heart, whose works are in the dark." They are the deeps whose death by which they are dead in spirit is likewise hidden to physical eyes. The magnitude and depth of their sins and God's wrath against them are so hidden as in physical deep waters that no creaturely means could reach and expose them, unless by God. The revelation of the truth about their wretchedness under the Law opposes them, thus troubles and infuriates them. "Because truth begets hatred."[128] Luther quoted the preceding Psalm (Ps. 76:4–5): "Thou enlightenest wonderfully, more than ["different from"][129] everlasting mountains. Therefore all the foolish of heart were troubled."[130] The phrase "everlasting mountains" refers to teachers of "prey or of captivity."[131] "In an active sense," these teachers plundered the devil and captured people and nations for the church and faith; "in a passive sense," they themselves were snatched and held captive by the devil and the flesh.[132] "Tropologically they are the holy souls or theological virtues, which snatched up the senses of the flesh and the members of sin to make them members of righteousness, etc."[133] These so-called holy souls are the deep and the foolish of heart;

128. LW 11.31 (WA 3.544).
129. LW 11.3 (WA 3.519). See note 1 where Luther paraphrases the Latin *a montibus* with *plus vela liter quam*, "more than, or different from."
130. LW 11.3 (WA 3.522).
131. LW 11.3 (WA 3.522).
132. LW 11.3 (WA 3.522).
133. LW 11.3 (WA 3.522).

they live openly as though they were wise, but in reality, they are fools. The point of comparison is to highlight how wonderfully the Lord enlightens inwardly in spirit, "different from" what the carnal teachers do, namely, reveal outwardly in the flesh. "For the light shines in the darkness, and the darkness did not comprehend it" (John 1:5). While these teachers of prey lead us into the captivity of the flesh, the Lord leads us wonderfully out of it. This too is not open to the physical eyes except by God's revelation.

Luther's theology of the cross is a theology of revelation; it calls the thing what it really is. Thus thesis 21 of Luther's *Heidelberg Disputation* reads: "A theology of glory calls evil good and good evil. A theologian of the cross calls thing what it actually is."[134] The cross contradicts "the theological virtues," peeling off the superficial knowledge they have about themselves and stripping them of righteousness, which they claim to possess. God shines forth so effectively that they might see the magnitude of their darkness within and the certainty of their spiritual death. The outcome of this revelation is that they are angry because they cannot bear the true knowledge God reveals about them. This also happens to "the foolish Jews"[135] in spirit, as it happened to Pharaoh in the flesh. "Hence the psalmist here makes known the appearance of the Lord in the flesh; Christ as God was seen by the Jews, and He appeared in the flesh. But because of that Herod was troubled, and all Jerusalem with him (Matt. 2.3), and then this prophetic sense was literally fulfilled."[136] The Jews were

134. LW 31.53.
135. LW 11.31 (WA 3.545).

troubled after having been exposed of the depth of evil, as this Psalm was read on the feast of the Epiphany. So the Jews under God's reproof have slept in spirit, just as Pharaoh faced the physical sleep of death in the sea. Therefore the entire Exodus story applies in spirit to the Jews, who in a mystical way completed in themselves that which happened literally to Pharaoh. Just as Pharaoh could not escape the terrifying wrath of God, which no one can withstand, so also the Jews were not exempted from it.

Tropological sense exposes the systemic condition of a sinner under Law, namely, under God's wrath so that he is made ready to hear the Gospel, namely, God's mercy triumphs over his wrath, if only he believes. It calls for abandoning human works as a preparation for the effectiveness of grace and clears the way for a reception of God's works fulfilled in Christ or God's way hidden in Christ.

The Efficacy of Faith in Christ: God's Power, Hidden and Spiritual

Verses 13–14 say, "Who is a great God like our God? Thou art the God who workest wonders." The greatness of God is known in the great works he has done, the ones on which the psalmist has meditated. Commenting on how "all Thy works" are great and wonderful, Luther wrote: "All thy works must necessarily be great and wonderful, because they have been prefigured by wonderful and great things. But if the literal and death-bound and transitory works were

---

136. LW 11.31 (WA 3.545).

wonderful, how much more will *their truth and realities signified* be wonderful and great?"[137] These works were perceptible to the senses; hence they were reflected upon and praised. But here the psalmist calls for a consideration of God's works in spirit, namely, meditating on the spiritual elements, which no human mind could grasp. Only faith can perceive how much more wonderful and great are *"the truth and realities signified"* in the amazing and mighty works of God. As a result, what was done in the past becomes wonderful to us in the present through faith. Thus the psalmist says: "Thou are the God who workest wonders." Where faith is wanting, one is incapable of seeing, and being seized by, the wonders of these great mighty works, such as healing and justifying a soul. Faith is the condition of efficacy of a "true" miracle; or else it would be a "shadowy" one.[138] For the Lord in the gospel never performed a miracle apart from people's faith. This is evident in the gospel of Mk. 16:17: "These signs, however, will follow those who believe in Me" and Matt. 11:15: "The blind see." Faith enables us to perceive the great and wonderful works of God so that we despise everything visible and pin our hope on the heavenly or invisible things.

"But since this power is hidden and spiritual,"[139] says Luther, the psalmist declares in verse 14: "Thou hast manifested Thy might known among the peoples." Here Luther extends the power of God to the future; it is at this

---

137. LW 11.28 (WA 3.542). Italics are mine.
138. LW 11.28 (WA 3.542).
139. LW 11.28 (WA 3.543).

place where Luther speaks of faith in Christ as the condition of possibility for apprehending God's might, hidden and spiritual. "This is faith in Christ, for we preach Christ crucified, the power and wisdom of God (I Cor. 1:23f.)."[140] Faith and Christ are used interchangeably, for the very object of faith is nothing but Christ and him crucified. This reflects Luther's theology of the cross, in which God hides himself in the efficacious activities of the crucified Christ, by which we are constituted as the object of his love. Luther wrote:

> It ["Christ, that is, faith in Christ"] accomplishes these great things. What, indeed, is greater than conquering the whole world and its prince? What is greater than overcoming all good and evil things in this life? What is greater than crushing eternal death? Than for the soul to rise from sins and become daughter of God as heir of the heavenly kingdom, a brother of Christ, an associate of angel, a friend of the Holy Spirit?[141]

Thus of the three works we are to be mindful of, Luther considered the redemptive works of Christ "most wonderful."[142] The great things God has done in Christ are "incalculable and so wonderful and truly great that the ancient miracles are barely shadows and figures of these."[143] Because the physical mind cannot perceive God's power, and being ignorant of this power, Christ the Lord has declared it to His people. The words "Thy might" is set in contrast to "the strength of the flesh"; the former is "truly the power of God which performs the works of God."[144] Nevertheless,

140. LW 11.28 (WA 3.543).
141. LW 11.28-29 (WA 3.543).
142. LW 11.10 (WA 3.530).
143. LW 11.29 (WA 3.553).

FRUIT FOR THE SOUL

sinful persons considered God's might "nothing,"[145] but the might of the flesh, which ultimately sends them to sheer despair, unless they cling to God's might, the basis of their victory. The purpose of Christ's work on the cross, said Luther, is "precisely that Christ destroyed ["the strength of the flesh"] in order to raise up His own. Therefore the strength of the works is His."[146] The marvelous victory that Christ won for us in the cross become ours, or becomes real in us, by faith. As support, Luther quoted several texts: 1 John 5:4: "For this is your victory which conquers the world, namely, your faith"; John 6:28: "What shall we do that we may work the works of God?"; and Mark 9:23: "All things are possible to him who believes"; and Matthew 2:21: "If you have faith and say to this mountain, 'Be taken up and cast into the sea,' it shall be done."[147] Faith conquers all contraries—sin, evil, wrath, death, flesh, the world, the devil, enmity against God, and inaccessibility of the heavenly sanctuary.

Worship as God's Work: Christ's Priestly Mediation

The external righteousness of the flesh vitiates worship, for the external works of righteousness are not the works of God "in the holy place" (v. 13). As Luther said: they are done "not in the spirit, but in the letter" (v. 13).[148] Our righteousness does not prepare us for efficacious worship; it keeps us, said Luther, "in the court outside the temple."[149]

144. LW 11.29 (WA 3.543).
145. LW 11.29 (WA 3.543).
146. LW 11.29 (WA 3.543).
147. LW 11.29 (WA 3.553).
148. LW 11.26 (WA 3.542).

The word *holy* denotes the spirit, which was formerly hidden but is now revealed, as the tabernacle symbolizes. At that time, just as the holy place was hidden, so also was God's way. Thus he later declares, "Thy footsteps will not be known" (v. 19). "Thy way (which includes "the works of God, the wonders and inventions of God") is in the holy place."[150] Being spiritual, "Thy way" is hidden to the physical eyes but revealed to the eyes of faith. The way of God in which the saints walk is a "holy place," that is, "in spiritual things, in faith," and not in the righteousness of the flesh.[151] And "Thy way" is hidden definitively in Christ, whose perfect sacrifice secures for us a righteous standing before God and thus grants us free access to the holy sanctuary:

> In the holy place, that is, in spiritual things, in faith, where man does not see but God sees. Not those who walk about openly in the flesh and in the righteousness of the flesh. Hence Heb. 13:11 says: "The bodies of those animals whose blood is brought into the sanctuary by the high priest… are burned outside the camp." Therefore also our blood is brought in through Christ, and He Himself offers us, killed in the flesh, to God.[152]

Latent in the above text is Luther's theology of worship in which the accent is on the mediation of Christ, not the priest's sacrificial offering, as the basis of true worship. The significance of Christ's priesthood and mediation consists in the fact that God descends to us in Jesus Christ as human, vicariously doing for us and in us what we cannot do for

149. LW 11.26 (WA 3.542).
150. LW 11.27 (WA 3.542).
151. LW 11.26 (WA 3.542).
152. LW 11.28 (WA 3.542).

ourselves. Therefore worship is grounded in the theology of radical reversal, in which God must begin and "lay the first stone, without any entreaty or desire of man—must first come and give him his promise."[153] Necessarily the reversal of direction entails the divinely ordained means by which we ascend to God—that is, not by way of Christ's divinity but his lowly humanity, "that holy ladder."[154] Althaus rightly discerned a movement in Luther's Christology: "from below to above."[155] He who wants to meet God must observe his "well-known rule,"[156] which Siggins elucidates: "He who wants to encounter God must encounter Him where He may be grasped as He cannot be grasped in His majesty: in the incarnate God, who lives in His mother's lap, and in the crucified God. To cling solely to Christ as He goes through death to the Father is the only way to God."[157] This Luther elaborated in his *Lectures on Hebrews* 1:1 (1517–18):

> One should also note that he mentions the humanity of Christ before he mentions His divinity, in order that in this way he may establish *the well-known rule* that one learns to know God in faith. For the humanity is *the holy ladder of ours,* mentioned in Gen. 18:12, by which we ascend to the knowledge of God. Therefore John 14:6 also says, "No one comes to the Father but by Me." And again, "I am the Door (John 10:7). Therefore he who wants to ascend advantageously to the love and knowledge of God should abandon the human metaphysical rules concerning knowledge of the divinity and apply himself

153. LW 35.81-82 (WA 6.355). Also quoted in my *Gifted Response,* 106–7.
154. LW 29.111 (WA 57, III. 99).
155. Althaus, *The Theology of Martin Luther,* 186.
156. LW 29.111 (WA 57, III.99).
157. Ian D. Siggins, *Martin Luther's Doctrine of Christ* (New Havens: Yale University Press, 1970), 84.

first to the humanity of Christ. For it is exceedingly godless temerity that where God has humiliated Himself in order to become recognizable, man seeks for himself another way by following the counsels of his own natural capacity.[158]

The vicarious function of Jesus as the High Priest for humanity is the foundation of worship, that in his person and act we by faith, in our person and act, enter the holy of holies. Because of sin, we cannot offer acceptable worship to God, although we should. The gospel consists in this: that God provides for us, in our High Priest Jesus, the very worship we could not offer. The worship God requires of us, and that we could not offer, is already accomplished by Christ, our representative. Grace means that God comes to us as one of us, freely and unconditionally, to mediate to us the efficacy of his worship via his priesthood in which we now participate by faith. In relation to us, God hides in his humanity to reach us; in relation to God, we too hide in his humanity by which we ascend to the heavenly sanctuary. Thus worship is God's causative work, drawing us into the temple through "Thy way," namely, Christ's priestly mediation. "The right hand of the Lord leads the saints wonderfully," from below to above: from Christ through death to the Father.

It is through Christ's blood that we are counted righteous, not of our own. Aristotle held that righteousness is acquired by doing righteous acts, just as skills are acquired by practicing: "Anything that we have to learn to do we learn

---

158. LW 29.111 (WA 57, III.99). Italics are mine. Also quoted in Kenneth Hagen, *A Theology of Testament in the Young Luther: The Lectures on Hebrews* (Leiden: E. J. Brill, 1974), 92.

by the actual doing of it: people become builders by building and instrumentalists by playing instruments. Similarly we become just by performing just acts."[159] However the cross has altered everything, reversing what Aristotle had taught, that righteousness before God comes not by doing but by believing, or faith in the finished work of Christ on the cross. It is not the righteousness of the flesh but the righteousness of faith, which Christ's blood acquires and communicates to us. This concurs with what Luther later taught in thesis 25 of his *Heidelberg Disputation*: "For the righteousness of God is not acquired by means of acts frequently repeated, as Aristotle taught, but it is imparted by faith, for 'He who through faith is righteous shall live' (Rom. 1: [17]) and 'Man believes with his heart and so is justified' (Rom. 10: [10])."[160]

The Wonderful Road: Christ's Way and His Leadership

Of verse 19: "Thy way is in the sea, and Thy paths in many waters," the "waters" here Luther interpreted as a figure for "people."[161] Following Augustine,[162] Luther gave a christological interpretation, that Jesus walked on the people "spiritually," as he did in his body "figuratively" (Matt. 14:25).[163] So the proper meaning of Christ walking on the

---

159. See Aristotle, *Ethics* 92, as quoted in Forde, *On Being a Theologian of the Cross*, 105. See also Notger Slenczka, "Luther's Anthropology," in *The Oxford Handbook of Martin Luther's Theology*, edited by Robert Kolb, Irene Dingel and L'ubomir Batka (Oxford: Oxford University Press, 2014), 212-32.
160. LW 31.55.
161. LW 11.32 (WA 3.545).
162. Augustine, "Expositions on the Book of Psalms," in *A Select Library of the Nicene and Post-Nicene Fathers*, First Series, volume VIII, edited by Philip Schaff (Grand Rapids: William B. Eerdmans, 1956), 366.

people lies in the gracious activities of Christ in us, not our works, magnifying him as "the leader," who causes us to go forward on his way, not ours.

> This He did in this way when His works were done in the people. The works of Christ and of righteousness and faith are the very way of Christ according to which He walks and goes forward in us, that is, He causes us to go forward. For it is He who performs all good works in us, and not we ourselves. Hence the psalmist said earlier (v. 13): "God, Thy way is in the holy place." And Exodus has this in a figure. For the way through the Red Sea and through the wilderness is the way of Christ. He himself was the leader of the journey, leading them on His way. And thus His way was there in the sea [that is, He did these works in the sea and on the way, which He made for His people], and in many waters. He designated the way by which He goes and rules in the midst of the world, in the midst of His enemies. In like manner He leads His own on the same spiritual way.[164]

What is prefigured in the Red Sea is the wonder of salvation Christ wrought for us. The way of Christ in the sea and the path in many waters consists in this: "His own life and conduct and that of His own is in the midst of the world and among people of this world, who are the sea and the many waters, as the crossing through the Red Sea prefigured."[165] The waters on the right are those who enjoy a prosperous life; the waters on the left are those who are hostile and prone to persecution. Likened unto a wall on both sides, they may

---

163. LW 11.32 (WA 3.545).
164. LW 11.32 (WA 3.545). Parenthesis is Luther's, which accentuates the redemptive work of Christ.
165. LW 11.32 (WA 3.546).

indeed threaten the church "in plain sight and in motion to the sense,"[166] but cannot envelop them. Sin and its evil passions may assault the faithful souls from both sides but cannot endanger them, for their lives are hidden in Christ, in whom is no condemnation. Of this, Luther explained:

> Also tropologically, in like manner. The sea and the many waters are the flesh with its senses, full of every tempest of evil motions and cravings on the left and on the right. But to them who are Christ's there is no condemnation, who do not walk after the flesh (Rom. 8:1), though the soul, on its path of strength toward God, moves forward in the flesh, namely in the midst of it and all its senses. For the Lord provides for the faithful souls that, though the flesh amuse itself and full of cravings on the left and on the right and be moved by desires in opposition to the spirit, it will not rule through sin or entangle the soul, as it does for the men of Egypt and the world.[167]

Sin and the desires of the flesh continue to abide in the Christian life. Like the waters on the left and on the right in the sea, they surely roared but did not reign; they surely attacked, but they did not rush in. Thus one must move in the midst of temptations, "feel and see and experience the good things and the evil things of the flesh,"[168] without succumbing to them. "So is the lily among thorns (Song of Sol. 2:2), like Daniel in the midst of the lions (Dan. 6:16). Thus we sing, 'Thy saints, O Lord, have followed a wonderful road, so that they might be found unharmed in the healthy waters. The dry earth appeared, and a way in the Red

166. LW 11.32 (WA 3.546).
167. LW 11.32–33 (WA 3.546–47).
168. LW 11.32 (WA 3.546).

Sea, etc'."[169] Just as "the wonderful road" is literally apparent in the Red Sea, so it is also in spirit.

Hiddenness of God and His Works: The Weakness of the Flesh and the Cross

Here Luther is not speaking of the hidden God (*Deus absconditus*) but of the revealed God (*Deus revelatus*) hiding himself under the appearance of opposites. To speak of the hiddenness of God and his works, Luther linked verse 20 ["Thou hast led Thy people like sheep"] to verse 19 ["Thy footsteps will not be known"]. The way of God is veiled to the carnal, in what seems to be folly, error, or stumbling block to them. The carnal perceive their own way and their lives, not the way of God in which the saints walk (1 Cor. 2:14). So though Pharaoh and his people clearly saw the way in which the children of Israel went, they failed to understand that this was the way of God, hidden but wonderful, until they were submerged. Unless the Holy Spirit reveals, we remain in utter ignorance of God and his way (cf. John 3:8); no one could perceive the wonderful road that the saints travel. What Christ does in us remains outside of us unless the works he does are utterly divine. It is of no avail, like the killing letter, if the works are done solely by some weak men. Luther wrote:

> [The psalmist] had said above about the incarnate God that the waters (people) would see Him, and that He would appear in the flesh as a man among men. Therefore, lest we think of

169. LW 11.32 (WA 3.546).

Him exclusively as a man and not also as the One who was there before, he says, "Thou are the One who has led Thy people," as if to say, "You have now become visible and appear in weakness, and You do Your works in humility, and so You are now not known by the proud; you are not working in majesty and power, but from hidden strength. Therefore your footsteps are not known, nor, for that reason, are you, that You are God. Your work are veiled in humility, so that they are not believed to be Your works but those of some weak man. Nevertheless, You are the One who of Old worked in majesty and manifest strength by the hand of Moses and Aaron."[170]

Just as the divinity was veiled beneath the flesh of weakness, so His works were veiled beneath the weakness of the cross. The works that the cross has achieved for us are exclusively God's, which eventuates in "the casting down of the devil, victory over the world, destruction of hell, the gaining of heaven, the sanctification of the world, and the killing of flesh."[171] These incalculable results of the cross are hidden to physical eyes, the devil, and the world, except perceived by faith.

Therefore His footsteps were not known, nor did any man see His way which He then walked. And neither the world nor the devil understood what He was doing. Nevertheless this does not mean that He was therefore not the same God who anciently led the people in open strength, but *it means that He then administered the letter and now administers the spirit of the letter, which was hidden in the letter. And so we are again forced into a spiritual understanding of the psalm.* Though ... this ignorance was demonstrated in the figure of the exodus, since Pharaoh did not understand that this was the way and work of

170. LW 11.34 (WA 3.547).
171. LW 11.34 (WA 3.547).

142

God, yet we think it better to understand that the prophet is speaking from the opposite, as if he were saying: "At that time Your strength was manifest, and Your wonders were visible, and the footsteps of Your strength were known to all. But now, when You were about to make the spirit of this manifest letter hidden, Your works are so hidden, Your works will be so secret, that they may not be recognized in any way unless they are perceived by faith. Indeed, unless faith teaches that Your suffering accomplishes such great works, they will seem to be the works of some extremely weak man."[172]

Not reason but faith alone apprehends the victory of the cross, that "the devil has been conquered, death killed, and heaven opened."[173] God has so veiled these works under abject weakness of suffering that by faith He might also veil reason and render foolish the wisdom of the world. For this reason Luther considered verse 19: "Thy footsteps will not be known," as that which proceeds against the Jews. Neither do the Jews know or want to know his footsteps because of unbelief. They did not expect a Messiah to be found in the humility, weakness, and suffering, but only in power, strength, and glory. Luther juxtaposed the Septuagint version of Isaiah 53:8: "In humility His judgment was taken away,"[174] and the Vulgate version of Isaiah 53:8: "He was taken away, from distress and from judgment."[175] Through unbelief, Christ was hidden and taken away from the Jews; this is due to "distress," namely, the affliction of suffering, and

---

172. LW 11.34–35 (WA 3.547). Italics are mine, stressing that Luther retains the Augustinian Salvation historical model in this lecture on psalm.
173. LW 11.35 (WA 3.547).
174. LW 11.35 (WA 3.548). He cited this version according to Acts 8:33, based on the Septuagint: *In humilitate iudicium eius sublatum est.*
175. LW 11.35 (WA 3.548). The Vulgate version reads: *De augustia et iudicio sublatus est.*

"judgment," that is, the condemnation which he bore on the cross, both of which were repugnant to the Jews. Furthermore "Christ was taken away" could mean his exaltation, that he was lifted "on high to the right hand of the Father in the humility of suffering and the distress of weakness."[176] Because of his suffering and obedience unto death (Phil. 2:8–9), God has exalted him above all things and given him the judiciary power to judge the living and dead. The Jews only apprehend the weak things they find in him, and thus they deny that he is their true God, the one they always look for till the present day. They not only fail to see God veiled under the humanity but also fail to see God's works veiled in his opposites. Of verse 20, "Thou hast led Thy people like sheep," Luther had the psalmist say that he is "the very same God" who of old led the people by the hands of Moses and Aaron, "no one else, but the One who only hid his works in weakness and then did not do manifest wonders in the strength of majesty but hidden wonders in the humility of suffering."[177] Through unbelief, the Jews in ancient times were under the administration of "the letter" and thus were ignorant of God's paradoxical works in Christ prefigured in the Exodus account; but now God "administers the spirit of the letter, which was hidden in the letter" so that the hidden christological spiritual sense will be disclosed to the minds of those who are his. Here Luther is interpreting the distinction between the letter and the spirit not eschatologically and existentially, as two words of God that wage the struggle

176. LW 11.36 (WA 3.548).
177. LW 11.35 (WA 3.548).

144

against Satanic deception by killing the sinner and making the new creature in Christ alive. Rather he used the terms to reflect the Augustinian salvation historical model that posits gospel as the law amplified, Jesus' improvement on Moses.[178]

The Transition from Remorse to Joy: Lament to Praise

For the reformer, the Jews are principally rebuked for extolling the works of righteousness and forgetting the works of God. Neither do they show regard for the works of faith or understand salvation through grace on account of Christ and in the church.[179] Thus verse 14 says: "Thou hast manifested Thy might among the people." That is, God has done so by showing to all that his power is "not in the flesh and earthly might but rather that the weakness according to the world is pleasing to Him, for his power is spiritual."[180] Contrary to human reason or expectation, God has chosen the weak to shame the strong (1 Cor. 1:27). The powerful and the

---

178. Lohse, *Martin Luther's Theology*, 269, argues that "Luther's distinction (between Law and Gospel) not only differs from the tradition (Augustinian) insofar as it is no longer structured in salvation-historical but in dialectical fashion." Quoted in Paul R. Hinlicky, *Luther and the Beloved Community. A Path for Christian Theology after Christendom* (Grand Rapids: William B. Eerdmans, 2010), 112. The study of this Psalm proves otherwise.

179. LW 11.13 (WA 3.533). See LW 11.88 (WA 3.596) for Luther's view of the Jews, as quoted in Gritsch, *Martin Luther's Anti-Semitism*, 50. The reason for Luther's basic polemic and scatological language against the Jews, Gritsch notes, was because of their opposition to Christ as the Messiah. This is borne out in his comment on Psalm 78:66: "He put them to disgrace": "But at this place, what seems to be more expressly denoted is that their *recta*, their innermost bowels, are sticking out through the rear, because the rear is different from the buttocks on which we sit…. Their *recta* stick out, that is, the innermost feelings of their heart and their desires in opposition to Christ they display to the present. Therefore, the *recta* sticking out means that their will to harm and do evil appears, since they are not able to vomit the feces of evils against Him."

180. LW 11.13 (WA 3.533).

strong do not act in God's strength; they act in their own, which is of the world. God's delight is not in the efforts of people or in the strength of the horse (Ps. 147:10), but rather in the poor and weak, the lowly and despised, in whom God's power is made perfect. The knowledge of God and the knowledge of human beings coincide. Only when one acknowledges God as a great God (v. 13: "Who is a great God like our God?") will one humble oneself and recognize one's poverty before God. God is foolishness to the Gentiles and weakness to the Jew; but He is power, wisdom, and glory to the saints. That is why Luther said: "The right hand of God leads the saints wonderfully" (Ps. 45:4).[181] The wonder of God is revealed in a hidden way, or in his opposites: the Most High is present in the lowest; the might of God is hidden in weakness. The Jews fail to perceive the wonderful way in which God accommodates himself to reach us, not by the might nor power of the world, but through God's might hidden in its opposite. God is wonderful in the saints who acknowledge their feebleness and sinfulness because they alone proclaim the greatness of God. As support, Luther quoted several Psalms, including Ps. 51:13–15, "I will teach transgressors Thy ways.... My tongue will sing aloud of Thy righteousness.... And my mouth will show forth Thy praise."[182] The transition from remorse to joy, repentance to faith, lament to doxology, has occurred. This is not our works but an act of God's creation, similar to the first creation, which occurs *ex nihilo* and through the Word upon which

181. LW 11.19 (WA 3.544).
182. LW 11.36 (WA 3.549).

the psalmist meditates. Luther concluded his study of this Psalm as follows:

> Thus the aim of the whole psalm seems to me to be that any righteous man, and the whole human nature, seeing its wretchedness and filled with remorse, cries to the Lord for deliverance. After this, having been heard and delivered and changed so that he is now a true *Jeduthun*, leaping out of wretchedness into the status of salvation, as an act of thanksgiving he promises and proposes that he will always praise God and tell His works also for the instruction of others.[183]

Concluding Reflections

This chapter would not be complete without further clarification on two major themes: Luther's hermeneutic and the idea of conscience (*synteresis*).

Literal or Christological Hermeneutic: Christ as the Center and End of the Scripture

For the reformer, all that we find in the Scriptures must be interpreted in terms of Christ and his significance for salvation.[184] The three senses are subordinate to the literal (christological) sense, and they must find their basis on Christ. This is clearly stated in his *Preface to the Glosses* of the *First Lectures on Psalms*: "In the Scriptures, therefore, no allegory, tropology, no anagogy is valid, unless the same truth is expressly stated historically elsewhere. Otherwise Scripture

---

183. LW 11.36 (WA 3.548). *Jeduthun* means victor or conqueror.
184. Lohse, *Martin Luther,* 156.

would become a mockery."[185] The fourfold interpretation "flow(s) together into a large stream,"[186] namely Christ, the principal sense. As Bouman commented: "Christ is in all interpretations the beginning."[187]

For Lefèvre,[188] there are two literal senses: the literal "historical" and literal "prophetic" sense. Drawing on Augustine's letter-spirit dialectic, he identified that the literal-historical and the literal-prophetic senses correspond to the false, "literal-carnal" and true, "literal-spiritual" senses respectively.[189] The former applies the words of the psalmist or prophet only to the specific historic context, as the Jews did; the latter interprets the words as referring to Christ. To confine the words of the psalmist or prophet to a series of historical narratives dealing with the historical context at the time of writing is to deprive the text of the deeper meaning, intended by the Holy Spirit. For Lefèvre, the only literal sense of any significance is the christological (prophetic-spiritual).

With Lefèvre, Luther also endorsed a double literal sense: the literal "carnal" and literal "spiritual" senses, which correspond to the literal-historical and literal-prophetic senses

185. LW 10.4 (WA 3.11). See McGrath, *The Intellectual Origins of the European Reformation*, 159.

186. LW 10.52 (WA 3.46). See Parsons, *Martin Luther's Interpretation of the Royal Psalms*, 4–6.

187. Herbert Bouman, "Introduction to Volume 10," LW 10.xii.

188. See Jacques Lefèvre d'Étaples, *Quincuplex Psalterium* (Paris: Henri Estienne, 1509), fol. 159 A. Also quoted in McGrath, *The Intellectual Origins of the European Reformation*, 157. See Heiko A. Oberman, *Forerunners of the Reformation* Illustrated by Key Documents (Philadelphia: Fortress Press, 1981), 286ff; David Steinmetz, *Reformers in the Wings* (Philadelphia: Fortress Press, 1971), 43–52.

189. McGrath, *The Intellectual Origins of the European Reformation*, 157; Lienhard, *Luther*, 39.

respectively.[190] For him, the Jews possess a "carnal" understanding of the Psalms and apply the Psalms to "ancient history [historical] apart from Christ," that is, apart from "spiritual" [prophetic] understanding.[191] Luther avowed: "Every prophecy and every prophet must be understood as reference to Christ the Lord, except where it is clear from plain words that someone else is spoken of."[192] The distinction between literal-historical and literal-prophetic also corresponds to the distinction between letter and spirit.[193] The hidden christological spiritual sense will be revealed to the minds of those who are His so that they can understand the Scriptures. Luther was wary of the danger of mistaking shadow for substance and the sign for the thing that is signified. Christ is the very substance that is foreshadowed in the Old Testament; Christ—his life, death, and resurrection—is the very thing that is signified by the law. To reinforce his christocentric hermeneutic,[194] Luther opens his exposition of the Psalter with a *"Preface of Jesus Christ, the Son of God and our Lord in the Psalter of David."*[195] It was of Luther's position that the Old Testament must be

---

190. LW 10.3 (WA 3.11). See McGrath, *The Intellectual Origins of the European Reformation,* 159. In Luther's *Preface to the Glosses,* the historical is part of the literal sense. See LW 11.414 (WA 4.305), where the prophetic belongs to the literal sense.

191. LW 10.3 (WA 3.3).

192. LW 10.7 (WA 3.13). Ebeling, *Luther,* 280.

193. LW 10.4 (WA 3.11).

194. LW 10.4 (WA 3.11).

195. LW 10.6 (WA 3.12). Also cited in E. G. Kraeling, *The Old Testament Since the Reformation* (New York: Harper & Rows, 1955), 18 and William L. Holladay, *The Psalms Through Three Thousand Years* (Minneapolis: Fortress Press, 1996), 194. For further discussion, see James G. Kiecker, "Luther's Preface to His First Lectures on the Psalms (1513): The Historical Background to Luther's Biblical Hermeneutic," *Wisconsin Lutheran Quarterly* 85 (Fall, 1988): 287-95.

interpreted by the New Testament. "If the Old Testament can be interpreted by human wisdom without the New Testament, I should say that the New Testament has been given to no purpose. So Paul concluded that 'Christ died to no purpose' if the Law were sufficient (Gal. 2:21)."[196] Unlike Lefvere,[197] Luther did not ignore the historical contexts in which the letters of the Old Testament were written; nevertheless he regarded Christ as the center of the Psalter.[198] Christ was the subject matter of the Psalter and the object of the faith of the patriarchs. To read the Old Testament with profit is to read it christologically. This he wrote in his *Preface to the Old Testament*: "Here you will find the swaddling clothes and the manger in which Christ lies. Simple and little are the swaddling clothes, but dear is the treasure, Christ, that lies in them."[199]

Hence when Luther assigns the tropological sense as the principal meaning of Psalm 77, this in no way means he alters his view and rejects the literal or christological interpretation of the Scripture. Vogelsang wrote of Luther: "Even where the tropological interpretation is completely indicated, it can be communicated within only by the Christological sense."[200]

---

196. LW 10.6 (WA 3.13). See n. 2.
197. See David S. Dockery, "Martin Luther's Christological Hermeneutics," *Grace Theological Journal* 4 (1983): 477, who observes that Luther followed Lefvere's "use of the letter and spirit by both emphasizing the need for the Spirit's illumination and seeking the Christological meaning in the Old Testament, although he did not devalue the historical senses, as Faber [Lefvere] did."
198. Lohse, *Martin Luther's Theology*, 52–53; Gerald Bray, *Biblical Interpretation. Past and Present* (Illinois: IVP, 1996), 198.
199. LW 35.236 (WA DB 8, 12).
200. See Vogelsang, *Die anfänge von Luthers Christologie*, 26, as quoted in Lienhard, *Luther*, 41.

The tropological sense of existence must be understood in light of Luther's hermeneutical axiom: the christological sense. In his commentary on Psalm 64, Luther sharpened the christological witness of the plain, literal sense of Scripture:

> Because all the works of creation and of the old law are signs of the works of God, which He does and will do in Christ and His saints, therefore *all those already in the past are as signs which are fulfilled in Christ.* For all of them are transitory, symbolizing those things that are eternal and enduring. The latter are works of truth, while all the former are *shadows and works of foreshadowing. Therefore Christ is the end and center of them. To Him they all look and point, as if they were saying, 'Look, He is the One who is in reality, but we are not; we are only signs.*[201]

The literal sense, for Luther, is the starting point of his exegesis. This is also borne out in his commentary on Psalm 119, where the christological sense reigns over the others: "[T]he prophetic sense, that is, the literal sense, is the foundation of the rest, the master and light, the author and foundation and origin."[202] Tropologically, whatever is said of Christ is applied to the believers (soteriologically); literally, there is nothing in the lives of the believers that does not find its basis on Christ (christologically). To interpret a text according to the tropological sense consists in appealing to faith, not human works, and announcing to the believers the victory, which has its basis on Christ. Therefore the tropological sense flows into Christ, "the end and center" of Scripture; for it is Christ, the head, to whom all look and

---

201. LW 10.311 (WA 3.368). Italics are mine.
202. LW 11.414 (WA 4.305).

point. When the tropological interpretation is tied to, and comprehended by, the christological interpretation, it steers away from moralism so that Christ is apprehended not so much as a moral example to be imitated, but as a Savior to be believed. For the saving encounter that the saints have with Christ is primarily of the order of faith, not of imitation.

The Murmuring of Conscience (Synteresis)

Meditation on "all Thy works" effects mortification in order to achieve vivification; it crucifies all human works so that all God's works shine. We reap justification by faith, the fruit of such meditation: that I may be perfectly God's beloved, not of my own righteousness. What Luther rejected as the theology of glory was the self-glorification of works righteousness. What is taught here in this Psalm later appears in thesis 24 of the *Heidelberg Disputation*, where Luther indicated that without the theology of the cross, our sinful condition "misuses the best in the worst manner," seeking to draw near to God through good works.[203] "(This) sort of wisdom which sees the invisible things of God in known good works simply inflates a man, and renders him both blind and hard."[204] Luther elaborated: "It is impossible for a person not to be puffed up by his good works unless he has first been deflated and destroyed by suffering and evil until he knows that he is worthless and that his works are not his but God's."[205]

203. LW 31.55.
204. WA 1.362, 21–22; *Martin Luther, Early Theological Writings*, in The Library of Christian Classics, vol. 16, trans. and ed. James Atkinson (Philadelphia: Westminster Press, 1962), 290.
205. WA 1.362, 21–22; *Martin Luther, Early Theological Writings*, ed. Atkinson, 290.

The cross, then, is directed against works righteousness and human efforts to do what is morally good so as to merit justification which only faith in Christ makes possible. Thesis 25 of *Heidelberg Disputation* asserts: "He is not righteous who does much, but he who, without work, believes much in Christ."[206] This thesis, as Pannenberg argues, "rejects the Aristotelian notion of justice (as) that (which) is acquired by developing the appropriate attitude or habit of action."[207] Thereby it repudiates the attitude of anyone who boasts that he is wise and learned in the law. With this, Luther would have rendered the murmuring of conscience (*synteresis*) impotent to achieve point of contact with God. The grace and fervor of God reigns above all, and because of this, the murmuring of conscience is quenched.

Gordon Rupp observed that Luther had already made frequent citation of the *synteresis* in his lectures on the Psalms (1513–1515).[208] As late as 1515, especially in his early lectures on Psalms and sermons, Luther was still subscribing to the necessity of doing one's best as a predisposition to the reception of divine grace. In his commentary on Ps. 115, Luther averred: "Hence, just as the law was a figure and preparation of the people for receiving Christ, so our doing what is in us [*factio quantum in nobis est*] disposes us to

---

206. LW 31.55.
207. Wolfhart Pannenberg, "A Theology of the Cross," *Word and World* 8, no. 2 (1988): 162.
208. Gordon Rupp, *The Righteousness of God* (London: Hodder & Stoughton, 1953), 151. For a detailed study of conscience, see Randall C. Zachman, *The Assurance of Faith: Conscience in the Theology of Martin Luther and John Calvin* (Minneapolis: Fortress Press, 1993). For further discussion on faith and *synteresis*, see Loewenich, *Luther's Theology of the Cross*, 52–58.

grace."[209] Like Biel,[210] Luther believed that human nature possesses a "residue of former goods," which is inextinguishable (Ps. 79).[211] The same thought occurs in his commentary on Ps. 42, where he said: "And there is such a natural desire in human nature indeed, because the *synteresis* and desire of good is inextinguishable in man, though it is hindered in many. God surely hears the desire and above all also answers it after Christ has made Himself the mediator for such a person."[212] On some occasions, s*ynteresis* was used in connection with the murmuring of conscience, as in his commentary on Ps. 11: "For there is nobody so bad who does not feel the murmuring of reason and the voice of conscience."[213] And here in Ps. 77: "For the remnant (that is, reason and the conscience [*synteresis*]) which go on murmuring, always cry to the Lord, even if, forced by sin, the will should sin."[214] At the beginning of his lectures on Romans (1515–16), Luther was somewhat inclined toward using *synteresis* as a valid category. This is evident in his remarks on Romans 1:20, where Luther comments: "the theological *synteresis* is in every man and is incapable of being

209. LW 11.397 (WA 4.262).
210. For more discussion of the Bielian premise, doing what lies in us, see Heiko Oberman, "Facientibus Quod in se est Deus not denegat Gratiae: Robert Holcot and the Beginning of Luther's Thought," in *The Reformation in Medieval Perspective*, edited by Steven Ozment (Chicago: Quadrangle Books, 1971), 119–41; and his "Notes on the Theology of Nominalism," *Harvard Theological Review*, 53 (1976): 47–76.
211. LW 11.94 (WA 3.603).
212. LW 10.99 (WA 3.94). Also cited in Rupp, *The Righteousness of God*, 151.
213. LW 10.99 (WA 3.94).
214. LW 11.17 (WA 3.535). Here I follow Rupp's translation. See his *The Righteousness of God*, 151.

obscured."[215] However, this scholastic idea was later rejected by Luther: "this concupiscence (original sin), is always in us, and therefore the love of God is never in us unless it is begun by grace."[216] Already in his comment on Romans 3:10, we find Luther's contradistinction to scholastic anthropology and moral theory: "We are so entirely inclined to evil that no portion which is inclined toward good remains in us."[217] It was not until late 1516 (or early 1517) that Luther broke with the nominalist concepts of merit and grace and came to recognize in his famous *Disputation Against Scholastic Theology* (1517) that "on the part of man, however, nothing precedes grace except ill will and even rebellion against grace."[218] "This is said in opposition to Scotus and Biel,"[219] according to whom doing what lies in us prepares us for a reception of grace.

Luther's increasing awareness of the depth and intensity of human wretchedness enables him to break with the scholastic concept of *synteresis* as the point of contact with God.[220] This break was evident in his exposition of the penitential psalms, such as Ps. 6 and Ps. 51 dealt with previously (chapters 1 and 2 of this book). Furthermore, based on Luther's commentary on Ps. 90 (chapter 4 of this book), Zachman writes of Luther's negative view of conscience: "The conscience can recognize sins (acts), but it cannot of itself, even under the external

215. LW 25.157 (WA 56.177).
216. LW 25.262 (WA 56.275).
217. LW 25.222 (WA 56.237).
218. LW 31.11.
219. LW 31.10.
220. Rupp, *The Righteousness of God*, 151; George, *Theology of the Reformers*, 67.

revelation of the law, acknowledge the person as sinner (nature). The subjective ability to feel oneself a sinner and to sense the wrath of God on sinners is thus a gift of God, and not an ability of conscience."[221] Justification is solely God's work *ex nihilo*, not out of any preexistent salvific matters including human accretions, the murmuring of conscience, etc. It is precisely this that the next chapter (Psalm 90) will bear out.

---

221. Zachman, *The Assurance of Faith*, 47.

4

———

Psalm 90: Moses Being "Most Mosaic": A Minister of Law, Sin, and Death

Moses wrote only this one Psalm, Luther argued, for it has a title, that is, "A Prayer of Moses," while the rest do not. Moses' authorship is supported not only by "the title but also the language itself, the subject matter, and the whole theology of the Psalm."[1] Luther's second lecture on the Psalm is the focus of this chapter. His introductory remarks in the lecture speak of the whole content of the Christian faith. The entire human race has fallen from grace in Adam. Thoroughly blinded by original sin, Adam's posterity know neither themselves nor

---

1. LW 13.79. Written in 1535, Ps. 90 was Luther's last lecture series before the massive study of Genesis occupied him for the remaining years of his life. Luther's first lectures the Psalm deal with Jews and Christ's coming and do not substantially contribute to the discussion. See LW 11:195–207.

God. They suffer indescribably great misery transmitted to them from the first parents. The fallen race does not know how miserable their condition under sin is, although they feel it and languish in it. "He neither understands its origins nor does he sees its final outcomes,"[2] unless by divine revelation. Neither human "reason nor the power of human nature" can expose the reality and extent of our misery caused by original sin.[3] Moses, imbued with the Holy Spirit, is given the knowledge of the dreadful miseries, in which we too participate by following his example in believing and praying. Moses' words ought to be read as possessing divine authority, as sayings that proceed from God. This is the touchstone of the Reformation, that Word and Holy Spirit are not opposed but juxtaposed, not separated but united. The "inseparable companion"[4] of Holy Scripture is the Holy Spirit, who moves our hearts more than one way, sometimes through the law to humble the smug and at other times through the gospel to console the one afflicted.

"Moses had to be Moses": His Prime Office

Moses taught us the proper way of reading the Scripture (2 Tim. 2:15), in which one must deal with arrogant and smug sinners in one way (i.e., by law) but in an entirely different way with those who already have been terrified (i.e., by gospel). His prime concern is that "the root bearing poisonous and bitter fruit" (Deut. 29:18) in the smug must be

2. LW 13.75.
3. LW 13.75.
4. LW 13.111.

smothered by the law before new life might emerge. This is Moses at his "most mosaic,"[5] when he describes intensively the annihilating knowledge of the law. The opposite of the gospel must be revealed in order that the most terrified under the law might receive the proper fruit, "the exceeding abundant consolation" of the gospel.[6] God judges sinners and abandons them to death but not so that he might condemn them so completely that they are beyond hope and the reach of God, whom Moses called, "our Dwelling Place from generation to generation" (v. 1). The introductory verse, for Luther, is a valid inference from his *Large Catechism* in 1530, the First Commandment, which speaks of God as "the true God" to whom our hearts cling for all good.[7] "Dwelling place" and "grace" Luther used interchangeably.[8] Hidden in the terrifying knowledge of the law is God's grace, which extends from generation to generation. "This introduction" (v. 1) with which Moses began his prayer psalm, Luther asserted, "breathes life and is relevant to the sure hope in the resurrection and life eternal."[9]

"Moses had to be Moses," fulfilling his special office as "a minister of death, sin, and damnation."[10] Moses' peculiar aim was to put the arrogant and unbelieving despisers of God under the law and set squarely before their own eyes the horrible reality of their sad condition. He peeled off the

---

5. LW 13.77.
6. LW 13.98.
7. "The Large Catechism," in *The Book of Concord*, 365.
8. LW 13.93.
9. LW 13.83.
10. LW 13.78.

masks of sin, death, and wrath and showed them in their true colors, without cover up and pretense. This is Moses at the height of his power as the minister of law. But this in no way means he completely ignores the ministry of the opposites, namely life, righteousness, and grace. He does so in "an obscure way," directing the one afflicted away from the condemnation of the law to the consolation of the gospel of divine redemption. The gospel of Christ was veiled and anticipated in the Old Testament. By declaring that God is our dwelling place, Moses accentuated that those who pray have the assurance that their hope is grounded in God, both of the Old and New Testament:

> In this way Moses calls attention to the resurrection of the dead and the hope of life over death. True, he does not employ very clear words; nevertheless they are very meaningful. It was necessarily reserved for Christ, and properly so, publicly to proclaim in the New Testament era the remission of sins and the resurrection of the dead, truths which were presented in the Old Testament era, one might say, in veiled language.[11]

Luther then proceeded from his comment on the hidden nature of the gospel in the Old Testament to what he considers to be the chief aim of Moses: "men might learn to fear God and are terrified by God's wrath and death, might humble themselves before Him and be prepared for the reception of divine grace,"[12] for the simple reason that they would not fear God unless they are first shown God's

11. LW 13.85.
12. LW 13.85.

wrath, the result of sin (Rom. 4:15). Luther harnessed his understanding with examples from Scripture:

> Therefore the people who were assembled at Mount Sinai became terror-stricken at those pearls of thunder and the fearful tempest, for these reminded them of their sins and made the Divine Majesty unbearable for them. This humiliation, or this fear, was pleasing to God. This is the way to deal with hardened and smug sinners who disregard the Word of God, who are callous at one time to all punishments resulting from impiety and at another time to the reward of piety.[13]

The distinction between God's promises and his threats must be kept without confusion. Both are aspects of the one and same God, who assures the terrified with his promise and terrifies the smug with his threats. He elaborates:

> For this reason also Paul enjoins on Timothy "rightly to divide the word of God." God's promises and threats must not be intermingled. This the Jews were in the habit of doing many centuries ago. The papists do it in our own day. Although the prophets threatened them with every kind of plague, the Jews nevertheless disregarded these threats and relied on the promises. Because of this they stifled the fear of God and became presumptuous and ungovernable. On the other hand, in the papacy the tyrannical doctors and tormentors of souls heaped on troubled consciences every imaginable outburst of anger and abuse, whereas these souls should have been encouraged and dealt with in the most loving way. And thus he sins in both directions who does not divide the Word of God rightly.[14]

One must observe the proper timing and contexts in which

13. LW 13.85–86.
14. LW 13.86.

the ministry of law and gospel occurs in order to reap soothing consolation as the proper outcome. This is autobiographical for Luther, who at one point failed to grasp this Psalm aright and sank into despair. Luther confessed:

> It often happened to me, when I was a monk, that when reading this psalm I had to lay it aside. For I did not know at that time that these frightening truths were not intended by Moses for a terrified soul. I did not know that Moses most to be preached to the hardened and self-assured masses, who are neither concerned about nor understand God's wrath, death, and all their own miseries.[15]

This Psalm, Luther claimed, surpasses the writings of pagans in a twofold sense: "Moses kills through his ministry by exposing sin and its punishments, nevertheless, by calling this psalm a prayer, he indicates in veiled but unmistakable language the remedy against death."[16] The heading "prayer" suggests that the hope of a remedy is to be found in the God to whom Moses is praying. Moses not only *teaches* the law that terrifies but also *prays* to God who comforts the one afflicted with "the hope and assurance of the forgiveness of sins and of eternal life."[17] The proper outcome of reading this Psalm aright is that smug sinners are terrified by the voice of Law, and trembling sinners are cheered by the voice of the gospel.

15. LW 13.86–87, note 20 indicates that the young Luther experienced the same feelings when he came across the story of the flood in Genesis 7. Hence Luther is referring to an earlier encounter than what is recorded in his comment on the Psalm.
16. LW 13.81.
17. LW 13.83. The italics are Luther's.

Contraries Revealed: Sin, Wrath, and Death

Commenting on verse 8, "Thou settest our iniquities before Thee, the sins unknown to us in the light of Thy Countenance," Luther underscored that the magnitude of sin is beyond adequate analysis and satisfactory verbalization. "Even as God's wrath, even as death, is infinite, so sin also is infinite."[18] Sin, wrath, and death must be exposed for what they really are, namely the infinite triadic miseries that threaten human life. "The basic total picture of man's existence," Elert wrote, "is developed by Luther exhaustively but also with unparalleled gloom."[19] Human reason is incapable of exposing the triadic miseries. Not only is reason unaware that unbelief and despair of God is sin, but it also knows nothing of the duty to fear, trust, and love God. Reason is impotent to understand the true nature of God's law and its demands and thus fails to grasp the gravity and burden of death. Hardened in its blindness, it has become totally insensitive to sin and its destructive consequences. The office of Moses is essential in lifting this blindness and abolishing the human presumption that sees outward actions as the sum total of God's demands on his people.

The dreadful miseries that confront us remind us "God is a God of wrath."[20] In Aristotelian language, God in his wrath is both "the efficient cause" and "final cause" of death.[21] Death,

18. LW 13.117.

19. Werner Elert, *The Structure of Lutheranism*, translated by Walter A. Hansen (St. Louis: Concordia, 1962), 18.

20. LW 13.77. See footnote 7, where Aristotle, *Metaphysics*, V. 2 was cited. The efficient cause refers to "that from which change or the resting from change first begins"; the final cause means "that for the sake of which a thing is."

both physical and eternal death, to which we are subject, is the consequence of God's wrath over sin. Death does not come as a result of human weakness or illness. It is a divinely wrought disaster, which occurs as a result of God's own verdict that he executes upon the sinner. Elert wrote of sin and God's response to it:

> If sin were only disobedience, that is, deviation from the norm, the damage could be repaired forthwith by obedience, and the problem of destiny would be solved by 'composure.' In reality, however, sin in the strict sense, is 'enmity against God,' that is active opposition to the will of God, which, to an equal degree, is active against sin. God replies to sin with a judgment that can only terminate in our death.[22]

The contraries—horror of sin and the terror of divine wrath—are to be revealed in their starkness. Not only did Moses pray in verse 8, "Thou settest our iniquities before Thee, the sins unknown to us in the light of Thy countenance," he also prayed in verse 7, "For we perish because of Thy wrath, and we are terrified because of Thy furious anger." Humanity's condition under sin is one under divine wrath, which ultimately leads to death. Moses' intention is to speak of death in the context of the terror of divine punishment so as to drive fear into the hearts of those who are smug and hardened against such an idea and to bring comfort to those who are already terrified and are in need of respite from their drooping spirits. The second part of verse 7, "and we are terrified because of Thy furious anger," refers

21. LW 13.77.
22. Elert, *The Structure of Lutheranism*, 27.

in reality to fear when one is facing death. Without fear, death would be so dead that it could not haunt us, like a dead serpent with form, but without poison. Death struck terror into the hearts of people, and "this terror is truly the poison of death."[23]

Luther so highly reveres the paradoxical work of God that he avers: "This is the name of God: 'He kills and restores to life. He brings down to hell and raises up' (I Sam. 2: 6)."[24] God corresponds to himself in this apparently contradictory state of affairs: he judges in order to redeem. Moses was at the height of his power as the minister of law, who communicates to us a "truly awful revelation" of God as "an outraged God."[25] He studiously presented a knowledge of God that is nothing but damning in order to terrify smug and impenitent sinners. The frightening truth of a death-causing God was not intended by Moses for a terrified soul. Moses preferred most that it be preached to those who are callous at the Word of God and heart-hardened against God. Only by terrifying them with the tyranny of God's wrath and death would they humble themselves before God and be prepared for a reception of God's grace.

Death under Divine Wrath: A Far Greater Calamity

People have sought ways to reduce the gravity of death. Some mitigate the evil of death by heavily indulging in the pleasures of this life, like the Epicureans. Thus in the attempt

---

23. LW 13.115.
24. LW 13.97.
25. LW 13.94.

to soften the punishment of sin, the wise men of the world end up committing greater sins. Some follow the example of street bandits or soldiers, who with courage but jokingly wish upon others various kinds of misfortune. Others view death as part of the natural order. When death is understood as an instance of the transitory nature of existence, the solution is to disregard or scorn it. Luther considers it "pagan blindness and the result of original sin," when theologians of his time offer insensitive advice in their funeral sermons against grieving over death as if it were evil.[26] They minimize death as a kind of "haven," in which they are securely shielded from the pain and misfortunes of this world to which we are all subject.[27] This is tantamount to defending evil as if evil is not real, while they experience and feel the opposite. Luther writes:

> [T]his is the worst blindness and a further disaster – also a result of original sin when we thus minimize sin and death, together with all other sorrows of the human race; when we thus oppose the universal judgment of mankind, yes, experience itself; and when we flatter ourselves with the most superficial and meaningless thoughts. This is not the way to talk about death.[28]

Against the foolish discourses on death, Luther outlines what he believes to be the intent of the Psalm's author, Moses, according to whom death is "the gravest and most horrible punishment of sin," frequently accompanied by acute fearful afflictions.[29] Moses magnifies maximally sin and death so that

---

26. LW 13.76.
27. LW 13.76.
28. LW 13.77. Also quoted in Pless, *Martin Luther,* 90.
29. LW 13.76.

sinners before God (*coram deo*) see death for what it actually is. At this point, Moses, in keeping with his calling as a lawgiver, is "most Mosaic, that is a stern minister of death, God's wrath, and sin." Luther elaborates:

> In a magnificent manner, therefore, he performs the ministry of the Law; he depicts death in the most repulsive colors and in this way demonstrates that God's wrath is the cause of our death. Yes, he shows that even before we physically die, we have been put to death and are overwhelmed with dreadful miseries.[30]

The death of a person is a far greater calamity, an event that elicits immense sadness than the slaughter of a cow, because he dies due to God's wrath. The animal's death is not a divine punishment but "a temporal casualty" ordained by God. But "the death of human beings is a genuine disaster. Man's death is in itself truly an infinite and eternal wrath."[31] Humanity's death is not accidental, and neither is it an aspect of temporality. It was "threatened by God and is caused by an incensed and estranged God."[32] Originally death was not intrinsic to a person's nature. Because of the fall, he succumbs to death like the animals. "He dies because he provoked God's wrath. Death is, in this case, the inevitable and deserved consequence of his sin and disobedience."[33] Gripped by this grim reality, Luther wrote soberly: "Is it not a frightening

---

30. LW 13.78. See also Martin Brecht, *Martin Luther: The Preservation of the Church 1533–1546*, translated by James L. Schaaf (Minneapolis: Fortress Press, 1993), 156–71.
31. LW 13.94.
32. LW 13.94.
33. LW 13.94.

statement and a most terrible wrath—that he dies because of God's wrath?"[34]

In his commentary on Psalm 118, Luther asserted that "death always appears in the company of sin and the law."[35] The terrible triad—death, sin, and law—always attacks us. "Because Christians know of law and sin," Lohse writes, "they sense more strongly than others the horror of death."[36] No species of living beings are ever tormented by the frightful burden of death the way human beings are. However Christians, the God-fearing ones, feel even more the depth of it. He writes:

> Truly our death is not only more terrible than the deaths of all [other creatures], but also more terrible than that of other human beings. What of it when Epicurus dies? He not only does not know that there is a God, but also fails to understand his own misery which he is experiencing.... Christians, however, and God-fearing people know that their death, together with all other miseries of this life, is to be equated with God's wrath. Hence they find themselves warring and battling with an incensed God in an effort to protect their salvation.[37]

The terrible reality of death is made worse by meditating on its opposite, namely the blessed estate we lost through the fall. Humanity was originally created to be "noble," to surpass all other living creatures. Created in the image of God, each one is "to live and rule."[38] A good and perfect being created for life and to have his dwelling place in God is now destined for

---

34. LW 13.94.
35. LW 14.83.
36. Lohse, *Martin Luther's Theology*, 331.
37. LW 13.112.
38. LW 13.95.

the opposites—death and wrath. This shocking, inescapable news so crushed Moses' heart that he lamented the loss of his blessed estate through sin. Death renders insignificant God's most significant act, the creation of human life. By way of contrast, he describes the horrible reality of humanity's condition under divine wrath: "that which was created for life is now destined for death."[39] Death is laid upon us by God. The one who creates the world and us by his word now condemns the one who falls from grace. "Therefore this is a profound saying," Luther wrote, "when Moses prays in verse 2: 'Thou causest men to die'," referring to God as the cause of our death. "It is He who plunges [sinners] from life to death."[40] Both creation and condemnation, contradictory activities, are done by the one and same God—he who speaks the creative word at birth now declares death at the end of the person's life. Just as life comes as a result of God's design, so death occurs as the result of God's wrath.

Most Terrible Misfortune: Lacking Awareness of Death

The fourth verse, "For a thousand years are in Thy sight as yesterday when it is past, and like a watch in the night," looks at life as God sees it. The assumption that living a long life, like Methuselah did, is a sure sign of blessing and cannot be the object of God's wrath is a fallacious one. For none can escape God's wrath, which is "not merely wrath but rather his speedily executed wrath."[41] Even if Methuselah did live a

39. LW 13.96.
40. LW 13.96–97.
41. LW 13.100–101.

thousand years, from God's perspective, his life is short, for a thousand years are like a passing yesterday. Time understood by us is inapplicable to God. Life is a good creation of God. Because life passes away with a fearful rapidity of death, we rightfully deplore our terrible condition. We die too fast and cannot take comfort in the thought that we can defer and mitigate death. The "most terrible misfortune" besetting people is the lack of awareness of the fearful condition, namely, that of God's wrath and the brevity of human life, even though they experience it and see it with their naked eyes. The sobering truth is reflected in this: "Today a person dies who yesterday had hoped to live another forty or more years."[42] Death follows us everywhere and is at all times our nearest neighbor. Being insensitive to the terror of death, we go about our tasks as if we are going to live forever. Luther explains:

> This is the most terrible of all disasters and the one most deserving of tears—when people who are about to die still imagine they will go on living; when, overwhelmed by miseries, they still dream of happiness; and when, in the most critical perils that surround them, they are deliriously self-assured.[43]

It is necessary for original sin and the punishment of sin to be revealed for what they really are so people are compelled to reflect on life—its brevity and wretchedness. In verse 9, "For all our days pass away under your wrath, we live out our years as though they were speech," Moses employs the image

42. LW 13.100.
43. LW 13.129.

of sound to speak of the brevity of life. His complaint is that neither do we know the beginning of life or its end. "Just as a noise or sound vanishes to a place where nothing was before and where nothing remains afterwards, so, says Moses, is our life."[44] From God's perspective, a life of seventy years or more is like a sound of a speech that vanishes as nothingness; from a human perspective, life, even an extended one, is like a flight in which there is nothing but toil and trouble (v. 10). Thus Moses prayed in verse 12, "Teach us to know the number of our days, that we may be guided by wisdom as we go about our tasks."

This life, exceedingly short, is subject to manifold evils, including physical sufferings and eternal sorrows. The cause of the miserable and tragic life under divine wrath must be revealed in order that we might know the cure for it and rejoice in it. Thus Luther insisted that the knowledge of original sin must not be kept as a secret. Of this, he illustrated: "To be afflicted with original sin is not like being afflicted with leprosy, which feels nothing; rather, it is like being a stone."[45] We live our lives, not in the sense that we wish to know the exact moment of our last hour on earth, but that we might be disturbed by, and feel, the fearful perils of our miserable condition. Unfortunately the vast majority of humanity are practical atheists, going about their tasks as though there were "no death, and for that matter, no God."[46]

44. LW 13.120.
45. LW 13.128.
46. LW 13.128–29.

Life under Divine Mercy: An Exceedingly
Abundant Consolation

Moses ascribed wrath not to a different God but to the Creator, the one eternal God who is "our dwelling place, from generation to generation" (v. 1).[47] It is not the devil but God who reduces sinners to naught: "Thou Thyself does this, Thou, who hast existed before there was a heaven and an earth." Here Luther's doctrine of God is contrary to Manes's, according to whom there are two gods, the good god from whom all goods originate and the evil god from whom all evil things proceed.[48] This is a false notion propagated by Manes, which the earlier Augustine also held for almost nine years.[49] No comfort is derived from taking refuge in the evil God of the dualists, because death, something sinners justly deserve, abides as a perennial assault and cannot be averted.

Moses was principally concerned that we rightly refer both good and evil to the one God and learn how evils may be defeated. It is God who causes death in the sinners; it is this God, too, who commands them to return and receive life through him. Thus Moses had God say in the latter part of verse 2, "Return, Children of men." To appreciate the force of Moses' intention, one must observe the order: "Thou causest men to die" is logically prior to "Return, children of men." After having disclosed the true character of our condition under divine wrath, Moses immediately shifted the attention to the significance of our condition under divine

47. LW 13.83–84.
48. LW 13.96. See footnote 34 where Luther mentioned the heresy of Manichaeanism.
49. LW 13.96, footnote 35 where Augustine, *Confessions*, Book IV, ch. 1 was cited.

mercy. There the one afflicted reaps "exceedingly abundant consolation in the thought that death comes first and life follows."[50] Just as law must be accompanied by gospel, so also the repulsive picture of divine wrath as the cause of death must be followed by a delightful offer of divine mercy as its cure.[51]

The source of the abundant consolation is God, as borne out in verse 1, "Lord, Thou art our Dwelling Place from generation to generation." God is, in Luther's rendering, "the Place of Refuge," to which the one afflicted flees for security.[52] "From generation to generation" means God remains the dwelling place, from which people receive the assurance that "God has never deserted His own"[53] Those who pray to this God, in whom hope of a remedy against death resides, are assured of this: "they are not needlessly afflicted, and they will not die, since God is their Place of Refuge and the Divine Majesty, so to speak, their Dwelling Place, in which they can rest securely throughout eternity."[54]

Comfort Derived from Creation *Ex Nihilo*: Born out of His Word

Moses is being "a real Moses" when he expatiates freely on our miserable condition under sin, wrath, and death. From verse 2, "Before the mountains came into being, or earth

---

50. LW 13.98.
51. Althaus, *The Theology of Martin Luther*, 405–25, where Luther's view of dying is seen in the light of law and gospel.
52. LW 13.82.
53. LW 13.85.
54. LW 13.84.

and world were created," Luther derives a biblical doctrine of creation. Neither is creation out of God's essence, nor is it out of preexistent matter. It is purely out of nothing (*ex nihilo*) that creation occurs. Luther found support for creation *ex nihilo* in Moses' saying, "Before the mountains came into being [were born]." The Hebrew word "birth," Luther argued, denotes a miraculous origin, likened unto another body born from a human being, or trees that are born from the earth, out of nothingness, as it were. "Everything in creation appears to have been more truly born than formed and created."[55] Mountains are born, and God is the one who begets, without the use of any antecedent materials. By that Moses wanted to reflect in his Psalm the saying in Gen. 1:3: "He spoke, and so it was." That God's Word creates all realities is a center point of Luther's theology. All things exist through the causality of the Word, without the help of any instrumental causes. The verb "to be formed" also suggests an idea of begetting, as an embryo being formed in the womb without any instrumental means. Luther argued that Moses employed these words, "birth" and "formed," to suggest that the creation of the world is a kind of begetting or birth that happened at the command of God. This gives "prominence to the greatness of the Person," at whose speech or command springs reality into being.[56] "Being born is obviously a very easy thing. The birth of a tree does not involve labour."[57] The knowledge of how easy it was for God to beget the

55. LW 13.92.
56. LW 13.99.
57. LW 13.92.

universe by his word, Luther wrote in a superlative, is "most consoling,"[58] especially to trembling hearts in all trials and miseries. He wrote:

> The God who does such marvellous things is our God. This God we worship. To this God we pray. He is that God at whose command the whole universe was born. Why, then, do we tremble if this God is kindly disposed toward us? Why should we be afraid even though the whole world were angry at us? If this God is our Dwelling Place, will we not be secure even if heaven itself were to cave in? We have a Lord who is greater than the whole world. We have a Lord who is so powerful that at His Word all things were born.[59]

Effective Pastoral Care: Lamentation with Profit

Effective pastoral care is nothing other than the ministry of law and gospel. It is learning how and when to administer the law, whose office it is to accuse, and the gospel, which can only be heard as good news by those who are already broken by their sin. Reason purports to rid one of the feeling of God's wrath, either by way of disdain or blasphemy of God. It inevitably judges God's works as unjust and challenges God's wisdom and goodness for the throes of miseries and death. The one afflicted ends up either insane or incredulous. However, Luther reaps from Moses a remarkably realistic and pastoral method of lamentation with profit to the one afflicted. He wrote:

> We must learn to regulate and control the complaint which issues from our heart when we are overwhelmed by God's

58. LW 13.92.
59. LW 13.92.

wrath and death. There is nothing wrong with feeling of God's wrath this way, though we must not fall into the foolish error of disdaining or blaspheming God because of tribulation....

And yet it is not a bad sign to be incensed. But we must govern and control eruptions with a sure hand. An adolescent feels sexual desire; but God forgives it, provided that he checks and keeps it under control or marries. So also Christians are troubled by agitation of a muttering, blaspheming, and doubting heart; but these agitations must be controlled lest they eventuate, as they do in the case of godless people, either in disdain of God or despair.[60]

Luther did not deny, or reduce the fury of, the experience of being overwhelmed by God's wrath and death. With this disaster, he discerns the element of protest in lamentation. "Even the innocent creature cannot bear its sufferings without intense protest."[61] Just as "a hog that is slaughtered expresses its revolt and distress by its squeal," so the lamenter will revolt:

Who can continually give thought to God's wrath and not mutter disapproval? ... Therefore, how can human nature bear to think of God's wrath without tears, without muttering, without the most vigorous objection? How can it be indifferent to death, since it knows that it must die because of sin and as a result of God's wrath?[62]

Not only is God the target of lamentation, but he is also the reason for it. The one afflicted becomes so charged with a feeling of God's wrath that he is deprived of peace, and

60. LW 13.106.
61. LW 13.107.
62. LW 13.107.

thus he murmurs within himself: "Why has God burdened us with eternal miseries?"[63] The mutterings of the one afflicted "include at least an element of blasphemy," as in the case of Job, who cursed the day of his birth (Job 3:1–3), or Jeremiah, who became bitter because God did not destroy him in the womb (Jer. 20:17).[64] Luther cited Augustine who complained against God: "It is positively far better to be than not to be. Yet if you reason with yourself, you might say that the opposite is more desirable."[65] Such thought, Luther commented, is "not far removed from blasphemy," and is precisely that all the more if one gives way to it.[66] However this kind of complaint is not "evil,"[67] nor is it "a bad sign," if it is done in the light of God's grace and does not eventuate in utter despair or profane disdain of God. When harassed by agitation of a doubting and blaspheming heart, self-control is necessary.

The inexperienced or the fainthearted ones could not bear the thoughts of blasphemy without being consumed by them. Just as in temptation when a person is aroused by an intense sexual desire, his whole being is captured by it, so that he could not but dwell on what that desire suggests, so it is with complaint when his whole person is overwhelmed by it and its concomitants: anger, hate, anxiety, and other passions. At such times, complaint must be kept under control, or else it

---

63. LW 13.114.

64. LW 13.109.

65. Augustine, "De libero arbitrio," Book III, ch. 7, *Patrologia, Series Latina*, XXXII, 1280–1281 as quoted in LW 13.108–09, n. 53.

66. LW 13.109.

67. LW 13.116.

might erupt. "Such control is effective," Luther stressed, "only if one firmly believes that God has not rejected him," even when haunted by the terrifying thoughts of blasphemy.[68] For God not only is kindly disposed to the adolescent who feels sexual desire but also is friendly toward those who complain against him. Conversely when we are persuaded that God is "our kind and lovable friend," who will not deprive us of life and remission of the residual sins in us, we too must remain friendly and kindly disposed toward him.[69] This attitude, over which God rejoices, prevents a degeneracy of complaint to disdain of God or despair.

The negative thoughts of blasphemy not only originate in us due to our own weaknesses but also in a cause outside us, namely Satan. He is fully alive and unceasingly active in assailing us with thoughts of despair and dejection. When Satan tempts the saints with the spirit of blasphemy, one must leave the problem alone, lest he will overpower them. Luther illustrates this by an example of a barking dog, whose barking will become increasingly vicious and furious if we try to silence it with our own devices.[70] Likewise the sting of this temptation is made worse if we try to foment the thoughts of blasphemy by giving way to them. The one afflicted should hold Satan's accusations in contempt by holding onto the "Thy work." Commenting on verse 16, "Let Thy work be manifest in they servant," Luther had Moses saying, "We are the most abject slaves of demons. Therefore give us Thy

68. LW 13.109.
69. LW 13.138.
70. LW 13.113.

work as compensation in lieu of the work of Satan."[71] The pronoun "Thy" Luther interprets christologically, referring to "an emphatic accent" on the divine work that Christ does. This is "Moses' manner of speech and meaning," which, for Luther, reflects the victorious work of Christ over Satan as in 1 John 3:8: "The Son of God appeared to destroy the works of the devil."[72]

Satan causes us to lament excessively, without moderation, and sometimes contrary to our wish. At such times, we should console our troubling hearts with the assurance that God knows our infirmities and is not incensed at us. Not only should we give heed to the devil's fury but also God's design: he promises grace to the wounded and lays upon us such humiliation so that we might "sigh"[73] and pray to God. The troubled believer takes comfort in the thought that these attacks of Satan are "merely sufferings" of a child who is chastened by his loving father, but not "ultimate realities" of divine disfavor.[74] Consequently a person afflicted bans from his mind the thought of blasphemy and looks beyond himself and Satan for recovery. The proper outcome of lamentation includes humility, that we receive a humiliation that pleases God, and empathy, that we might console those overwhelmed with the same assault.[75] Hence lamentation can work for our benefit.

---

71. LW 13.135.
72. LW 13.133.
73. LW 13.114. See a separate section on "sigh" as a way of dealing with lamentation with constructive fruit.
74. LW 13.110.
75. LW 13.110–111.

Luther places a tremendous weight on the word spoken by another from Scripture as a means of consolation when facing perils. Focusing on the weaknesses of the church does not bear holy fruit as it might lead to pride, causing people to sit in judgment on others; or to despair, causing them to abandon the church and by implication, the word of God, the mark of a true church. Manifested sins might offend the Papists and Donatists, who could not bear to see faults but demand spotlessness as the essence of the "holy" church. However these sins do not offend God because God remains the dwelling place. Because God's grace extends from generation to generation, there will always be some who are the members of the church. God's grace admits sinners to the church, and it keeps them there in spite of faults and flaws. The creative word of God, with which we console, will sustain one another in distress and keep the church alive, despite her hiddenness and impurity. The task of a theologian is not to judge and measure human hearts, which are transparent only to God, but to teach and console by means of the Scripture, which expressly exhorts us to "encourage the fainthearted" (1 Thess. 5:14), and that "a dimly burning wick should not be quenched" (Isa. 42:3) but rather strengthened.

Both Aristotle and the monks deem meditation on death as the remedy that makes death less frightening. However, meditation alone does not dissipate the fear of divine wrath, unless it is accompanied by the assurance of divine mercy.[76] To engage in meditating on the evil of death where this

---

76. LW 13.81.

assurance is absent is to remain under the condemnation of the law, where no comfort is found, except utter despair and sheer terror. Where there is no hope of relief, being an Epicurean, indulging in one's body, is obviously more desirable than being an ascetic, vainly tormenting oneself with cares about that evil from which one cannot break free.[77] Lamentation over death is indeed a pitiable and lost cause, for the lack of the assurance of life and God's mercy. A fruitful meditation on death not only must be accompanied by this assurance but also must observe the proper timing in which it is done. In daily life, the feeling of fear and terror is necessary, as it works in us a mortification of the flesh; it awakens the old Adam lest "he snore in perfect smugness."[78] However in the last hour when death is most terrorizing, we pray that it will not surface lest we wallow in sheer despair. Moses is a "real Moses" when he tutors the readers, particularly the pastor, in the ministry of both law and gospel for the sick and dying. Pless writes aptly of Luther:

> The Ministry to the sick and dying will always be the ministry of both Law and Gospel. The Law is proclaimed to convict and condemn those who would shield themselves from the reality of death as God's judgment, while the Gospel is heralded to those who are terrorized by death on account of their sin. Luther sees Psalm 90 as tutoring the Christian pastor in this very work.[79]

Negative Theology: The Theology of the Cross

Luther's treatment of Ps. 90 confirms that he continued to

---

77. LW 13.81.
78. LW 13.115.
79. Pless, *Martin Luther*, 91.

apply aspects of his "theology of the cross" that he had begun to formulate in the late 1510s. Luther's critique of Dionysius occurs in the context of what constitutes a true definition of "negative theology." "Affirmative theology" reflects on the positive affirmations by which the more one takes flight upward the more one departs from the intelligible world altogether and becomes one with God, who is ineffable. Correlative to affirmative theology is "negative theology," which seeks to know God *via negativa*, by way of negating the possible affirmations that can be predicated of God. This mystical way of Dionysius results in the union of divinized minds with God. It is an experience that occurs in the cloud of unknowing, devoid of sense and meaning. The goal of this union is the cessation of intellectual activity.

The negative experiential knowledge of God Luther did not deny, but he defined it in terms of a completely different psychological content. Forde observes in Luther an affinity to and distance from mysticism.[80] Indicative of this is the following text, where he discusses the experience of God through the negative:

> Therefore such thoughts of blasphemy are indeed terrifying. But they are nevertheless good, provided that one controls and uses them to one's advantage. They include those "sighs too deep for words" (Rom. 8:26) which "pierces the clouds" (Ecclus. 35:21) and, as it were, compel the Divine Majesty to forgive and to save.

---

80. Gerhard O. Forde, "When the Old Gods Fail: Martin Luther's Critique of Mysticism," in his *The Preached God: Proclamation in Word and Sacrament*, edited by Mark C. Mattes and Steve D. Palson (Grand Rapids: Eerdmans, 2007), 65–66.

These thoughts can be felt, like all other thoughts. But they cannot be expressed in words, and they can be learned only through experience. Therefore Dionysius who wrote about "negative theology" and "affirmative theology" deserves to be ridiculed. In the latter part of his work he defines "affirmative theology" as "God is being." "Negative theology" he defines as "God as non-being."

But if we wish give a true definition of "negative theology," we should say that it is the holy cross and afflictions in which we do not, it is true, discern God, in which nevertheless those sighs are present of which I have spoken.[81]

For Dionysius, it is by the negation (*via negativa*) of positive affirmations of God that one arrives at union with God. "Negative theology," for Luther, is the theology of the cross, according to which God is found precisely in places where human reason least expects—that is, in "the holy cross and the afflictions." This negative theology, that God is found in his opposites, not in power but in weakness, not in majesty but in the lowliness of the cross, is what Luther wants us to learn of. It prohibits any attempt to understand the almighty God as he is in his inscrutable self but leads us to the locus where he wills be to found, namely, in the redemptive story of the crucified Christ. Thus Moses' petition in verse 16, "Let Thy Work be manifest to Thy servants, and Thy glory to their children," points to the advent of Christ into the flesh, apart from whom prayer cannot be realized. God is pleased to be clothed in the person of Christ, whom we behold with pleasure. In Christ, we apprehend "the glorious God, God clothed in His

81. LW 13.110–11.

glorious and gracious works."[82] By the efficacious activity of the incarnate Christ, who is "Consummate Grace, Life, Salvation, Redemption,"[83] the negative feeling of wrath is negated.

This negative theology is a theology of negation, in which negation is achieved not by natural knowledge or experience of God but by the glorious and gracious works of the crucified Christ. On the cross, both the horror of sin and the terror of divine wrath are revealed and finally conquered for those who believe. Christ interposed himself in the path of law, bearing the just punishment for sin so that the wrath of God may be dissipated. Christ bore our sin by suffering it, and finally conquered it. "With this ransom, by which Christ made payment for sins," he achieved for us the "plenteous redemption" (Ps. 130:7).[84] Christ is the remedy against God's all-embracing wrath over sin. "And so all saints feel God's wrath," Luther wrote, "but they overcome this feeling through Christ,"[85] not through any speculative peering into the being of God.

Certain thoughts cannot be articulated but are felt and learned only through experience, as opposed to reason. The terrifying thoughts of blasphemy that arise from the experience of rejection are negated only by the knowledge revealed in the story of the crucified. This is something Dionysius's mystical theology cannot do, and thus, Luther said, it "deserved to be ridiculed."[86] The God of grace finds

82. LW 13.137.
83. LW 13.137.
84. LW 13.134.
85. LW 13.115.

above all the ungodly and meets them in the word of death and life, the cross and resurrection of Jesus Christ. The negative experience of God leads the one afflicted into the terrifying abyss of nothingness, a condition where no comfort is gained, unless one prays, which moves God to be kindly disposed to him. So the negative experiential knowledge of God may be causally useful, if it causes the one afflicted to cleave to God for deliverance. Human reason cannot negate the haunting specter of wrath. But a life oriented toward a childlike sigh for the loving Father, as Moses did, succeeds in delivering us in the hands of a gracious God.

The Sacred Text: Negation and Affirmation

Not that Luther repudiated negation in one's experience of God, but he redefined it in accordance with his theology of the cross. The negation of which Luther speaks is performed by the sacred text itself, not by a mystical ascent to God. The text defines the experience and performs the task of divine negation, for the text possesses its own efficacy in accomplishing the work of God in the life of the hearer through threat and promise, law and gospel. Pseudo-Dionysius described Moses as one who "renounces all that the mind may conceive" and "plunges into the truly mysterious darkness of unknowing."[87] Rather than seeing Moses as the

---

86. LW 13.111.
87. Pseudo-Dionysius, *The Complete Works.* The Classics of Western Spirituality, trans. Paul Rorem (New York: Paulist Press, 1987), 49, as quoted in Gordon Isaac, *In Public Defense of the Ministry of Moses: Luther's Enarratio on Psalm 90* (Milwaukee: Marquette University PhD Dissertation, 1996), 244, n. 57.

exemplar of Dionysian mystical piety, Luther presented Moses as "the man of God,"[88] the mouthpiece of God. Moses is an appointed instrument of divine power through which the word of God in law and gospel comes. Thus the sacred text is not the occasion for contemplation about the hidden God, the being of God as it exists beyond all knowing. It is not from the sacred page from which one could abstract a theology of ascent and descent. Rather the sacred page is the occasion in which the voice of the living God comes, vanquishing the voice of the law with its accusation in order to beget a new life of freedom. Through preaching, Christ's righteousness, life, and strength break into the closed circle of death and annihilates it so that through him sin ceases to be "the sting of death."[89] Christ has done what the law could not. In an attempt to deny or redefine death, human reason is incapable of delivering the promise of the resurrection. Only faith dares to risk viewing death for what it actually is—namely the consequence of God's indescribable wrath over sin. But death is not the final word, though it is, apart from the gospel. Where the law announces there is no life, the gospel pronounces, "Even though you die yet you shall live." The gospel counters the terror of death and negates the condemning voice of the law so we might receive divine consolation.

The text is where God speaks, and by this word, the deed is done. Because the text is primarily about God who speaks and acts in the lives of his people, it centers on the story of exodus,

88. LW 13.80.
89. LW 35.242 (Preface to Old Testament).

exile, incarnation, cross and resurrection, and eternal life. The fundamental truth of Scripture is that God has descended in human flesh, through which we ascend to God. This precludes all human attempts, mystical or otherwise, to grasp God as he hides in himself. For Scripture leads us away from God as he is in himself to God as he wills to be found, namely in "the holy cross and the afflictions," the actual history of the crucified Christ.

Dionysius and Luther differ in their understanding of the word "experience."[90] For Dionysius, the experience of God occurs in the darkness beyond all knowing, quite apart from words; for Luther, the experience of God occurs within the life of the believer, who hears the word of God. It is an experience of rejection and affirmation of God through the voice of law and gospel. For Dionysius, the experience is one of ecstatic union with the being of God; for Luther, the experience is centered not so much on the being of God as it exists beyond all knowing as it is on his deed where God wills to be known. This spells the death of all human speculations about the inscrutable being of God. "The question of what God might or might not do," Forde says, "is already answered in what he actually does."[91]

The text is where we hear God addressing us, doing his work in us through God's threat, his alien work, and his promise, his proper work. This is evident in another text:

90. Isaac, *In Public Defense of the Ministry of Moses*, 246. I am indebted to Isaac for his insight on the different definition of the word "experience."
91. Gerhard O. Forde, *Where God Meet Man. Luther's Down-to-Earth Approach to the Gospel* (Minneapolis: Augsburg Publishing House, 1972), 26.

> Moses rightly refers death to God himself. He wants to warn us
> not to look frantically for help anywhere except to Him who
> has caused the evil. "For He has torn, the same will also heal"
> (Hos. 6:1). This is the name of our God: "He kills and restores
> to life; He brings down to hell and raises up" (I Sam. 2:6).[92]

The experience of rejection is God's creation, that he
performs an alien work of damning us in order to lead us to
the proper work of saving us. The result of such paradoxical
work is that the old Adam is crucified, and the new person
of faith is made alive. God performs a negative work—by
exposing the negative experiential knowledge of God
(wrath), before which all smugness in us is uprooted so he
might perform his positive work—by leading us to the
positive, saving knowledge of God (mercy). The force of the
annihilating knowledge of divine wrath comes to an end, as
the negative voice of the law is negated by the voice of the
gospel. What is ended is not the contents of the law but the
condemnation under the law.

Instead of pondering the positive affirmations of God as
a way to banish the thought of blasphemy, Luther directs
our attention to the word of the Scripture in which this
negative thought is both felt and negated. The Word creates
the negative experience of wrath in us so that we feel it. It
also communicates to our hearts that the God who creates
this negative experience is indeed the same who negates it,
if only we believe that this is done for us. "It is enough of
an evil to perish. But to perish because of God's wrath is
something human reason is not wise enough to overcome

92. LW 13.97.

unless instructed by the Word of God and assisted by the Holy Spirit."[93]

The text defines one's experience of wrath and determines the remedy against it. The Christian not only stands under God's law, where God's severe no is heard, but also under the gospel, where God's mighty yes is heralded. Even as God meets sinners in his wrath, the condition where they hear a terrifying no of God, he seizes them in his mercy, a condition where they hear a consoling yes of God. Those who have heard, and are captured by, the yes of God know that their sin, the sting or power of death, is forgiven and divine wrath dissipated. The sacred text exposes a true knowledge of human existence before God. It describes the negative experience, that we, due to sin, are under divine wrath, about which we cannot do anything, save cling to the cross. As such the text also determines the remedy against it, namely Christ. This is to be interpreted to our hearts by the Holy Spirit, Scripture's "inescapable companion" that divine wrath is negated not by means of mystical ascent, nor by means of merits but purely on account of Christ's work we apprehend by faith. This brings into focus the major pillars of Luther's theology: by grace alone (*solo gratia*), Scripture alone (*sola scriptura*), Christ alone (*sola Christus*), and faith alone (*sola fide*). Hence the ascent to God is trinitarianly grounded—purely by the grace of God revealed in Jesus Christ, as attested in the Scripture and appropriated by faith in the power of the Holy Spirit.

93. LW 13.115.

Sigh as Prayer (Oratio): Govern Our Lives with Sigh

Luther anchors his meditation in concrete experiences, in the narrative of Moses' life. After having been thoroughly terrified under the law, Luther advises the terrified soul to sigh to God for mercy.

> This is the climax of the drama which God enacts with us. His intention is that we play our part in full awareness of our sins and of death. Yet it is not an evil thing, so I have shown above, to have this awareness, to complain about our miseries, and to conclude that there is nothing within us but damnation. Indeed, one should complain and sigh this way. One should also try to arrange and govern one's life in accordance with such sighing. Then it will happen that one becomes aware of salvation.[94]

Moses was so overcome by grief and sorrow that his sighs had caused the division of the Red Sea and its drying up, the drowning of Pharaoh with all his accomplices, and the salvation of the Israelites. Not knowing for what or how he should pray, in this case, not knowing how the deliverance might come about, Moses uttered a cry from his heart that was found acceptable to God. In lieu of blasphemy or smugness, Moses exhibited a childlike sigh that preserved him from despair. However, to govern one's life in accordance with sighing, as Luther wrote, is not to flee but to engage with the struggle and win through the blasphemous thoughts to an apprehension of a gracious God. This is something reason cannot attain. The emphasis here is not so much on

94. LW 13.116–17.

the speculative as it is on the affective, viewing sighing as the appropriate manner with which one approaches the divine majesty. Luther included in the terrifying thoughts of blasphemy sigh, a deep-felt emotion with which one engages with God.[95] These terrifying thoughts that arise from the experience of rejection can be useful, if they move us to cling to God, not with words but with sighs, which will not go unnoticed by God. Instead of giving way to these terrifying thoughts, in his nude and helpless condition, the one assailed flees to God with "sighs too deep for words" that penetrate heaven, compelling the divine majesty to respond. This is precisely what Moses did:

> [H]e clings to this childlike sighing for the heavenly Father. He does not turn away his face from God. He does not underrate God. He does not blaspheme. He rather murmurs and complains with an honest face and in childlike fashion.[96]

The characteristics of a childlike sigh include authenticity, honesty, naivety, and dependence, all of which God delights in.

Luther accepts the monastic orientation toward the affective or experiential encounter with God. Unlike the monastics, he disavows sighing as a prerequisite for the reception of grace. For him, sighing is not a spiritual exercise that leads to the affective union with God. Rather it arises from one's negative experiential knowledge of God (i.e., God as he is hidden in his wrath). Sigh, in this regard, is the result

95. LW 13.110.
96. LW 13.118.

of an encounter with God, not a preparation for it. Sigh is not to be treated as preexistent salvific material we could foster or facilitate so as to move us toward the good. Just as prayer (*oratio*) makes a good theologian out of Luther, so it is with sigh (*gemitus*), which marks our absolute nothingness, total impotence, and hence total dependence on God.[97] Like prayer, sighing is a means of grace, through which the one assailed receives the plenitude of heavenly blessings.

God is revealed to those who sigh not because they twist by force the hands of the Almighty God through a cleansing action of their own or perceive the divine majesty with the aid of an intact remnant desire for good, but because God, despite their flagrant faults, continues to be their God. Luther considers with approval the exercise of sighing, not because he is a thorough-going Dionysian mystic but because it is scriptural. By sighing, Moses did not perish, nor did the people in the Red Sea. Thus Luther insists that the Holy Spirit "composed this psalm" in order to instruct us concerning our sorry condition, in which there is no relief unless we sigh to God as Moses did.[98] In the midst of afflictions and sufferings, the one under assault clings to God's grace and hopes for "the eternal weight of glory beyond all comparison" (2 Cor. 4:17). Sighing is an act of faith that waits eagerly for God to act mercifully. It is part of Luther's theology of the cross in which the one assailed refuses to abandon belief in God, despite

---

97. Heiko Oberman, "Gemitus et Raptus: Luther und die Mystik," in *The Church, Mysticism, Sanctification, and the Natural in Luther's Thought*, ed. Ivar Asheim (Minneapolis: Fortress Press, 1967), 58.
98. LW 13.81.

the contrary appearances. Sighing is the form in which the theologian of the cross utters his hope. He lays bare before God and engages with him by sighing, which penetrates through miseries and contraries (sin, death, and wrath) to heaven from where proceeds the "most loving things" of God: righteousness, life, and mercy.[99] The question of revolt, "Why has God burdened us with such miseries?"[100] is already resolved in the sigh, the condition of the possibility of hope, as it moves the divine majesty to descend with grace.

The Efficacy of Sigh: Faith and Holy Spirit

The efficacy of sigh (prayer) lies not in itself but in faith, the fruit of the Holy Spirit. Commenting on verse 1, "Thou art our Dwelling Place," Luther taught that no one can pray from the heart "without faith and without the gift of the Holy Spirit."[101] True prayer necessarily proceeds from the heart, as in Moses, who, "in true faith of the heart," prays, "Thou art our Dwelling Place."[102] Faith and prayer form such a seamless unity that if "we conclude our prayer with the word 'Amen' spoken with confidence and strong faith, it is surely sealed and heard."[103] Where faith is lacking, our prayer becomes ineffectual. Not only do we pray in vain, but our prayer also becomes a sin. We anger and blaspheme God, supposing that God will not hear us. Faith is the condition of an effective prayer. Luther explained,

99. LW 13.86.
100. LW 13.114.
101. LW 13.87.
102. LW 13.87–88.
103. LW 42.76.

If faith is present, we triumph. Because of faith in Christ our prayer is acceptable and pleasing to God and is also effective. If you believe that this God is your Dwelling Place, He is truly a Dwelling Place for you. If you do not believe this, He is not.[104]

These audacious statements do not mean that faith determines its object, totally devoid of the objective reality of God. True prayer done in faith must be directed to God himself, not to any earthly agencies of help. Luther advised us to cultivate these two virtues: "to have God and to hold on to God."[105] Faith lays hold of a gracious God, for whoever possesses faith has this gracious God. Therefore his prayer, together with his works, are God-pleasing. The objective reality of God's love is, for Luther, a necessary foundation of faith, that by which we truly hold on to God and are not snared by Satan, who tempts us in various ways to rely on human agencies of help rather than the true God. Those who sigh to God must believe and hold on to this reality: "Thou, Lord, art our Dwelling Place." Otherwise, idolatry is the outcome.

Luther defends the ministry and office of Moses as lawgiver. He also acclaims Moses as the one who follows the leading of the Holy Spirit. He juxtaposes Moses' sigh with Paul's in Romans 8:26, which speaks of the intercessory work of the Holy Spirit. The Holy Spirit aids us in our weaknesses, and in our helpless situation when we cannot pray, although we ought to, he intercedes for us with "sighs too deep for words." Just as we orient our lives in accordance with Moses' sigh, through which we become aware of our salvation, so we

104. LW 13.88.
105. LW 13.88.

also live in the Holy Spirit, through whom we become aware of God's consolation. Thus Luther asserted: "Who would now deny that it is the Holy Spirit who prays best in those who are His own?"[106] Not by merits or intercessions of the saints but by the gift of the Holy Spirit is the yearning of hearts found pleasing to God. We pray by the Holy Spirit, whose knowledge of us is deep and accurate and surpasses our own, and who presents our prayers with sighs too deep for words that reach heaven. When assailed by unfathomable thoughts of evil, the believer comes to the end of words, at which point the Holy Spirit aids as the consoling agent who presents our cries to God. Just as the stirrings that go on in the hearts of lovers are beyond the scope of analysis and articulation, so it is with the sighing of one's encounter with God. The end of words is not the end but the beginning of hope, as words are replaced by sigh, which will surely be heard by God. Complaint is not where we stay as a perpetual state; rather it moves us from ventilation of anger to sighing of it to God and finally to relinquishment of it.[107]

Movement from Complaint to Trust: Oceanic Mercy and Unending Joy

By a childlike sigh and through Christ, the one who is given for us, the negative experiential knowledge of God dissipates. The movement from the negative to the positive is the

---

106. LW 13.87.
107. Brueggemann, "The Costly Loss of Lament," 58, where he wrote: "Israel moves from the articulation of hurt and anger to submission of them to God and finally to relinquishment of it."

gracious action of God in his Word. As a result of God's salvific act, the movement from wrath to mercy, death to life, affliction to joy, lamentation to trust, has been made. God then ceases to be the problem, so to speak; he is the remedy to those who sigh to him in distress. Consequently the one lamenting changes his view of the situation about himself, that though most terrified, he is most assured of deliverance. This is borne out in his exposition of verse 13: "Turn Thy countenance upon us at last! Be merciful to Thy servants!"

> We should always cling to the truth that it is not a damnable thing to feel God's wrath, but that this feeling is the beginning of deliverance, which cannot be gained without constant prayer. This feeling is a singular gift, which reason does not grasp or understand.[108]

After having complained, governed our complaint, and received God's comfort by way of a childlike sigh, we are to live our lives that reflect the awareness of the oceanic immensity of mercy more than the distress caused by manifold evils in the course of our lives and manifest hearts filled with unending joy and gratitude. Thus Moses prayed in verse 14, "Satisfy us in the morning with Thy forgiving love, and we shall rejoice and be happy all our days." Luther explains:

> Therefore he [Moses] means to say: "God, grant us overflowing mercy, not a particular mercy by which the empire or health is preserved. We ask for a plenitude and abundance of Thy mercy. In our misery, which lies on the entire human race like a heavy burden, a particular and, as it were, droplike ...

108. LW 13,130.

mercy does not suffice, but rather a deluge and an ocean of mercy which completely assuages our feverish thirst.... For that mercy alone which frees us from sin and assures us of certain and eternal salvation brings about unending and true joy, thankfulness, and thanksgiving."[109]

Although God's oceanic mercy has freed us to serve him freely and live as saints in joyful obedience to God's Word, the remnant of sin is still left in us because of the flesh. By contrast, Moses was more certain of God's overflowing mercy than his awareness of the dregs of sin and its manifold afflictions. With this conviction, Moses voiced his petition in the final verse of the Psalm, verse 17: "Let the favor of the Lord, our God, be upon us, and establish Thou the work of our hands. Yea, the work of our hands establish thou it." Sins and the punishment of sin abound in daily life, which are enough causes for sorrows and the frailty of faith. Even so, the good news prevails: "When our hearts are troubled with sorrow, truly God Himself sorrows, who died that we might be justified, and full of joy."[110] The freedom of the justified saint is the heart of the matter. When our works fail, God nevertheless remains our God, whose favor rests on those to whom he reveals his work. That God is pleased with what we are, and what we have is indeed a cause for inexpressible gratitude and unending joy, instead of a perpetual complaint against God.

109. LW 13.133.
110. LW 13.138.

Final Words

Luther's earthiness is reflected in that he neither denies the anxiety over the physical pain of death nor undermines the turmoil of psychological feeling of loss. He does not sanitize or sentimentalize death by severing it from sin, law, and wrath. Luther's prime concern, which he derives from Moses, is a theological one, which speaks of the fearful reality of death as a confrontation between God and an individual. The cognition that leads from a mere awareness as an individual to a self-understanding as one who is opposed to God and stands under divine wrath is supplied by the sacred text. Only those who are seized by the word of the Scripture are awakened from perfect smugness to a consciousness of their terrible condition before God and finally cleave to God as their only remedy against it. The disclosure of human miseries (sin, wrath, and death) is not the final word but the display of God's most loving things (forgiveness, mercy, and life). And nothing can undo it!

5

Psalm 94: Praying against the Enemies: Negative Capability and Positive Agency

In 1526, Luther wrote *Four Psalms of Comfort* and dedicated them to Queen Mary of Hungary.[1] The impetus behind Luther's commentary on these Psalms was the bitter and difficult lot of the Royal Majesty. She was favorably inclined to the cause of the Reformation. As a result she was severely restrained by the wicked bishops in Hungary. Furthermore she was widowed so early in life. The misery and loss of the Royal Majesty presents a field for Luther's concrete application of the concept of alien work, a significant aspect of Luther's theology of the cross. As alien work, God

1. LW 14.x; 209. The four psalms of comfort include Pss. 37, 62, 94, and 109.

permitted these misfortunes to befall her, not because he was displeased with her but because he intended to teach her where the ultimate trust lies:

> Through this experience Your Royal Majesty should learn to trust solely in the true Father who is in heaven, to find your comfort in the true Bridegroom, Jesus Christ, who is also our Brother, indeed our flesh and blood, and to take delight in your real friends and true companions, the holy angels, who surround us and take care of us... [T]he Scriptures, especially the psalms, will give Your Royal Majesty a great deal of comfort against this and show you in detail the sweet and kind Father and Son, in whom certain and eternal life lies hidden (Col,. 3:3). And certainly anyone who has come to the point that he can see and feel in the Scriptures the Father's love toward us will easily be able to bear all the misfortune that there may be on earth.[2]

The imprecatory Psalm 94 has been commonly used by "all the pious children of God and members of His Spiritual people," as they pray against the persecutors.[3] This has been the case, Luther insists, because from the beginning of the world the people of God have suffered from two groups of persecutors about whom this Psalm complains. The first is "the tyrants, who use force to persecute the body on the account of the Word"; the second is "the false teachers, heretics, and sectarians, who use lies and mockery to persecute the soul."[4] So vehement is this Psalm that it not only asks for divine vengeance against the persecution and perversion of the gospel but also curses the enemies who are

2. LW 14.210 (WA 19.533).
3. LW 14.243 (WA 19.581).
4. LW 14.243 (WA 19.582).

guilty of such activities. However, this Psalm also delineates the boundary when cursing is done—not on one's account but on the account of the Word of God, not for personal vengeance but for the sake of God's names or honor. It also sets the boundary for love, which must not be done for one's personal gain but for one's neighbors' interest, just as Christ himself did, not by virtue of his person but his office and the word of God. The psalmic imprecatory, though expressed in a mode that appears to be the psalmist's personal wish, is actually the prophetic judgment upon the wicked for striking at the gospel. Ultimately God's names and his salvific activities must shine, before which the enemies, together with their stubborn plans and wise ideas, vanish into nothing and are finally destroyed. The divine negative capability, that *"God cannot forsake his own,"*[5] is the ground of the fatality of the enemies; the divine positive agency, that *"God is our Stronghold,"*[6] is the ground of the victory of the faithful. Furthermore the alien work of God, that God permits the faithful to suffer so long under the oppressors, is penultimate; it clears the way in us for God's proper work. God creates despair in us as his alien work, not so we may be held bound by it but so we may be led to trust in God as his proper work. Ultimately grace wins, not sin; mercy triumphs, not wrath.

5. LW 14.252 (WA 19.590). Italics are mine.
6. LW 14.256 (WA 19.594). Italics are mine.

Reformation Reference: The Negative Effects
of the Proclamation

The message of the Psalm underscores a contemporaneity for the reformer, who also was confronted by the persecution and perversion of the gospel about which he wrote. Accordingly, Luther included in the first group the popes and bishops, the princes and lords who employ force to persecute physically those who uphold the gospel, and the second group, the sectarians who persecute spiritually by means of their perverted and false interpretation of the Scripture.[7] Luther makes full use of this Psalm to instruct his hearers in how to pray against them.

Like the psalmist, Luther also saw the need of comfort from the Scriptures in days of evil and of patience in persecution (Eph. 5:17). He warned about the negative effects of the proclamation of the gospel before the healing power of the gospel is felt. Before these assaults subside, they might magnify in greater intensity after the believer receives the gospel. This too was part of Luther's own experience, that suffering occurs not as the condition of salvation but as a result of faithful proclamation. The devil cannot stand it and stirs up many negative agents to battle against it. Circumstances might become bitter before they become better. This, to Luther, is "the usual course of the Gospel or the Word of God":

> When it arrives on the scene, days of trouble begin. The reason for this is that the devil cannot stand it and goes to work raising

7. LW 14.243 (WA 19.582).

up tyrants and heretics. Here there is never less peace, and there are never more wicked people and more offences than in a time of grace and peace. In other words, when the grace of God and peace are being proclaimed, which happens through the Gospel, it is amazing that people are more wicked than they used to be. But this is how it must be; for here you see him complaining about days of trouble and urging stillness and patience, which are unnecessary in good days.[8]

Correspondence: God's Identity and God's Act

In verse 1, "O Lord, Thou God of vengeance, Thou God of vengeance, shine forth," the psalmist mentions "the God of vengeance" twice, which indicates he is very earnest and wants to stir God into action. This God of vengeance is thoroughly approachable by the psalmist, and the intensely personal nature of Luther's understanding of God is brought into light. In the Hebraic way of speaking, God derives his names from the works he performs. Thus the name "the God of vengeance" is not to be treated as a statement about God's being *per se*, that God is, but about God's *way of being* in relation to his world, the way in which he acts.[9] God's identity corresponds to God's act, as God is known in the acts he does. His names perfectly reflect his acts, in correspondence. The identity of God is inseparable from God's operations. Accordingly, Luther's theology, says Braaten, prohibits any attempt to seek "the inner nature of

---

8. LW 14.251 (WA 19.590).
9. Italics are mine. God's *way of being* is God's way of acting. See Erich Zenger, *A God of Vengeance? Understanding the Psalms of Divine Wrath*, trans. L. M. Maloney (Louisville: Westminster John Knox, 1996), 71. Zenger rightly says that vengeance is not God's nature but God's way of acting.

God in some remote sphere above and beyond the structure of God's operations in and upon the world."[10] For the God at work is indeed the God revealed. This spells the death of speculation on who God is in essence, for what can be known of God is found in the acts he does for us.

God's true nature is love, not wrath. "Wrath is truly God's alien work," Luther writes, "which He employs contrary to His Nature [i.e., love] because He is forced into it by the wickedness of man."[11] God pours out his wrath against sin as his alien work through which God's redeeming love as his proper work is expressed. That God is wrathful against evil is proof that he cares. Hence God's wrath is most terrifying when the sinner is not punished but allowed to remain sinful. In Luther's own words:

> When God speaks, shows his wrath, is angry, punishes, gives us into the hands of the enemies, sends plaque, hunger, the sword and the other troubles, it is a certain sign that He is gracious to us. If however, He says "I will no longer punish you and be silent, withdraw my wrath from you, and let you go on and do whatever you want as you think best," this is a sign that he has turned away from us. But the world and our reason turn this upside down and think that the opposite is true.[12]

Vengeance is not God's nature but God's way of acting in response to evils. "The God of vengeance" means God alone

10. See Carl Braaten, "The Problem of God-language Today," in *Our Naming of God. Problems and Prospects of God-Talk Today*, ed. Carl Braaten (Minneapolis: Fortress Press, 1989), 31; and his "Let's Talk about the 'Death of God'," *Dialog* 26, no. 3 (Spring 1987): 209–14.

11. LW 2.134 (WA 42.356).

12. See WA TR 1.117 as cited in Dietmar Lage, *Martin Luther's Christology and Ethics* (Lewiston: Edwin Mellen, 1990), 66.

can and should take vengeance. Just as the name "God of steadfastness" is appropriate only to God, so also the name "God of vengeance" applies only to God. "Because no one but God can do such works, no one but God is entitled to the names that are based on such works. No one but God can give comfort, hope, patience, and the like; thus also no one but God can punish sin and avenge evil."[13] Since we cannot know all evil, we cannot avenge all evil. We often mistake evils as virtue when they ought to be punished. What human government cannot judge or avenge, that God does, so that it may be true that God alone judges fairly and avenges fittingly.[14] God alone is the Avenger and Judge (vv. 1–2), whom the psalmist calls upon to "shine forth," to "come out," to "become visible and evident" to all, or to "break forth" in wrath upon his enemies.[15] The God to whom the psalmist appeals is not some wildly abusive God who punishes out of a sadistic pleasure but a good God, who cannot stand by idly and allow evil to triumph. God's wrathful opposition against sin is generated not by some abstractly conceived divine justice, which demands unmitigated retribution for the broken law, or by a wounded self-esteem turned vindictive, or by a frustrated love turned bitter. Rather, God's wrath proceeds from a pure love that opposes anything that stands between God and his people so that their relationship will be preserved. God's love expresses itself in wrath, in a vengeful opposition against evil so that good and its love might shine

13. LW 14.244 (WA 19.583).
14. LW 14.245 (WA 19.583).
15. LW 14.244 (WA 19.583).

forth. In Luther's own words: "For love's anger seeks and wills to sunder the evil that it hates from the good that it loves, in order that the good and its love may be preserved."[16] Watson wrote of the wrath of a loving God:

> For the God whose nature is revealed in the Gospel as pure love and grace is no mild sentimentalist.... Love's wrath, however, is neither the evil passion of offended self-esteem, nor the cold severity of violated justice, but the intensely personal reaction of the Father's all-holy will against evil. Wrath represents the purity of the Divine love which, while it freely and fully forgives sin, never pretends that it is not sin and does not matter.[17]

The Psalmist's Complaint: The Apparent Inactivity of God

The apparent inaction of God constitutes the basis of the psalmist's complaint. It creates in the psalmist an earnest plea for God to break out of his concealment and make known himself in wrath. "If vengeance is Thy work and is also very necessary now," the psalmist lamented, "why dost Thou conceal Thyself in the darkness and make Thyself so invisible?"[18] Commenting on Moses' saying in Deut. 33:2: "The Lord came from Sinai, and dawned from Seir upon us; He shone forth from Mt. Paran," Luther writes:

> Tyrants and false prophets have the upper hand. They have come to the fore and have made themselves evident, and they are well-established. But Thou art altogether silent. Thou dost conceal Thyself as though Thou wert buried and unable to

16. LW 29.175 (WA 23.517, 2ff). Also quoted in Philip Watson, *Let God Be God: An Interpretation of the Theology of Martin Luther* (Philadelphia: Mühlenberg, 1948), 182.
17. Watson, *Let God Be God*, 159.
18. LW 14.244 (WA 19.583).

act, for Thou does not prevent or punish such wickedness. Therefore we ask Thee to shine forth, peek out, and let Thy countenance look out at them—and to do it soon! For Thou art a God of vengeance, and it is fitting for Thee to avenge and punish. Avenge Thyself then![19]

The psalmist complains that God has kept silent and permitted the enemies to continue soaring high and celebrating their victory. Yet the complaint, "O Lord, how long shall the wicked triumph?" (v. 3), is framed by the motif of trust, oriented toward the salvific actions that proceed fittingly from the God of vengeance to whom the complaint is hurled. The impetus behind the psalmist's lamentation is not rational speculation on what God might or might not do in times of trials but hopeful expectation in God, whose very name "a God of vengeance," precisely denotes what he should do for him in crises. For that is who He is, "a God of vengeance," in whom the psalmist trusts, and correspondingly, this is what God does appropriately, pouring out his hostility upon the enemies so that his name and salvific actions might loom large. The psalmist abandons himself to the God of vengeance, trusting that the present troubles are temporary, lasting only until God acts justly with his wrath, an alien work he does that is not basic to his nature.

A Description of the Enemies: The Proud and the Wicked

"The Proud" in verse 2, "Rise up, O Judge of the earth; render to the proud their deserts," refers to both "tyrants" and "heretics." In verse 3, "O Lord, how long shall the wicked,

19. LW 14.244 (WA 19.583).

how long shall the wicked exult?" the psalmist mentions "the wicked" twice to indicate the two groups of the enemies of the gospel about whom the psalmist asks for vengeance. The two words "tyrants" and "heretics" designate all the persecutors of the pious and God's word, past, present, and future.[20] Not only are they conceited in their hearts, but also they have gained the upper hand by either persecution or deceit. They act as though they had triumphed and smothered the pious, as though they were everything and we are nothing, as though they conquer, and God and his Word amounts to nothing. What is at issue here is not the existence of God, for they all acknowledge God, but "the word and works of God" which they repudiate.[21] So stiff, self-confident, and smug are they in their unbelief and teaching that they condemn the Word of God and regard the pious as fools and deceivers for affirming the Word. Just as a kettle runs over and spills out, so they run over and spill out all bragging words that fill their hearts (v. 4). They have become so smug that they are "boasting, rejoicing, singing, and dancing, as though we are done for."[22]

It irks the prophet and any pious ones when people refuse to "accept God whose Word is his boast."[23] The psalmist calls them "fools" and the "dullest of the people" (v. 8), though they appear to be wise and are considered outstanding teachers. They are fools and by their erroneous teaching are making fools of the people too. They are both blind and deaf

20. LW 14.246 (WA 19.585).
21. LW 14.246 (WA 19.585).
22. LW 14.246 (WA 19.585).
23. LW 14.248 (WA 19.586).

concerning God's Word and works. The fools blaspheme God by saying: "Your God neither sees nor hears; neither will he nor can he avenge for us." They attribute to God inactivity, impotence, and indifference, the very opposite of the true God whose names are "God of hope" (Rom. 15:13), "the God of steadfastness and encouragement" (Rom. 1:3), and "God of vengeance" (v. 1). Against the fools, the wise say:

> Our God, whose Word we have and whose work we proclaim, is the true God, Creator of all things.... If He is the true God, why would He grant to others the good and useful gifts of sight and hearing, and Himself be unable to see and hear what concerns Him, what is done against Him or for Him? Hence he would have to grant something that He does not have. But since He does grant ears and eyes, you must be utterly blind and mad fools not to know Him and to say that He does not see and hear.[24]

The wicked know how to bind, fasten, and distort consciences but fail to teach comfort as a balm to the afflicted soul. Though they sit on the seat of authority and are teachers who hold the keys to knowledge, they teach the opposite of the gospel. "So it is that their seat is utterly inconsistent with the Law and teaching of God."[25] They sharply clash with God not only in fellowship with him but also in their teachings about him. Instead of teaching comfort and relief, they offer misery and heartache and heap upon people trouble and all sorts of evil. They teach and live wrongly and are therefore accursed by God. The subject of their teaching is

24. LW 14.248 (WA 19.586).
25. LW 14.255–56 (WA 19.594–95).

"an old thing," which is ineffective in issuing forth freedom.[26] Instead of creating relief for the afflicted soul, they erect many laws, by whose commands they create more works for the people. Luther explains "they command labor by statute" (v. 20) by means of Christ's saying in Matt. 23:4, "They bind heavy burdens, hard to bear, and lay them on men's shoulders." Instead of preaching about the patience or the steadfast love of God, they attempt to remove the anguish and persecution by their own works, or they cling firmly to ceremonies or external rites they invented as the antidote to evil. Furthermore, "they band together against the righteous ones, and condemn the innocent blood" (v. 21) of those who refuse to obey them or speak against them.

Faith Active in Curse, the Opposite of Love: Eventual Outcome of the Enemies

Because God is the Avenger and Judge, the pious invoke God as both. They ask God to "rise up" (v. 2), that is, to assume his seat high up as both Avenger and Judge, and to demonstrate his power fittingly. For the person who is righteous by faith, the angry God is approachable. The psalmist is serious about praying against both the tyrants and the deceivers and proposes two ways to do it, respectively:

> Very fittingly, he asks for vengeance on the tyrants and for a judgment on the false teachers. For the tyrants operate by brute force, without any attempt to conceal it; therefore they

26. LW 14.247 (WA 19.585). For a major study of freedom of faith, see Brett Muhlhan, *Being Shaped by Freedom. An Examination of Luther's Development of Christian Liberty, 1520–1525* (Oregon: Pickwick, 2012).

deserve vengeance and are already condemned. But the sects dress themselves up and put on a fine front; therefore they must be condemned by means of a trial and a judgment.[27]

The enemies eventually obtain what they justly deserve—that is, the ultimate and certain judgment as the end. "Our God," whose word we speak and whom the wicked reject as God, "will bring back on them their iniquity and wipe them out for their wickedness" (v. 23). This Psalm culminates in curse, the eventual outcome of praying against the enemies. The psalmist's revolt against the wicked intensifies to the extent that it not only prays for vengeance, that the God of vengeance will not let their evil go unnoticed, but actually curses the enemies, that they will be wiped out totally.

But how could pious and spiritual people ask for vengeance when Christ commands us to pray for the persecutors and love our enemies? Desiring vengeance and punishment obviously conflicts with Christ's command to love, since we ought to do only good (Matt. 5:44; Rom. 12:17). Here Luther replies by a sharp distinction he draws between faith and love. Where "faith and the Word of God are at stake," he argues, "it is not right to love or to be patient but only to be angry, zealous, and reproving" as did all the prophets. In a situation when the enemies attack God's word and his honor, the believers themselves must manifest the contrary of love. Luther writes: "Faith tolerates nothing; love tolerates everything; faith curses, love blesses; faith seeks vengeance and punishment, love seeks reprieve and forgiveness."[28]

---

27. LW 14.243 (WA 19.583).
28. LW 14.244 (WA 19.583).

In the introductory summary of his exposition of Psalm 109, Luther further elaborates on the distinction between faith that takes vengeance and love that forgives. There he introduces the phrase "curses of faith"[29] to argue for the legitimacy of cursing on account of the Word of God. Faith is active not in love but in curse, the opposite of love. To fully grasp this, one must observe the distinction "between God and people, between persons and issues."

> Where God and issues are involved, there is neither patience nor blessing but only zeal, wrath, vengeance, and cursing. When the wicked persecute the Gospel, for example, this strikes at God and at His cause. We are not to bless them or wish them luck when they do this. Otherwise no one could preach or write even against heresy, because that is impossible without cursing. Anyone who preaches against heresy wishes that it be destroyed and tries as hard as possible to destroy it.[30]

Faith does not permit the Word of God to be destroyed or the heresy to stand. Instead it prefers all heretics destroyed, for heresy deprives one of God himself. When faith is under attack, not only is it "correct" but also "necessary" to curse and pray for vengeance against the distortion of the gospel and against those who are guilty of it.[31] Not on one's account but on account of the Word of God, one can take the name of God and curse by God, just as one swears and blesses by the name of God. His teaching on the subject of curse is interlaced with scriptural citations. They include 2 Kgs. 2:24, where Elisha cursed the children of Bethel in the name of

29. LW 14.258 (WA 19.595–96).
30. LW 14.258 (WA 19.595–96).
31. LW 14.258 (WA 19.595).

the Lord, resulting in the bear tearing them up; Zech. 3:2, where the angel curses: "The Lord rebuke you, O Satan!"; and Acts 23:3, where Paul curses: "God shall strike you, you whitewashed wall!"[32]

However when a person, not faith, is under attack, love is in charge. He should not avenge himself but rather bear all things and do good to his enemies. We are to be Christ to our neighbors, in accordance with Christ's command and the way of love.[33] Likewise, when people are under attack, a Christian may rise in defense, assume the role of a judge, and wish evil upon a murderer, as if God himself had done it. This he does not on his own behalf or for his own sake but on behalf of others and by virtue of his office, just as Christ himself does, not on account of his person but of His office and His word. "In short, it is permissible to curse on account of the Word of God; but it is wrong to curse on your own account for personal vengeance or some other personal end."[34] The psalmic imprecatory is not the expression of the psalmist's vindictive sentiments or personal wishes but the prophetic judgment against the wicked for striking at God and his cause.

---

32. LW 14.258 (WA 19.595).
33. For further discussion on Luther's Theology of Love, see Veli-Matti Kärkkäinen, "The Christian as Christ to the Neighbor: Luther's Theology of Love," *International Journal of Systematic Theology* 6, no. 2 (2004): 101–17. "In faith, the believer is given the whole Christ, who is fulfillment of the law. Christ as gift inhabits the Christian and makes the believer to act like Christ acts, in loving and caring. The works of the Christian are in the sense not the believer's own bur rather the works of the Christ present in faith, given to the believer through faith" (116).
34. LW 14.248 (WA 19.596).

Divine Negative Capability and the Fatality
of the Oppressors

It is the psalmist's conviction that his oppressors will not, and cannot, succeed in their campaign against God and his church. This is based on the constancy of God's character, which the psalmist understands by way of the opposite—that is, in what God cannot do. Intrinsic to the reliability of God's character is a sort of negative capability, that God cannot violate himself and must act reliably. This is specifically encapsulated in verse 14: "For the Lord *will not* forsake His people; He *will not* abandon His heritage,"[35] in which God responds to what the enemies aim to do, as in verse 5, "They will crush Thy people, and afflict their heritage." The negative capability of God, that "God *cannot ignore* a prayer which reminds Him that His people and His heritage are being destroyed," (v. 5)[36] is an assertion of the freedom of God in making promises to his people, not of his impotence. However God's promise never becomes God's own prison. The God who is free in making promises remains free in fulfilling them. That which God has ordained will occur, a contingent consequence of God's free choice. Thus Luther writes: "For the Lord *will not* forsake His people; He *will not* abandon His heritage."

What is in view, though Luther does not discuss it in his exposition of Ps. 94, is the Ockhamist distinction between the two powers: absolute power (*potentia absoluta*) and ordained

---

35. LW 14.252 (WA 19.590). Italics are mine.
36. LW 14.246 (WA 19.585). Italics are mine.

power (*potentia ordinata*). The former refers to the mode of power according to which God can do anything, without violating the law of contradiction; the second is that mode of power according to which God has chosen a certain course of action, thereby allowing himself to be limited by a free and uncoerced primordial decision of his own. "The significance of the distinction between the two powers of God," McGrath writes, "lies in the conception of necessity involved: how can God be said to act reliably, without simultaneously asserting that he acts of necessity?"[37] It is the ordained power (*potentia ordinata*) that is guided by necessity, not absolute but conditional, not coercive but consequential. That which God ordains is of conditional necessity occurs, or else the character of God is at stake. It is of divine scheme that God must be faithful to the order he has established, or else the reliability of God's action cannot be upheld. Therefore Luther insists: "God cannot forsake His Own"—this negative capability is a predicate of God's ordained order and is thus a consequential necessity.

God must act reliably in accordance with his promise, a free decision of God. In so far as an action is freely decided of God, God cannot be said to act out of absolute necessity but merely by a conditional necessity. For God is under no obligation to do anything; God is not of absolute necessity to preserve his own but of consequential necessity to fulfil what he has freely decided.[38] Because God cannot contravene

---

37. McGrath, *Luther's Theology of the Cross*, 56.
38. See Robert Kolb, *Bound Choice, Election, and Wittenberg Theological Method: From Martin Luther to the Formula of Concord* (Grand Rapids: William B. Eerdmans, 2005),

his own promise, he cannot forsake his own. This negative capability of God is a condition of possibility of the victory of the pious.

Conversely, the divine negative capability, that "God cannot forsake his own," is a condition of possibility of the fatality of the oppressors. Thus no matter how hard the wicked plot against the people of God, they must fail, "as certainly as God is God."[39] God knows that "they are but a breath" (v. 11), and in due course all eyes will see that their biggest and most ambitious plans are futile and fleeting. This knowledge is not open to human nature or reason, for they are incapable of revealing the true state of affairs. The knowledge that the magnificent appearance of the enemies at the beginning will come to naught at the end is not grasped by reason but is given by God, "a disciplinarian," who teaches it to us out of the His law, that is, the sacred Scriptures.[40] Therefore Luther resonates with the psalmist in verse 12: "Blessed is the man whom Thou dost chasten, O Lord, and whom Thou dost teach out of Thy Law."

Through the law, that is, God's instruction in Scripture on his person and nature, we are enabled to transcend our feelings and look, not at the present, but at their end when the eventual failure and falling of the wicked will come to pass. As support of this, Luther quoted several texts including

---

52–55 and 65, where he states that Luther largely shies away from the terminology of necessity after 1526. "Apart from a letter to Capito in 1537," Kolb writes, "Luther left no record of his enthusiasm for *De servo arbitrio*. Nor did he quote or argue from it" (65). This may be due to the fact that Luther's concept of God was just larger than the scholastic concept of necessity.

39. LW 14.252 (WA 19.591).
40. LW 14.250 (WA 19.588).

Ps. 33:10–11: "The Lord brings the counsel of the nations to nought. He frustrates the plans of the peoples"; Ps. 21:11: "If they plan evil against you, if they devise mischief, they will not succeed"; and 1 Cor. 3:20: "The Lord knows that the thoughts of the wise are futile." For the Scriptures offer no comfort or promises to the wicked, even though their sinister plans always fail. They instruct us not to look at how the wicked begin but to wait and watch the eventual outcome of their campaign. "Their plan is simply to wipe out the people of God and the Word of God. But then the tables are turned around; they are destroyed, while God remains with those who are His."[41] God is thoroughly against the enemies, though they think God is completely on their side. The enemies cannot rejoice, for they do not prevail over God and his Word. Our "joy and comfort" is that they will not succeed, for "God is laughing at them and all their smart ideas and fancy plans."[42] Should the supplicant's oppressors gain the upper hand and prevail ultimately, the fatality of the supplicant is guaranteed, and God's honor will be at stake.[43] The supplicant's complaint is not to the inscrutable hidden God, distant from his people and disinterested in them, but to the covenantal God who cannot do otherwise but fulfill his promises that his people and his heritage will be preserved against the oppressors. Thus the psalmist advises that in the

---

41. LW 14.251 (WA 19.589–90).
42. LW 14.249 (WA 19.587–88).
43. See Bernd Janowski, *Arguing with God, Theological Anthropology of the Psalms*, translated by Armin Stedlecki (Lousville: Westminster John Knox, 2013), 83–84, where he argues, on the basis of Psalm 13, that should the enemies claim to have prevailed over the faithful, it would imply Yahweh's loss of sovereignty as Lord over life and death, including the enemies.

days of trouble, we must manifest stillness and patience, not raging against the persecutors, and believe that their "pit or destruction" (v. 13; 2 Pet. 2:1) is at hand. Curse is the outcome of the enemies for striking at the gospel. But blessing is around the corner, if only the pious remain still and retain a good will toward God.

Verse 15, "For justice will return to the righteous, and all the upright in the heart will follow it," points again to the fatality of the enemies and the victory of the supplicant. As an all-powerful judge, God will see to it that justice will be returned to his people, whom he will not abandon. In the days of evil, might makes right; yet lies gives way to truth. Eventually injustice and deception will be swept away; justice and righteousness will reign at the end. Speaking of this, Luther cites the example of John Hus, who was condemned at the Council of Constance (1514–18),[44] violently and unjustly, but now is vindicated by righteousness, which prevails. The cause of the gospel is not hindered by the shedding of the innocent blood, that of Hus. The sixteenth-century Reformation reference is conspicuous, about which Luther wrote: "And everything the papacy has tried to do against him—all its excommunications, its preaching, its burning, its ranting—has been unable to prevent this; their plans have failed. The same things happened to the Jews in their plans against Christ and to the Romans in their plans against the Christians."[45]

44. George, *Theology of the Reformers*, 80.
45. LW 14.253 (WA 19.591).

Divine Positive Agency: The Triumphant End
for the Faithful

Knowing that God is on our side and considering the eventual outcome of the enemies impel us to be patient in the days of evil. "Whoever believes this and is instructed by God can be patient and permit the wicked to rage, for he considers their end and waits it out."[46] The historical context in which the psalmist found himself strikes a chord in the hearts of the reformer. What is discernible here is that Luther appropriated this Psalm for his own context, acknowledging that in the seeming uncertainty of the times confronting him, the one thing he is most certain of is who God is in relation to his people, that "God is my Stronghold" (v. 22). This metaphor Luther stresses twice, in order to accentuate it as the remedy against the persecution and perversion of the gospel:

> Let them preach, rage, and slaughter all they please! I am safe against them and mightily defended, for *God is my Stronghold*. Our teaching must abide, their fiction must pass away, for *God is our Stronghold*. Therefore we shall remain safe against them both here and hereafter, for our God is our Refuge; He makes us bold and secure.[47]

The repetition of the positive image of the divine stronghold adds to the certainty of hope, despite the contrary appearances: they preach, rage, and slaughter, but I am safe; their fiction will disappear, but my teaching abides; though

---

46. LW 14.256 (WA 19.594).
47. LW 14.256 (WA 19.594). Italics are mine. Also quoted in Parsons, *Luther and Calvin on Grief and Lament*, 105.

oppressed, we remain safe and secure in God's shelter, not only presently but also eschatologically, "both here and hereafter." The wicked will be done away with; the faithful will be mightily defended. With God's comfort and help, we can face the pressures of life with boldness and confidence. The divine positive agency, that "no one but God can give comfort, hope, patience, and the like,"[48] is a ground of the triumph of the supplicant. Victory is assured but only for those whose God is their stronghold, an assertion of his faithful character, and for those whom God cannot forsake, a contingent consequence of God's efficacious promise. Fatality is reserved for those who persecute the pious and pervert the gospel; their just desert is destruction, a pit prepared for them.

What matters most for the reformer is the Word of God that frees the heart, not the outward reform or implementation of additional pious activities, which lead people into further bondage. The assurance of the heart of the upright comes from justifying grace, not by ceremonial observances of religious rites. Genuine worship emanates from the heart that is touched by the word of God, quite apart from any forms of external piety. It is precisely the impact of divine revelation and grace that enables Luther to cut through the synthetic law-making of the enemies, crush the disastrous effects of human agency, and cure the afflicted hearts. Ultimately grace reigns, not sin; righteousness prevails, not evil; faith presides, not works.

---

48. LW 14.244 (WA 19.592).

The Cross and the Inefficacy of Reason: Faith Perceives and Receives the Contrary

The alien work of God, that God lets the oppressors triumph so long, is the ground of the psalmist's complaint. "Every genuine temptation," Luther argues, "has to bring a man to the point of despair, as though his enemies had won and he had lost."[49] The psalmist was brought so low that he felt as though his "life would be wiped out completely, like a man who is dead and buried."[50] To experience temptation (*anfechtung*) is to experience despair with no power to heal it, unless he turns to God for aid.[51] This reflects an aspect of Luther's theology of the cross already taught in the *Heidelberg Disputation* of 1518: "It is impossible to trust in God unless one has despaired in all creatures and knows that nothing can profit one without God."[52] Of God's sovereign will, the psalmist suffers under the assaults as God's alien work so that he might turn toward God for comfort and help as God's proper work. God permits the enemies to rejoice so long so he might induce his people to lament. "He lets them continue so long to make us ask Him."[53] Left to our own devices, we would have been destroyed, dwelling "in the land of silence"

---

49. LW 14.254 (WA 19.592).

50. LW 14.254 (WA 19.593).

51. See Karl Holl, *What did Luther understand by Religion?* (Philadelphia: Fortress Press, 1977), 75, where he described Luther's experience of temptation (*Anfechtung*): "...these *Anfechtungen* always took Luther by surprise. This confirms his view that genuine religion originates in an experience of the divine that is neither sought nor desired. Suddenly, unexpectedly, in the stillness of the night the Numinous is there!"

52. LW 31:48. Also cited in Paul R. Hinlicky, "Luther's Theology of the Cross—Part Two," *Lutheran Forum* 32, no. 3 (Fall 1998), 58.

53. LW 14.246 (WA 19.585).

(v. 17), like the silence of the dead, who are completely beyond reach, sight, and perception. Of this, Luther added an autographical note, as he reflected on his own situation:

> I would have been ruined, and the wicked would have achieved a splendid success against me; for everyone else deserted me, and my own heart was palpitating. *But it is God who gives me patience, who instructs me above and beyond my reason,* who topples the wicked. He permitted me to suffer so terribly at the hands of the wicked to teach me that I would be ruined without His help and that my own power is useless.[54]

Not reason but faith discerns the contrary: hidden in the apparent inactivity of God (the alien work) is the certainty of God's provision (the proper work); concealed in suffering is the grace of God. Luther stressed: "Whoever believes this"[55]—the paradoxical action of God—will reap the fruits of joy and comfort, the opposite of misery and affliction. In tribulations, reason is of no value in finding God; revelation is the key to assessing God's attitude toward us. Luther acknowledged: "*But it is God who gives me patience, who instructs me above and beyond my reason.*" Reason yields no comfort, for it inevitably ends up concluding that God does not exist, or if he does, he is a cosmic misanthrope. The theology of glory that focuses on reason always winds up calling good evil and evil good. However, the reformer took no interest in abstract theodicy that asks, "If God, why evil?" for God is not on trial. Luther's theology of the cross cannot be converted into a speculative theodicy,[56] for it is, as

---

54. LW 14.253 (WA 19.592). Italics are mine.
55. LW 14.256 (WA 19.594).

McGrath has written, "a theology of faith, and of faith alone."[57] To speculate about what the God behind the clouds really intends and why evil befalls is to lead those who suffer to doubt and distress rather than relief and comfort. A theologian of the cross does not know why suffering strikes an innocent, but he does not have to question how God regards him, for God has disclosed decisively in the cross of Christ that he is for us, not against us. Accordingly Luther's theology of the cross crucifies all human efforts in probing the darkness further and directs the afflicted ones to the cross, where the depth of God's love is revealed and where his faithfulness is beyond all doubt. In Kolb's apt words: "The search for answers ends where the search for God ends: at the cross, where God reveals his power and his wisdom in his own broken body and spilled blood."[58]

Luther was keenly aware of the hubris of human reason to repudiate the goodness of God when confronted by the

56. Robert Kolb, "Luther's Theology of the Cross: Fifteen Years after Heidelberg: Lectures on the Psalms of Ascent," *Journal of Ecclesiastical History* 61, no. 1 (January 2010), 80–82, where Kolb considers the theology of the cross as "Luther's version of a theodicy," in which the Christian simply holds fast to what the word revealed about God's true character—that God is good despite the contrary appearances. See also his *Bound Choice, Election, and Wittenberg Theological Method*, 62–63, where he argues that Luther's *theologia crucis* is a kind of anti-speculative theodicy, which does not seek to justify the ways of God to human beings. See also Jürgen Moltmann, *The Trinity and the Kingdom*, translated by Margaret Kohl (New York: Harper & Row, 1981), 49, where he questions the apologetic value of theodicy. Because the theodicy question assumes some belief in God, he says, "it is not really a question at all, in the sense of something we can ask or not ask, like other questions. It is faith and theology to make it possible for us to survive, to go on living, with this open wound. The person who believes will not rest content with any slickly explanatory answer to the theodicy." With this, Luther agrees.

57. McGrath, *Luther's Theology of the Cross*, 174.

58. Robert Kolb, "Luther on the Theology of the Cross," *Lutheran Quarterly* 16 (2002): 456.

myriad of evil.[59] Human experience consistently tells us that God is against us or absent from us; faith tells us the opposite, that God is with us, hidden in suffering. Faith is always at odds with experience.[60] Faith alone could withstand the unceasing attempts of the devil to deceive the pious into believing that God neither sees nor hears their struggles. He neither will nor can act justly, even if he wants to. Though the enemies say in verse 7: "The Lord does not see; the God of Jacob does not perceive," the faithful simply trust "beyond and above reason," as Luther did, in a God who loves us and promises his presence in the midst of afflictions. "Waiting on God in the midst of the shadows," says Kolb, "creates the patience that endures and fosters hope when believers can listen to his voice through the darkness. For they know their Master's voice and they have confidence in both his love and power."[61]

Speaking of faith, Luther acknowledges what he calls "the window of dim faith" through which God permits his goodness to be seen in one's painful situation, which in turn heals the despair one may have about God. This is borne out in his *The Treatise on Good Works* (1520):

> It is an art to have a sure confidence in God when, at least as we can see or understand, he shows himself in wrath, but to *expect better at his hands* than we now know. Here God is hidden, as the bride says in the Song of Songs (2:9), "Behold there he stands behind our wall, gazing in through the windows." That

59. For a major study of grace and reason, see Gerrish, *Grace and Reason*.
60. Rittgers, *The Reformation of Suffering*, 118. See also McGrath, *Luther's Theology of the Cross*, 224; Althaus, *The Theology of Martin Luther*, 33.
61. Kolb, "Luther on the Theology of the Cross," 457.

means he stands hidden among the sufferings which would separate us from him like a wall, indeed, like a wall of a fortress. And yet He looks upon me and does not forsake me. He stands there and is ready to help in grace, and through *the window of dim faith* he permits himself to be seen. And Jeremiah says in Lamentations 3:32-33, "He casts men aside, but that is not the intention of his heart."[62]

Though faith may be dim, the faithful can discern God in their sufferings and remain confident of God's favor. However the faithless, those who lack this "window of dim faith," despair of God's mercy, seeing in their afflictions only a sign of God's wrath. The faithless build their confidence on the shaky foundation of their pious works, which offers no assurance of God's favor. God is truly so, a good God cloaked in sufferings, as faith, even dimly, allows him to be. Lohse writes of the "authoritative significance" attached to Luther's view of faith:

> It is faith that ultimately gives God the honor. Faith is thus always and at the same time confession and "honor" done to God. Faith is also decisive in one's relation to God. Especially to be accented is the idea that when we honor him the Lord becomes in us such as he is in his person alone. This transformation or change occurs by faith.[63]

Faith perceives the goodness of God concealed under its

---

62. LW 44.28 (WA 6.208, 10-18). Also quoted in Rittgers, *The Reformation of Suffering*, 119. Italics are mine.

63. Lohse, *Martin Luther's Theology*, 61. Lohse quoted Ps. 104 to substantiate his claim that faith possesses "an authoritative significance." See LW 11.317 (WA 4.172): "Second, it applies tropologically, when we honor Him with acknowledgment of this kind and with praise and honor. For then He is already such a one in us as He is in person."

contrary, spiritual assaults. So from verse 16 onward, the psalmist begins to thank God for his providential care against the wicked and evildoers (v. 16), for the grace that God comforts him in the days of trouble. Just as faith perceives the contrary, it too receives the contrary: hidden in suffering is divine consolation. God is found in places where reason least expects. In places where God seems most absent, he is most present. When the psalmist begins to despair and to be convinced that he would be annihilated, and the wicked would triumph eternally, he discovers that the "steadfast love" of God is his "balm" (v. 18). When the despairing soul looks for various ways of healing, but to no avail, God comes to prop him up with his bountiful consolations through the stories and statements of the Holy Scriptures. Thus verse 19: "When the cares of my heart were many, Thy consolations cheered my soul."

Final Words

God's alien work is not "prescriptive"[64] but descriptive, which simply reveals the truth about a negative work God does, opposed to his very nature, and what happens when we come under that work. It seems as if God has abandoned us, but the truth lies in its opposite, that when we feel most abandoned, we are most embraced by him. Insofar as we despair in ourselves, we are made ready to count on God's grace to exalt us, in which we do not despair. Only when we are stripped of all powers within us would we ever cling

64. See Wengert, "'Peace, Peace ... Cross, Cross': Reflections on How Martin Luther Relates the Theology of the Cross to Suffering," 200.

to God, without whom nothing remains except ruin. Luther spoke of this experience: "[God] permitted me to suffer so terribly at the hands of the wicked to teach me that I would be ruined without His help and that my own power is useless."[65] Suffering is not a salvific act in and of itself; rather it is God's alien work, which prepares us for a reception of God's proper work of salvation. Sufferings may appear to separate us from God like "the wall of a fortress"[66] but actually draw us closer to the friendly heart of God.

Luther's pastoral sensitivity is evident, as he deems sufferings "the costliest treasures which no man can assess."[67] Though most distressed at the hands of the enemies, we are most blessed at the hands of God, from whom we *expect better*"[68] than we now know—this is revealed to the eyes of faith. In Ps. 94:18–19, Luther specifies the "better" things, namely, the balm of God's steadfast love and the cheer of God's consolation. Not only are they the antidotes to the afflicted hearts, but they also are the causes of the psalmist's doxology. Consequently a new vision of God is introduced: God, the target of the psalmist's complaint, becomes the source of his consolation; God, the ground of his complaint, becomes the reason of his praise.

---

65. LW 14.253 (WA 19.592).
66. LW 44.28 (WA 6.208:10–18).
67. LW 44.28 (WA 6.208:10–18).
68. LW 44.28 (WA 6.208:10–18).

6

Psalm 118: Soaring above Distress: The Efficacy of God's Right Hand

Since 1521 Luther had been outlawed and banned. From 1523 to 1532, Luther immersed himself in the tedious task of translating the Old Testament from Hebrew into German. On the border of the Saxony territory at the Coburg Castle, where he was safe, he corresponded with his colleagues at the Diet of Augsburg. During this critical time of internal turmoil and external persecution, Luther interrupted his translation of the Old Testament and wrote, among other things, an extensive commentary on Ps. 118, "the *Beautiful Confitemini*" of 1530.[1] Among several favorite Psalms, Luther

---

1. See Preface, LW 14.45 (WA 31, I.64). Robert Kolb, *Martin Luther as Prophet, Teacher, and Hero: Images of the Reformer 1520–1620* (Grand Rapids: Baker, 1999), 172. Kolb

229

had an especially strong connection with Ps. 118, for it has "proved a friend and helped [him] out of many great troubles."[2] This Psalm, the word of God, had become so dear to Luther that he was most unwilling to exchange it for all the wealth, honor, and power of the emperors and kings, the pope and the Turk, the wise and the learned. In his dedication to Psalm 118, Luther wrote: "This is my own beloved psalm. ... Sad to say, there are few, even among those who should do better, who honestly say even once in their lifetime to Scripture or to one of the Psalms: 'You are my beloved book; you must be my very own psalm'."[3] Luther invoked the word of God not only as a source of comfort but also of authority, even above a sovereign king. He condemns the neglect of the Scripture as one of the greatest evils in the world. For him, Holy Scripture is not "mere literature," whose content one could master quickly, without divine help; the words of the Bible are "words of life, intended not for speculation and fantasy but for life and action."[4] Thus he prayed that Christ our Lord would help us by his Spirit to love and hail his holy word with all our hearts.

While the first three verses of this Psalm focus on the temporal and spiritual gifts of our transient existence on earth, David devotes the rest of the Psalm to God's "comfort and help," a gift that is "higher and nobler," far transcending all

---

notes that the *Beautiful Confitemini* of 1530 enjoyed six printings before Luther's death. The Latin word *Confitemini* means confession.

2. LW 14.45 (WA 31, I.66).

3. LW 14.45–46 (WA 31, I.66–67). Also cited in Reinhard Slenczka, "Luther's Care of Souls for Our Times," *Concordia Theological Quarterly*, 67 (2003), 45.

4. LW 14.45–46 (WA 31, I.66–67).

creaturely gifts.[5] This gift is the causative agency of praise and faith, one no creatures could offer, not a single drop of it, even when they are fully endowed with all their goods, might, and skill. Not by human reason and strength but by the word and Holy Spirit could the distressed grasp the "real difference"[6] between the blessings of this temporal life and the blessings of everlasting life; the former is fleeting while the latter is eternal. By faith, a theologian of the cross perceives this certainty, that there is no other way to life eternal than the narrow path, which only those who come under affliction would find. It demands faith and grace to discern God's blessings hidden in distress and cling to God despite the contrary appearances. As Luther put it: "Faith has its Helper who is its Salvation."[7]

Grace-evoked gratitude occupies a paramount place in Luther's thinking. Gratitude is a response to the prior experience of grace, not a condition of it. This Psalm is a song of thanksgiving or gratitude amid internal stress and external affliction. The psalmist praises God "especially" for his greatest blessing he bestowed upon the world: "Christ and his kingdom of grace—first promised and now revealed."[8] He declares, in part: "The Lord is my strength and song. And He has become my salvation" (v. 14). "I shall not die, but live, and declare the works of the Lord. The Lord has chastened me severely, but he has not given me over to death" (vv. 17–18). The secret to soaring above distress lies in the

5. LW 14.57 (WA 31, I.90).
6. LW 14.58 (WA 31, I.91).
7. LW 14.81 (WA 31, I.141).
8. LW 14.47 (WA 31, I.68).

art of emptying the self and clinging solely to God's right hand. "Just as distress is a narrow place, which casts us down and cramps us, so God's help is our large place, which frees us and causes in us joy."[9] The tight narrow space in which God places us is an alien work of the law through which God performs the proper work of the gospel. Distress (law) is causally useful as it causes us to draw nigh to him, whose open wide spaciousness (gospel) is our salvation. Faith cleaves to God, who alone is our God, as the First Commandment teaches. All the great and lofty works of the right hand of the Lord are done so that we might proclaim the deeds of the Lord.

Luther and the Diet of Augsburg

It is noteworthy that at the time when Luther set about writing his commentary on this Psalm, he was keenly aware of the Augsburg Confession,[10] the theological document drafted by his colleagues that was about to be presented at Augsburg on June 25, 1530. In 1530, as the Protestant Reformation gained influence in Germany, Emperor Charles V summoned the Diet to meet at Augsburg and invited Protestants to present a summary of their statement of faith. Headed by Luther's trusted friend and colleague Philip Melanchthon, the Augsburg Confession promulgated the twenty-eight articles based on the teachings of Luther. Brecht called Luther "a participant *in absentia*"[11] at the Diet,

9. LW 14.59 (WA 31, I.93).
10. "Augsburg Confession," in *The Book of Concord*, 23–96.
11. Brecht, *Martin Luther*, 384.

for he did not sit idle at Coburg. A steady stream of exchanges flowed between Luther at Coburg and the Saxon party at the Diet. Elector John played the role of courier, which included missives from Luther designed to hold up Melanchthon's courage and spirit. Via courier, Luther received updated versions of the confession and returned with his recommendations for revision, if he had any. Luther acknowledged that since Melanchthon carried the burden of presenting the gospel in Augsburg, it would be inappropriate for him to interfere. Thus he did not "step softly and quietly."[12] The reformer was pleased with Melanchthon's work and did not see the need to do otherwise. This is recorded in his Letter to the Electoral Grace on May 15:

> Grace and peace in Christ, our Lord Most Serene, Noble Sovereign, Most Gracious Lord! I have read through Master Philip's *Apologia* or Confession, which pleases me very much. I knew nothing to improve or change in it, nor would this be appropriate, since I cannot step so softly and quietly. May Christ, our Lord, help [this *Apologia*] to bear much and great fruit, as we hope and pray. Amen.[13]

Luther's verdict remains the same, as he reiterated in his July 3 letter to Melanchthon: "Yesterday I carefully reread your whole *Apologia*, and I am tremendously pleased with it."[14] Citing Ps. 118:23, "This is the Lord's doing; it is marvellous

---

12. LW 49.297–98. See n. 13. The phrase "step so closely and quietly" might imply sarcasm or criticism in Luther's evaluation of Melanchthon's work. Whether that is the case or not, Luther did approve of Melanchthon's literary hand.
13. LW 49.297–98.
14. LW 49.343.

in our eyes,"[15] the reformer exhorted Melanchthon to trust in God's wondrous deed despite the contrary appearances.

In order to avoid political unrest and trouble between the opposing parties, the emperor demanded that the evangelical preachers refrain from preaching. For the sake of peace and unity, they complied with the Imperial Majesty. In the introduction to "Exhortation to All Clergy Assembled at Augsburg," Luther indicated how faithfully and firmly he had been against all factious spirits. He had always upheld law and order, "teaching the people nicely to maintain peace and to obey the authority."[16] In the same spirit, Luther advised the Elector John that he should submit to the emperor's order, if preaching were prohibited, since in Augsburg, as an imperial city, the emperor is the lord.[17]

A few days later, on May 20, Luther sent a letter to Elector John to console him, for he had suffered hostility exclusively for the sake of the word of God. The elector should take comfort in the fact that God's word was flourishing in his land, that it had the best pastors and preachers, that the youth were being built up in the Christian faith, and that he was supported by the faithful prayers of Christians. "Consequently Electoral Saxony is a paradise of God, and the Elector is the caretaker of this paradise."[18] As a result, "a large part of the kingdom of Christ is constantly being built up in Your

15. LW 49.343.
16. LW 34.14.
17. LW 49.297–98. See also LW 48.165ff. Luther's view remains the same. The emperor resided in Augsburg, an imperial city, and consequently he was lord there, just as Elector John was lord in Torgau.
18. LW 49.305.

Electoral Grace's territory through [the preaching of] the saving Word."[19] In contrast to these blessings of God, the trials the elector has undergone are of no importance. The elector should therefore not let the devil, "a doleful, sour spirit"[20] rob him of courage and peace amidst persecution.

Shortly after the hearing in Augsburg on June 25, Luther finally received a copy of the Augsburg Confession. Melanchthon requested further concessions to the papists, causing Luther to reply to him harshly on June 29:

> I have received your *Apologia,* and I wonder what it is you want when you ask what and how much is to be conceded to the papists…. For me personally more than enough has been conceded in this *Apologia.* If the papists reject it, then I see nothing that I could still concede, unless I saw their reasoning, or [were given] clearer Scripture passages than I have seen till now. Day and night I am occupied with this matter, considering it, turning it around, debating it, and searching the whole Scripture [because of it]; certainty grows continuously in me about this, our teaching, and I am more and more sure that now (God calling) I shall not permit anything further to be taken away from me, come what may.[21]

The reformer summoned Melanchthon to make the sacred and divine cause of the reformation his very own and face it with equal fortitude as did the princes and laymen. "If this is not simultaneously and in the same way your cause," Luther challenged, "then I don't want it to be called mine and imposed upon you. If it is my cause alone then I will handle

19. LW 49.310. Brecht, *Martin Luther,* 390.
20. LW 49.309.
21. LW 49.328. Quoted in Eugene F. A. Klug, *Lift High This Cross. The Theology of Martin Luther* (St. Louis: Concordia, 2003), 130.

it by myself."[22] Luther's contention is that the outcome of the Diet is a matter of faith, not of rhetoric or philosophy.[23] It cannot be converted into something that is perceivable and manageable. Faith lays hold of God, who is present in places least expected: "The Lord has promised that he would live in a cloud (I Kg. 8:12), and he has made the darkness his hiding place (Ps. 18:12)."[24] One has to suffer in order to possess Christ. However, on the contrary, one would be relieved of suffering if one were to deny and calumniate Christ. Faith enables the distressed to face Satan and the world. Should Melanchthon lack this faith, as Luther thinks he does, then he at least should garner strength from the faith of the believers and the church at large. Luther chastised Melanchthon's lack of faith in the form of several rhetorical questions, and in so doing, he made a brief confession of his own faith:

> For if Christ is not with us, where, I earnestly wish to know, is he then in the whole world? If we are not the church, or a part of the church, where is the church? Are the dukes of Bavaria [Eck's lords], Ferdinand [King of Bavaria and brother of Charles V], the Pope, the Turk, and those like them, the church? If we don't have God's Word, who are the people who have it? If God is with us, who is against us?[25]

Luther closed his letter, expressing his eagerness to come to Augsburg despite the imperial ban because Satan has made Melanchthon "so distressed and weak."[26] The truth that God

22. LW 49.330.
23. LW 49.331.
24. LW 49.331.
25. LW 49.331–32.
26. LW 49.332.

has appointed us to suffer for his word's sake has already been taught in a sermon Luther preached to the congregation that gathered at Coburg shortly before departing for the Diet at Augsburg.[27] There he exhorted every afflicted Christian to trust in the causative agency of God's word. "[E]ven though we are weak or timid both in life and faith," Luther confessed, "[God] will nevertheless defend his Word simply because it is his Word."[28] None can demolish it.

Luther considered Ps. 118 as a kind of personal confession, which complemented the confession Melanchthon was preparing for the evangelical princes and towns to present as a public statement of their faith and plans for reform. He interpreted this Psalm in all its richness, shying away from a purely contemporary, political interpretation. In so doing, he set forth his evangelical vision of faith, though far from devoid of political relevance.[29]

Gratitude and the Goodness of God

The divine agency of grace is the root of all human activities, including gratitude. In this, Barth's words might reflect Luther's thinking: "Grace evokes gratitude like the voice an echo. Gratitude follows like thunder lightning."[30] In his *A*

---

27. LW 51.205.
28. LW 51.205.
29. Brecht, *Martin Luther*, 392–93.
30. Karl Barth, *Church Dogmatics*, ed. George W. Bromiley and trans. Thomas F. Torrance (Edinburgh: T and T Clark, 1960), IV.1.41, as cited in Matthew L. Boulton, "'We Pray by His Mouth': Karl Barth, Erving Goffman, and a Theology of Invocation," *Modern Theology* 17, no.1 (2001): 70. Frank Senn, "Lutheran Spirituality," in *Protestant Spiritual Traditions*, ed. Frank Senn (New York: Paulist Press, 1986), 36. He concurs with Barth on this point: gratitude corresponds to grace.

Simple Way to Pray, Luther developed a four-stranded schema of prayer in a logical order: instruction, thanksgiving, confession, and petition.[31] The rationale for placing thanksgiving before confession is that grace has already been bestowed. Just as thanksgiving is logically prior to confession, so also grace is logically prior to gratitude. Any deviation from this pattern signals disaster, for it places us solely under the crushing weight of the law without the delightful consolation of the gospel. Because the psalmist has received the abundance of God's providential care toward him, he begins on a note of thanksgiving: "O give thanks to the Lord, for He is good. His steadfast love endures forever" (v. 1). The opening words of this Psalm should therefore echo in the heart and proceed out of the mouth of everyone daily. Luther stressed: "He must be aroused and trained to thank God for His daily goodness with a joyful heart and cheerful faith and to say to Him: 'Truly, Thou art a kind and benevolent God! For Thy kindness and goodness to me, an unworthy and ungrateful creature, are eternal, that is, unceasing. Praise and thanks are due Thee'."[32] These words "good" and "His steadfast love" must not be read with dull indifference, and neither should they be skimmed over as (in Luther's estimation) the nuns do or be bleated and bellowed as some do in churches. They are "vibrant, significant, and meaningful words"[33] that highlight one theme, the very

31. "A Simple Way to Pray," in LW 43.200. See Robin Maas, "A Simple Way to Pray: Luther's Instructions on the Devotional Use of the Catechism," in *Spiritual Traditions for the Contemporary Church*, ed. Robin Maas and Gabriel O' Donnell (Nashville: Abingdon, 1990), 164–66.
32. LW 14.49 (WA 31, I.73).

character of God: God is sheer goodness and steadfast love, the ground of divine providence and the basis of human dependence.[34] God is good, not by a goodness he receives from others as we are, but a goodness that he himself is. In his commentary on Genesis (1543), Luther wrote: "Wrath is truly God's alien work, which He employs contrary to His nature because He is forced into it by the wickedness of man."[35] The same appears in his exposition of Ps. 118:

> God is good, but not as a human being is good, from the very bottom of his heart, he is inclined to help and do good continually. He is given to anger or inclined to punish except where necessary and where persistent, impenitent, and stubborn wickedness compels and drives Him to it. A human being would not delay punishment and restrain anger as God does; he would punish a hundred thousand times sooner and harder than God does.[36]

This verse also serves as a source of comfort in every misfortune. God permits little evils to come upon us in order that he might awaken us from slumber, causing us to become aware of the incomparable and innumerable benefits we still possess. When compared with the countless blessings of God we still have, the evils we suffer are small, like a drop of water on a large fire. God wants us to consider the worst,[37]

---

33. LW 14.47 (WA 31, I.68).

34. Robert Kolb, *Luther and the Stories of God. Biblical Narratives as a Foundation for Christian Living* (Grand Rapids: Baker Academic, 2012), 152.

35. LW 2.134 (WA 42.356). Philip Watson, *Let God Be God: An Interpretation of the Theology of Martin Luther* (Philadelphia: Mühlenberg, 1948), 159.

36. LW 14.47 (WA 31, I.68).

37. See "Fourteen Consolations" (1520), in LW 42.119–66, where the same method of contemplation appears. Luther exhorted the Elector Frederick, who was easily exposed to the agents of evil, to marvel at the extent to which God limits their

meditating on what would result if God were to withdraw His love from us completely. By contemplating the opposite, a theologian of the cross sees through the eyes of faith how greatly he is favored by God. Consequently our hearts might "sing this beautiful *confitemini* and this particular verse"[38] in the spirit of Job: "Shall we receive good at the hand of God and shall we not receive evil?" (2:10).

Luther affirms a positive role suffering has in the life of the Christian. It causes despair of self-sufficiency so that he might cling ultimately to God. We are to view our little misfortunes not as a sign of divine disfavor but a lens through which God enables us to see "his steadfast love," or as Luther renders it, "his goodness in action" in numerous ways.[39] With this we comfort ourselves and love the words: "O give thanks to the Lord, for He is good; his steadfast love endures forever."[40] The Hebrew word "forever" denotes the goodness of God "continually," be it here or hereafter.[41] Even when this world is full of ingratitude, God's goodness never grows slack or weary. Just as God gives gifts to the wicked, he also does to the saints, in fact, much more. Instead of fulminating against God in a spirit of ingratitude, "the most shameful vice and the greatest contempt of God,"[42] the saints offer up praise and thanksgiving to God, "the believer's highest service both on earth and in heaven."[43]

powers. See chapter 3, "Gems for the Sick: Proper meditation on Evils and Blessings," in my *Luther as a Spiritual Adviser*, 48–80.

38. LW 14.50 (WA 31, I.74).
39. LW 14.50 (WA 31, I.74).
40. LW 14.50 (WA 31, I.75).
41. LW 14.51 (WA 31, I.75).
42. LW 14.51 (WA 31, I.76).

Doctrine of Divine Providence: Innumerable Gifts of God

Luther extends the doctrine of divine providence to the three groups or estates in society: the nobility, the clergy, and the citizenry.[44] This stratification forms the outline or the organizing principle of Luther's presentation of God's gifts for which gratitude is offered. God's goodness and benevolence were first understood elementarily: "God abundantly and convincingly proves His friendly and gracious favor by His daily and everlasting goodness, as the psalmist writes: 'His steadfast love endures forever'."[45] God is not only the redeemer but also the Creator, protector, and preserver of his own world and all that is in it. God unceasingly showers his best upon us daily, if only we have eyes to see, and hearts to feel after, his bountiful blessings. Luther wrote:

> What is all the money and wealth in the world compared with one sunlit day? Were the sun to stop shining for one day, who would not rather be dead? ... What would the finest wine or malmsey in the world amount to if we had to go without water for one day? What would our magnificent castles, houses, silk, satin, purple, golden jewelry, precious stones, all our pomp and glitter and show help us if we had to do without air for the length of one Our Father?[46]

Luther lamented that we are so accustomed to these gifts of God that we are no longer moved by them. They are the

43. LW 14.51 (WA 31, I.76).
44. LW 14.57 (WA 31, I.88). See n. 22.
45. LW 14.47 (WA 31, I.68).
46. LW 14.48 (WA 31, I.69).

greatest gifts but most despised. The devil works unceasingly to blind us to the knowledge that these immeasurable blessings are signs of God's goodness. We use them and accept them daily, as though we have a perfect right to them and hence see no need to thank God, the giver of gifts. The sins of the scoundrel would be more numerous than the leaves and grass in the forest if God were to demand an exact accounting for every hour of his ingratitude.[47] We should enjoy and use the gifts of God daily but do so with a heart of gratitude.

The second gift of God is "temporal government and blessed peace"—"the greatest of temporal gifts."[48] Verse 2 thus reads: "Let Israel say: His steadfast love endures forever." Israel as the kingdom was instituted by God, and only entrusted to King David, as Ps. 78:70–71 says, "He chose David, His servant, to be shepherd of Israel, His people." Scripture teaches that God makes both masters and subjects, but temporal government is essentially God's, as David testified in Ps. 18:40: "Thou didst make my enemies turn their backs to me." David, the foremost of all kings and princes, boasted not of himself but his utter dependence upon God, as Ps. 144:2 says: "He subdues my people under me." Although David had the advantage of the finest laws and customs of Moses to guide him, together with the prophets who had anointed and confirmed him as king, he had learned by experience that "neither human power nor skill, but God alone governs the world."[49] Kings, princes, and subjects should learn that peace

47. LW 14.49 (WA 31, I.72).
48. LW 14.51 (WA 31, I.76).

and order in the land are purely God's gift, which is bestowed "out of nothing but His pure goodness."[50] Accordingly David not only thanks God for this kingdom entrusted to him but also urges others to join him in thanksgiving for God's continual preservation. A nation without God's "special show of power"[51] could not stand on its own, and the present peace she enjoys hangs by a silk thread and would be lying in ruins in due course. Here, of course, Luther cites Germany as an example. This verse counsels Israel to thank God for the manifestation of his power, even when there is "precious little" of it,[52] lest she rob God of his honor through strutting and bragging. It also stirs Israel to pray that his steadfast love, as in the past, must remain with her continually, for the temporal government is solely in God's hands, above and beyond human wisdom and will and despite the irascible raving of all the devils.

Verse 3, "Let the house of Aaron say: His steadfast love endures forever," is the psalmist's prayer of thanksgiving for the third gift, namely, spiritual government, which includes the ministers of the word: priests, preachers, and teachers. In brief, this particular gift of God is "the precious Word of God and the holy Christian Church."[53] Just as so little could King David by his own will and wisdom rule his

---

49. LW 14.52 (WA 31, I.77).
50. LW 14.54 (WA 31, I.83). Kolb, *Luther and the Stories of God*, 152. See also Heinrich Bornkamm, *Luther and the Old Testament*, translated by Eric W. Gritsch and Ruth C. Gritsch (Philadelphia: Fortress Press, 1969), 9, where he described King David as "the authentic image of the true ruler."
51. LW 14.54 (WA 31, I.83).
52. LW 14.54 (WA 31, I.83).
53. LW 14.55 (WA 31, I.84).

earthly office, so also so little could the high priest Aaron by his own strength and wisdom govern the kingdom of Israel spiritually, even when he was endowed with the law of Moses, which ought to aid him in ruling spiritually over heart and soul. Like David, Aaron also learned by experience that neither temporal power nor human wisdom but Christ himself, out of pure grace, could preserve his own word and holy kingdom, "this great treasure of eternal life," for whom our thanks are due. Luther explained:

> Christ Himself brought us the Word; we did not invent it. He must preserve it, for we cannot do so with our might and skill. Christ instituted, founded, and built Christendom. He must also protect and promote it. Our wisdom and might will not do it; neither will sword and fire, as Paul says (I Cor. 3:5-9): "You are God's field, God's building. We are the servants; but neither he who plants is anything, nor he who waters, but God who gives the growth."[54]

The fourth gift of God, for which thanksgiving is offered, is "the true assembly," which includes the elect children of Israel and all the genuine Christians on earth.[55] Luther lamented that the previous three groups—the clergy, the nobility, and the citizenry—show no fear of God, abuse the gifts of God, and are self-serving. In the spiritual ministry, there emerge many heretics, sectarians, and priests who abuse the priesthood to satisfy their fleshly desires, just as the temporal rulers shamefully abuse God and all his gifts. However the order remains intact, not to be destroyed because of its abuse.

54. LW 14.56 (WA 31, I.86).
55. LW 14.56 (WA 31, I.87).

The common people also abuse their position, trade, skill, and money and do not use them for the benefits of their neighbors but themselves. Gleaned from these three groups is this "little group,"[56] who reveres God: pious, God-fearing ministers of the word, pious princes or lords of the land, and godly artisans, farmers, or servants. Because there abides residual piety in them, God preserves and bestows as much good on them. Were it not for these, the world would have been wiped out instantly, as Sodom and Gomorrah were.[57]

Performing the Art of Faith: "The Skill above All Skills"

While the first three verses of this Psalm focus on the temporal and spiritual gifts of transient existence on earth, the rest of the Psalm zoom in on God's comfort and help, a higher gift that far transcends these gifts of the first three groups, for it meets every kind of misfortune. Suffering and affliction from the devil, the world, and our flesh are the outcome of honoring, teaching, confessing, and practicing his word. As Paul says in 2 Tim. 3:12, "All who desire to live a godly life in Christ Jesus will be persecuted." The pain so overwhelms the little pious group that it fails to grasp the steadfast love of God hidden in it. "Therefore it demands skill and grace to discern this secret and hidden blessing, especially since the psalmist praises its eternal character and devotes so many lavish words to it.... The flesh would rather have evident, temporal consolation and help, and be above anxiety and need. But it must not and cannot be otherwise."[58] The

56. LW 14.57 (WA 31, I.88).
57. LW 14.57 (WA 31, I.88).

favor God bestows upon the afflicted seems to be nothing but eternal wrath, divine punishment, and torment. The situation is made worse by the provoking sight of God showering immeasurable blessings upon the ungodly in the three groups. By contrast, the ungodly appear to be God's very beloved because they are so amply provided with the visible, temporal, and manifold blessings of God. Luther knows keenly of the hubris of human nature to identify prosperity and well-being with God's grace and misfortunes with God's judgment. The self-righteous so prate their good works that they fail to apprehend God's goodness beneath the unfriendly circumstances. In Luther's words:

> [H]uman nature cannot acquire this skill. As soon as God touches it with a little trouble, it is frightened and filled with despair, and can only think that grace is at an end and that God has nothing but wrath toward it. The devil also adds his power and trickery, in order to drown it in doubt and despondency. The situation is aggravated by the provoking sight of God showering abundant blessings on the other three groups. Then human nature begins to think that the others have only the grace of God and none of His anger. Then the poor conscience becomes weak; it would collapse were it not for the help and comfort that come from God, through pious pastors, or by some good Christian's counsel.[59]

Luther's theology of the cross is faith-centered. Belief in God against all contrary appearances comes not out of human reason and strength but divine agency. Human nature cannot acquire God's consolation hidden in suffering and would

---

58. LW 14.58 (WA 31, I.91).
59. LW 14.59 (WA 31, I.93).

become weaker and eventually collapse, unless God's aids come. The eternal blessing of God, though completely hidden from the world, is revealed to the eyes of faith. Not self-actuated, faith is the action of the Holy Spirit, through whom the afflicted see the goodness of God in everything and trust in God despite the contrary appearances. "[T]his is skill above all skills. It is the work of the Holy Spirit alone and is known only by pious and true Christians."

> Note the great art and wisdom of faith. It does not run to and fro in the face of trouble. It does not cry on everybody's shoulder, nor does it curse and scold its enemies. It does not murmur against God by asking: "Why does God do this to me? Why not to others, who are worse than I am?" Faith does not despair of the God who sends trouble. Faith does not consider Him angry or an enemy, as the flesh, the world, and the devil strongly suggest. Faith rises above all this and sees God's fatherly heart behind His unfriendly exterior. Faith sees the sun shining through these thick, dark clouds and this gloomy weather. Faith has the courage to call with confidence to Him who smites it and looks at it such a sour face.[60]

Faith enables the afflicted to apprehend this certainty, that the only way to life eternal is the narrow path, which only the small God-fearing remnants find. In the event when we feel most forsaken, we are most seized by God. This is the art of faith, which opens our minds so that we might see God's benevolent heart behind his malevolent exterior,[61] and

---

60. LW 14.59 (WA 31, I.93).
61. Miikka E. Anttila, "Music," in *Engaging Luther: A (New) Theological Assessment*, edited by Oli-Pekka Vainio (Eugene: Cascade, 2010), 219: "Moreover, seeing the beauty of the world is an act of faith because the world does not look beautiful in many aspects. Praising God and believing in him means that one delights in the fact that there is anything beautiful at all, however small. The Beautiful *Confitemini*,

which emboldens the faint heart to lay hold of God amid life's agonies and stake on the certainty of God's grace. Of faith, Kadai wrote:

> It does not seek support in reason, philosophy, or metaphysical speculation. One apprehends salvation, healing, and new life through faith alone. The affairs of the world may often confound the Christian, but he can – and this in spite of what he may see or hear – believe by grace in God's gracious presence.[62]

Word and Spirit in Unity: The Source of Comfort

The word of God that is given us and placed in our mouths instructs us to recognize God's presence and his goodness, and to cling to them and be held by them. Unlike the sectarians who seek God's comfort directly without external means, that is, without the Word, Luther taught that God comforts us, not without but in unity with his word. In Althaus's words: "The Holy Spirit comes to us through the external, physical, sensible means of the word, of the human voice, and of the sacraments. All these words and sacraments are his veils and clothing, masks and disguises with which he covers himself so that we may bear and comprehend him."[63]

a commentary on Psalm 118 from the year 1530, is a call to praise God that there is not merely bloodshed and war in the world, but also at least some moments of peace. Likewise, it is a source of great praise that there are not only heretics and sects in the Church, but the word of God and the sacraments are there... Faith opens the human mind to see and appreciate the goodness of God in everything. Thus, faith is a deeply aesthetic way to look at the world." However the art of faith, for Luther, involves more than perceiving the beauty of the world and the goodness of God in everything; it involves unwavering confidence in God despite the contrary appearances.

62. Heino O. Kadai, "Luther's Theology of the Cross," *Concordia Theological Quarterly* 63, no. 3 (1999): 201.

The word is the substance of the Holy Spirit; the Holy Spirit is the dynamism of the Word. Both the Word and Spirit work together efficaciously in hearts: "Comfort does not come to us without the Word, which the Holy Spirit effectively calls to mind and enkindles in our hearts, even though it has not been heard for ten years."[64] Having reaped the comfort, the psalmist leaps with eternal joy. With courage, he meets the world's defiance with defiance, and says in verse 6, "With the Lord on my side I do not fear. What can man do to me?" Concerning comfort, Luther had the psalmist say:

> "Although troubles still continue, I now have a mighty, strong, powerful Defender, who is with me and supports me. This makes it pleasant and easy to bear my yoke (Matt. 11:30). What is this? It is the Lord Himself upon whom I called. In my sore distress He came to me through His eternal Word and Spirit. I scarcely know that I have been troubled."[65]

Misery and sorrow are like "feeble and temporary dark cloud and angry little wind," in the light of God-given comfort, "another, lovelier vision, to light my way, like the sun, into eternal life."[66] The Lord is the Cornerstone, before whom all forces of this world stagger and are crushed, and because

---

63. Althaus, *The Theology of Martin Luther*, 22.
64. LW 14.62 (WA 31, I.99). Jane E. Strohl, "Luther's Fourteen Consolations," in *The Pastoral Luther. Essays on Martin Luther's Practical Theology*, edited by Timothy J. Wengert (Grand Rapids: William B. Eerdmans, 2009), 321, where she sees in Luther the importance of the unity of the Word and Spirit in assisting believers to become indifferent to whatever the earthly conditions (joy or pain) in which they find themselves.
65. LW 14.62 (WA 31, I.99).
66. LW 14.62 (WA 31, I.100).

of whom the psalmist boldly boasts: "As long as the Lord remains with us, we shall stand, though they slay us. They have not killed the Lord who is with us; as long as He remains, and wherever He remains, we shall be with Him, as He says, 'Because He lives, you shall live also' (John 14:19)."[67]

Verse 7, "The Lord is on my side to help me; I shall look in triumph on those who hate me," extols how wonderful God is toward us. Not only does God stand by us in the hour of trials, comforting and supporting us by His Word and Spirit, but also he helps us win and overcome our enemies. Either the enemies are converted by grace, which brings the greatest joy to all the saints on earth, or they remain hostile and bitter toward us, thus "in God's name come under wrath and perish in the devil's name, while the Christians survive."[68] Whoever regards this verse as the word of God should rest assured that our enemies will not reach their intended goal but will completely be destroyed. This verse has outlasted the evil plans and the many plots of the enemies against the pious. That the enemies will perish, not our doctrine, is fulfilled in this verse, which is God's word. The majestic word of God reigns, irrespective of one's experience or lack of it.

When compared to God-given comfort, mere human comfort is of "a miserable and uncertain" kind.[69] To rely on human aid is likened unto a pitiable and poor soul who has no god. This also is borne out in Ps. 146:3–4, where David says, "Put not your trust in princes, in a son of man, in whom

67. LW 14.63 (WA 31, I.102).
68. LW 14.64 (WA 31, I.103).
69. LW 14.64 (WA 31, I.106).

there is no help. When his breath departs, he returns to his earth; on that very day his plans perish." The mighty devil prevents us from believing that life is uncertain and brief, and human comfort or earthly help must give way to death. In reality, God frequently takes the pious to himself early in life, and any plans and confidence based on them also vanish.[70] Hence the psalmist declares twice, in verses 8–9: "It is better to take refuge in the Lord." The princely office and temporal government, which God institutes, are gifts of God for our proper usage and enjoyment. But we should not place our trust, hope, and confidence in them. "To trust and to use are two different things. The former is appropriate to God; the latter is appropriate to creatures."[71] All human devices or wisdom fail to comfort and uphold a sorrowful heart. "They are all less than nothing, even in the trouble caused by one little everyday sin, unless God's Word gives counsel and comfort."[72] This was the spirit with which Luther encouraged Elector John and Melanchthon to stake on God's word in the cause of the reformation at Augsburg.

70. Neil R. Leroux, *Martin Luther as Comforter. Writings on Death* (Leiden: E. J. Brill, 2007), 218, where he quotes Luther's consolation letter to Elector John the Steadfast, the brother to the deceased Elector Frederick the Wise: "And without doubt God has taken away our leader in order that He may himself take the deceased man's place and draw nearer to Your Grace to give up and surrender your comforting and tender reliance upon that man and draw strength and comfort only from the goodness and power of Him who is far more comforting and tender." See Theodore G. Tappert, ed., *Luther: Letters of Spiritual Counsel.* Library of Christian Classics. Vol. 18 (Philadelphia: Westminster, 1955), 55.

71. LW 14.69 (WA 31, I.114).

72. LW 14.66 (WA 31, I.108).

The Efficacy of the Name of the Lord: First and Second Commandment

Commenting on the First Commandment in *The Small Catechism* (1529), Luther wrote: "We should fear, love, and trust in God above all else."[73] The fundamental proposition—fearing, loving, and trusting in God alone—constitutes a core of what it means to be human. Every subsequent commandment, according to Luther's *Small Catechism,* speaks of the proper and improper human activities that flow out of the proposition that "we are to fear, love, and trust in him." However in his *Large Catechism* (1529), Luther's explication of who we are centers on the word "trust."[74] "To have a god is nothing else than to trust and believe that one with your whole heart... It is faith and trust alone that makes both God and idol."[75] Kolb describes how this passage "understands being human as proceeding from the Creator's word and centering on trust in him as the ultimate source of 'all good' and the 'refuge in all need' that human action presupposes."[76]

The motif of trust is further stressed in *A Simple Way to Pray* (1535), where Luther taught people how to pray the Ten Commandments.[77] As part of the explanation of the Frist Commandment, Luther wrote:

Here I earnestly consider that God expects and teaches me to

---

73. "The Small Catechism," in *The Book of Concord*, 242.
74. Ibid., 365.
75. Ibid.
76. Kolb, *Luther and the Stories of God*, 66.
77. LW 43.200–09.

trust him sincerely in all things and that it is his *most earnest purpose to be my God.* I must think of him in this way at the risk of loving eternal salvation. My heart must not build upon anything else or *trust* in any other thing, be it wealth, prestige, wisdom. Might, piety, or anything else.[78]

Trust as an expression of what it means to be human inescapably links us to the Creator, whose "most earnest purpose" is to be our God. As part of God's design, our identity is founded and forged in his word. It is predicated upon God's command that his human creatures place "true faith and confidence of the heart" in their Maker and that their faith and confidence "fly straight to the one true God and cling to him alone."[79] Luther's intensely personal understanding of God shines when he has God say, "See to it that you let me alone be our God, and never seek another…. Whatever good thing you lack, look to me for it and seek it from me, and whenever you suffer misfortune and distress, come and cling to me. I am the one who will satisfy you and help out of every need. Only let your heart cling to no one else."[80] God is not only the source of our being but also the sustenance of our well-being. The authentic self is not the autonomous self; it is a relational self, as defined in relation to God, from whom we derive the core of our identity, that we are His creatures. The heart cleaves to God alone for all good, and in so doing, it permits God's most earnest purpose to be our God to be realized in us.

---

78. LW 43.200. Italics are mine.
79. "The Large Catechism," in *The Book of Concord*, 365.
80. Ibid.

Luther was cognizant of this, that it "remains a rare and remarkable skill not to trust in men or princes."[81] People are more willing to trust all kinds of false deities, except the one true and faithful God, and as a result, they reject God and trample his First Commandment underfoot. "Idolatry does not consist merely of erecting an image and praying to it. It is primarily in the heart, which pursues other things and seeks help and consolation from creatures, saints, or the devils. It neither cares for God nor expects good things from him sufficiently to trust that he wants to help, nor does it believe that whatever good it receives comes from God."[82] The psalmist not only exhorts us to take refuge in the Lord but also laments the opposite, that those who put their confidence in man and princes are poor, miserable souls and that they have no god. "God does not, should not, and cannot tolerate it. It is idolatry that would rob God of His divinity."[83] Whoever undertakes anything godly must begin with God's help and wager on his goodness, or else he may be put to shame (Ps. 25:3). Victory resides in "the insignificant and little word 'God'." Of this, Luther illustrated:

> I have heard story about that noble Bishop, Frederick of Magdeburg, who was also Count of Beichlingen not long ago. Duke Frederick of Saxony, his sworn enemy, was preparing to fight against him. He sent a spy to the bishop's court for the purpose of learning his defense operations. The spy returned jubilantly to the Saxon prince and informed him that the bishop was making no preparations and that the victory was theirs.

81. LW 14.66 (WA 31, I.109).
82. "The Large Catechism," in *The Book of Concord*, 367.
83. LW 14.67 (WA 31, I.110).

The prince asked: "What does the Bishop say about the war?"
The spy replied: "He says nothing more than this, that he is
interested in discharging his duties, visiting the cloisters, and
hearing the cases of the poor. He would let God fight for him
since He would take care of the war." When the prince heard
this, he said: "If this is what the bishop says, then let the devil
fight him in my stead!" He gave up the war, for he was afraid
to fight against God. Now who was it who helped the bishop
so quickly and easily, and so completely changed the mind of
the prince? Only the name of the Lord. The insignificant and
the little word "God" accomplish such great things as quickly,
so powerfully, and so easily.[84]

The meaning of "the name of the Lord" concurs with
Luther's exposition of the first two commandments in *The
Large Catechism*.[85] The God of the First Commandment is
almighty, before whom all the heathen are reduced to naught.
This God does not permit his name to be blasphemed or
let this sin go unpunished, as the Second Commandment
teaches. When our enemies malign us on account of our
honoring his name, they are actually persecuting God
Almighty himself and his name, and as a result, they incur
upon themselves the sentence or plague of God. Here Luther
endorsed the legal principle regarding agency, that whenever
one does anything in accordance with someone's advice or
command, it is actually done by the one who advises and
commands.[86] Prayer is the instrument of divine power,
through which the Christians crush their enemies, while God

---

84. LW 14.67–68 (WA 31, I.112–113).
85. "The Large Catechism," in *The Book of Concord*, 365–75. Friedrich Mildenberger,
Theology of the Lutheran Confession, trans. Erwin L. Lueker and edited by Robert C.
Schultz (Philadelphia: Fortress Press, 1986), 143–45.
86. LW 14.74 (WA 31, I.127).

actually does it for the sake of his name, which we invoke and honor. By these words, "I shall crush the world," Luther meant: "I will confidently ask God to hallow His name. Then I have already done it, for He will hear me, as this psalm says in verse 5: 'The Lord answered me'."[87] Thus David slew his enemies, not by his physical sword but the efficacy of the name of the Lord, the Almighty God. Luther elaborated:

> When he [David] honoured, hallowed and involved the name of God and prayed for the sake of God's glory, his sword became more than a hundred thousand swords. The name of the Lord is effective if we honor and call upon it. And when we fail to call upon His name, it is still effective. Of course, there will be no benefit or meaning for us, since we are not interested and do not call upon it. He punished the heathen, even though this brings no deliverance to the faithful, as the Romans destroyed one another and thereby carried out his sentence.[88]

The numerous, powerful, furious, and "holy"[89] heathen persisted with their siege, as the psalmist says in verse 13: "I was pushed hard, so that I was failing." But they are limited by these words: "The Lord helped me." God preserved him from their wiles and restrained their evil deeds, so that they could not accomplish their hearts' desires. Though they can torture, they cannot exterminate. They can hinder, but they cannot prevent. The word of God endures forever (Isa. 40:8), just as God and his name abide forever. God will not forsake

87. LW 14.75 (WA 31, I.127).
88. LW 14.75 (WA 31, I.127).
89. LW 14.75 (WA 31, I.127). The word "holy" is not a reference to the doctrine of imputation. It is merely a description of the self-sufficient.

his word, for which the saints suffer. No amount of raging, raving, blasphemy, or cursing will alter this. Here Luther added an autobiographical vignette as an application of this truth. When he first attacked indulgences, all the world was shocked and felt that he had overdone it. His prior and sub prior urged him not to disgrace his order by such actions. In utter dependence upon the goodness of God, Luther responded:

> Dear Fathers, if this work has not been begun in God's name, then it will soon fail. But if it has been undertaken in his name, then leave it to him (Acts. 5:38-9). They had nothing more to say. The work continues and, please God, with continue even better until the end.[90]

The mighty weapon is not the physical sword, but "the name of the Lord." When suffering numerous evils, Christians should not defend themselves with the sword, which is the opposite of a proper Christian spirit. Instead they should "diligently keep and promote peace."[91] This is consistent with the advice Luther offered to the Elector John at Augsburg that should His Imperial Majesty demand that preaching be banned, he should submit to the emperor's order, given that Augsburg is the imperial city. He must not resort to a political revolution but trust in God alone, as the psalmist did: "Now our Lord is a God who permits the faithful to suffer, ... but still does not forsake the pious in their need, and finally overthrows the monsters and rescues his own."[92]

---

90. LW 14.67 (WA 31, I.111).
91. LW 14.75 (WA 31, I.129).
92. LW 14.68 (WA 31, I.113). Brecht, *Martin Luther*, 392.

Distress and Prayer: God's Command and Promise

Distress is a predicate of the psalmist's condition. Prayer emerges out of the crucible of life under the cross. This is verified in verse 5 of this Psalm: "I called on the Lord in distress; the Lord answered me and comforted me." Concerning the etymology of distress, Luther explained:

> In Hebrew the word "distress" means "something narrow." I surmise that the German noun for distress (*angst*) is also derived from an adjective meaning narrow [*eng*]. It implies fear and pain, as in the process of clamping, squeezing, and pressing. Trials and misfortunes do squeeze and press, as is indicated by the proverb: "The great wide world is too narrow for me." In Hebrew "in a large place" is used in contrast to "distress." "Distress" means tribulation and need; "in a large place" denotes consolation and help. Accordingly this verse says: "I called upon the Lord in my trouble; He heard me and helped me by comforting me." Just as distress is a narrow pace, which casts us down and cramps us, so God's help is our large place, which makes us free and happy.[93]

On his *On the Councils* (1539), Luther taught that following the pattern of Christ's sacrifice on the cross constituted the seventh sign of a true church.[94] That suffering is a mark of a true church has already been stressed in this Psalm, where Luther wrote: "In short, we could never be or remain true Christians. Trouble and distress constrain us and keep us within Christendom."[95] Therefore the experience of distress is

93. LW 14.59 (WA 31, I.93).
94. LW 41.164–65 (WA 50.651–52). See Robert Kelly, "The Suffering Church: A Study of Luther's *Theologia Crucis*," *Concordia Theological Quarterly* 50 (1986): 3–17.
95. LW 14.60 (WA 31, I.95).

as primal as life itself, and is "much more necessary and useful" than the material possessions of this world, as it drives one to pray. Distress, "a narrow place," squeezes us and casts us down in sheer despair. But God's help, "our large place," frees us and lifts us up with joy so that we become "a falcon and soar above distress."[96] The tight narrow space in which God places us is an alien work, which is causally useful, as it causes us to cry to God, whose open wide spaciousness is our hope. Luther insists that we learn this: "God does not send him this distress to destroy him," but "to drive him to pray."

> [God] wants to drive him to pray, to implore, to fight, to exercise his faith, to learn another aspect of God's person than before, to accustom himself to do battle even with the devil and with sin, and by the grace of God to be victorious. Without this experience we could never learn the meaning of faith, the Word, Spirit, grace, sin, death, or the devil. Were there only peace and no trial, we would never learn to know God Himself.[97]

Distress is also Luther's experience. He remained in Coburg when the elector and his theologians left for Augsburg. Luther was still under the imperial ban and the threat of burning at the stake for his supposed heresy. Prayer arises out of being squeezed by tribulations and needs. The one under distress must be active, calling upon the Lord. He must not sit idly by himself, bemoaning in self-pity or brooding on his wretchedness or worthlessness. Nor should he attempt to

96. LW 14.60 (WA 31, I.95).
97. LW 14.60 (WA 31, I.95).

liberate himself from suffering or misery. Instead he should say to himself:

> "Come on, you lazy bum; down on your knees, and lift your eyes and hands towards heaven." Read a psalm or the Our Father, call on God, and tearfully lay your troubles before Him.... Here you learn that praying, reciting your troubles, and lifting up your hands are sacrifices most pleasing to God. It is His desire and will that you lay your troubles before Him. He does not want you to multiply your troubles by burdening and torturing yourself. He wants you to be too weak to bear and overcome such troubles. He wants you to grow strong in Him. By His strength he is glorified in you. Out of such experiences men become real Christians. Otherwise, men are mere babblers, who prate about faith and spirit, and are ignorant of what it is all about or of what they themselves are saying.[98]

Luther elaborated further the posture of prayer. When we come to God, we must not doubt that God is keenly aware of the condition in which we find ourselves. We must not pray aimlessly, like shouting into the wind. We lay hold of the efficacious promises of God, even when they are contradicted by experience.[99] To pray aright is to pray with a certainty that God indeed hears our prayer, as the psalmist did in the latter part of verse 5: "The Lord answered me and set me free." The devil might cause us to lose the assurance that our prayers are heard, simply for the lack of holiness, piety, and worthiness. As antidote, Luther advised us to make a sign of the cross and know for sure that we are the creature of "the only one God, of saint and sinner, worthy and unworthy, great and small."[100]

---

98. LW 14.60–61 (WA 31, I.96).
99. Pless, *Martin Luther*, 64.
100. LW 14.61 (WA 31, I.97).

Luther framed prayer within the paradoxical action of God's command and his promise, that the God who commands us to pray is the one who wants to help us. The God who accepted David's prayer, regardless of his holiness, is the same who will accept us, unholy and unworthy, as David himself was. At his command, David called upon God, and to him was promised God's forgiveness. God who offered mercy to David has promised it also to us, if only we beg for it. He has commanded us to demand, seek, pray, and knock (Matt. 7:7). Just as God's command that we ought to pray obligates us to come, so also his promise that he will hear us draws us to pray. At his command and promise we prostrate before God, raise our countenance to heaven, and plead for help. We pray in obedience to divine command, and in so doing God is honored as the true God. Luther averred, "He who does not call on God or pray to Him in trouble certainly does not consider Him to be God."[101] In Arand's apt words, "In prayer, the hegemony of God is at stake in our lives."[102] By calling upon God, we make known the peculiar significance of his place and standing as God in our lives. Prayer is the exercise of the First Commandment. That is, we allow him "alone" to be our God, worthy of trust and praise.[103] In prayer, we indicate how much God is worth to us (Is he alone worthy of my trust?) as well as how much we value the First Commandment (Do I take it as seriously as I take God?). Therefore the psalmist exhorts us to

---

101. LW 14.61 (WA 31, I.98). Charles Arand, "The Battle Cry for Faith. The Catechisms' Exposition of the Lord's Prayer," *Concordia Journal* 21 (1995): 42–65.
102. Arand, "The Battle Cry for Faith," 50.
103. "The Large Catechism," in *The Book of Concord*, 365.

trust and hope in God, as the First Commandment teaches. "Such trust is good, noble, and wholesome here in time and hereafter in eternity. It is the most acceptable offering to God and the finest service and honor we can render him."[104] Concurrently, he warns us against placing our trust, hope, and reliance on men and princes, thus violating the First Commandment. "This is evil, shameful, and destructive, here in time and hereafter in eternity. Besides, it is the greatest dishonour, contempt, and robbery to God."[105]

The Psalmist's Own Experience: A Pedagogical Example

In verses 10 through 13, the prophet utilizes his own experience of distress as a pedagogical tool by which he exhorts us to put our reliance in God, not in men.

> All nations surrounded me; in the name of the Lord I cut them off! They surrounded me, surrounded me on every side; in the name of the Lord I cut them off! They surrounded me like bees; they were extinguished like a fire of thorns; in the name of the Lord I cut them off! I was pushed hard, so that I was falling; but the Lord helped me.

His own example serves only to accentuate that God comforts, sustains, and strengthens the faithful in all their afflictions by His word and Spirit and does not forsake them. His experience applies to all the saints, before and after Christ. The psalmist refers to himself and to his people, since at the outset of the Psalm he speaks of Israel and Aaron. All

104. LW 14.68 (WA 31, I.113).
105. LW 14.68 (WA 31, I.113).

surrounding heathens attacked the Jewish kingdom vehemently wherever possible from all sides, especially in the days of David. However, David succeeded against the enemies, not by his own skill or might but by God's command and help. Thus he declares thrice, "In the name of the Lord I cut them off."

By "all nations," the psalmist described how great the danger is, and how numerous the adversaries are. They, with their mighty host, conspired against God and his Word and persecuted the anointed small group. Not only the enemies are powerful, but they also are determined in their relentless pursuit of the faithful until they ruin themselves. Therefore the psalmist repeats the same words twice in verse 11: "They surrounded me, they surrounded me." Even when they failed to accomplish their goal and were disgraced, the devil keeps them active in persecuting the saints and will not let them rest or relax. "Restlessness makes them furious, and fury makes them restless."[106] For this reason, the psalmist describes in verse 12: "They surrounded me like bees." An angry bee stings its enemy and leaves its sting there, without considering that it dies by this act or can never perform its task of producing honey. Its spiteful and vindictive spirit has resulted in the loss, in a shameful way, of its noble, sweet trade. "Henceforth it must be a water carrier for the other bees. Otherwise it could not eat with them. Among the other bees it is now a servant in the house."[107] Likewise the

---

106. LW 14.71 (WA 31, I.119).
107. LW 14.71 (WA 31, I.120). See note 35 where it is stated that Luther may have adopted some of the materials from the classics, for example, Pliny, *Natural History*, Book XI, ch. 57-60.

enemies would rather perish than fail to accomplish their goal. "Their wings buzz and whirr as they plunge their sting into Christ. They cool their fury with their own eternal harm and destruction."[108]

Furthermore in spite of the repeated failure, of which they must be deeply ashamed, and despite the lack of reason for being furious and vindictive, over which repentance is called for, they mask and camouflage themselves to their own detriment. They hurl their unreasonable and devilish attack on the Word of God, which does them no harm but rather offers them abundant blessings—good, grace, peace, life, and salvation. They forge a case, arguing that the word of God does just the opposite, that it creates sedition and is injurious to the peace of the community. The psalmist says in verse 12: "They were extinguished like a fire of thorns." Whenever the hedges and fences in a field catch fire, people must run to extinguish and save, lest the fire consumes the grain in the field and the vineyard and destroy the land, together with its people. The ranting and raving of God's enemies is likened unto this haste when fire breaks out. When one teaches the Word of God, one has set fire to the fences and hedges. When this occurs, everyone must run to help quench it, to kill the heretics and the rebels, to defend and save God's honor and people. This thought fuels in the enemies a laudable reason for murder and for raging against God. Should they fail, they obtain "the double distinction": one being holy martyrs in a praiseworthy deed and the other of

108. LW 14.71 (WA 31, I.120).

suffering severe opposition on the part of the devil. Luther exclaims: "What an excellent recipe for hardening a heart and making it impenitent!"[109]

The enemies strike fear into the hearts of the faithful and create affliction for them so that it is necessary for them to call upon the Lord. With Christians, the opposite is true as well: (1) The enemies are huge, embracing all the heathen and their might, the world, and all the devil; the Christians are alone and few; (2) The enemies are vehement, persistent, and restless, with no hope of grace; the Christians are weak and feeble; (3) though the enemies are bitter, furious, and spiteful, the Christians are gentle and patient; (4) Whilst the enemies are "the worst heretics in hell and the most dangerous people on earth," the Christians are "the greatest saints in heaven and most pious people on earth."[110] How do Christians meet all four points concerning the enemies? Where is victory? It is found in nowhere but in the right hand of God, this one efficacious weapon by which the enemies are subdued.

Comfort and Doxology: God's Right Hand

Having received God's comfort and help, the psalmist joyfully breaks into doxology, a short but beautiful song of praise to spite or scorn his persecutors and to glorify God. Verse 14 says, "The Lord is my Strength and my Song; He has become my Salvation." Luther highlights the intensely personal nature of God reflected in this fine, threefold summary of praise: The Lord is "my Strength," "my Song,"

109. LW 14.73 (WA 31, I.123).
110. LW 14.73 (WA 31, I.123).

and "my Salvation." The first indicates that God "alone" is the one the psalmist trusts wholly and completely, not himself and all the world's might, wealth, wisdom, and holiness. In him God is all in all: God acts, speaks, and quickens everything in him. Next, the psalmist cannot contain this good news and turns it into a psalm and sings. Faith cannot do otherwise but confess what it believes (Rom. 10:10). Third, that God is "his Salvation" indicates that God will abandon neither the singer nor his song. Here salvation Luther interprets as victory or help.[111] In his name and word God sustains him in life and death and grants him ultimate victory. Though the gates of hell and the entire world seek to exterminate the saints, God, in the end, will be our victory. The saints and their psalm and doctrine will survive, and all the persecutors will perish and go down in disgrace.

After having spoken of his own example about God's help in his life, he now proceeds to the common example of all the saints. Just as he was persecuted for the sake of God and his word, so also all the righteous were persecuted because they put their trust in God, not in humans. God helps them so that they sing praises to God. There is a unanimous chorus emanating from the Old Testament to the New Testament. We now sing along with the saints of the old hymns of salvation and victory, just as we are one in faith and trust in God and also participate in the suffering. St. Peter consoles us: "Knowing that the same experience of suffering is required of your brotherhood throughout the world" (1 Pet. 5:9). It

111. LW 14.79 (WA 31, I.136).

strengthens our hearts to know that St. Paul and the apostles possessed the same word, faith, and cross as we do. The pain the Christian undergoes is not unique to himself, and he therefore need not feel uniquely tormented. One of the benefits of the communion of the saints is the comfort we gain through knowing that we do not suffer alone. Luther wrote:

> It is frightening for a man with a special affliction to feel himself marked out for this distinctive suffering before all other men. Again, it is comforting when many suffer the same thing; for then a man does not get the horrible thought that he alone has been winnowed out and rejected. But still more comforting it is when all suffer the same and no one is exempt, as is the case among Christians.[112]

This Psalm focuses here not the suffering of the righteous but their victory, the ground of their joyful worship. He links the suffering of the righteous with the word "salvation." Just as the righteous have suffered sorely and fought valiantly in the battle of faith, they also will gain victory for which they could sing a song of joy. In order to increase our comfort, the psalmist portrays the jubilant picture of the redeemed, that in the end we will be able to sing as joyously as they. As sufferings abound, God's comfort and deliverance, singing and rejoicing among the righteous abound. Joyful songs and salvation truly belong to the righteous whose trust is in God; crying, wailing, reviling, cursing, and the gnashing of teeth (Matt. 22:13) inevitably belong to the wicked whose trust is in princes and humans.

112. LW 14.79–80 (WA 31, I.138).

What song of praise do the righteous sing in their tabernacles? The psalmist says: "The right hand of the Lord does valiantly."

> The right hand of the Lord is exalted, the right hand of the Lord does valiantly. I shall not die, but I shall live, and recount the deeds of the Lord. The Lord has chastened me sorely, but He has not given me over to death. (vv. 16–18)

This is the song of the righteous, not of the godless; it is sung by all the saints in their tabernacles. He who does not believe but places his reliance on people cannot sing this song; neither can he understand what he is singing about. Luther decried that this beautiful song, though it has been prominently used for Easter Day, has been shamefully mistreated and abused, as the godless prattle it in cathedrals and cloisters, or sing it as they have been taught. The godless sing in their hearts the opposite of what the righteous do: "The right hand of man does valiantly; the right hand of princes is exalted."[113]

The word "singing" includes not only making melody but also sermon or public confession by which God's work, grace, help, comfort, and victory are held out before the world. "God wants to be praised, glorified, honoured, and confessed by us in his works and wonders. Faith does it."[114] True faith cannot be silent but must break forth, speak, and proclaim that which seizes him. As support of this, he cites Ps. 116:10, which says: "I believed, therefore have I spoken."

113. LW 14.81 (WA 31, I.140).
114. LW 14.81 (WA 31, I.141).

True faith is never alone, without proclamation, or else it is not a true faith, even though it may suffer to be cursed, as the same Psalm continues: "I am greatly afflicted." However persecution does not prevent our salvation but actually promotes it, for God, who would not permit his name to suffer disgrace, is aroused to intervene, and the righteous are driven to pray to him for help. Hence Luther wrote: "Faith has its Helper who is its Salvation."[115] This concurs with what has been taught in verse 14, that God is indeed our salvation, if only we flee to him in the hour of need.

Self-sufficient, arrogant, and godless apostate Christians glorify their wisdom, strength, and holiness. However the righteous praise only God's grace, works, words, wisdom, and might as they are revealed to them in Christ. "This is their sermon and song."[116] In verse 16, "the right hand of God" is set in contrast with "the right hand of man," in order that we may know that nothing man does is effective before God. Human agency contributes nothing to righteousness, does not remit sin or produce a good work, or know or understand the true nature of salvation. Much less can it counsel and help in trials, danger, and hell. It delivers no life and salvation. "The work of man," Luther said, "is a rotten, ineffective, and vain delusion. Whoever relies on this builds a hell."[117]

The right hand of God, however, avails much. First, it does valiantly. "It is the power of God, that whoever believes and trusts in Him is thereby delivered from all sins, from a guilty

115. LW 14.81 (WA 31, I.141).
116. LW 14.81 (WA 31, I.142).
117. LW 14.82 (WA 31, I.143).

conscience, a sorrowing heart, error, lies, deception, and all the power of the devil, and is led to grace, righteousness, truth, understanding, consolation and true light."[118] All of these are the great, mighty, divine works and miracles, which no human reason, power, and might can comprehend and accomplish. "As a result, God is our power. We do not live in ourselves but in Him, and He acts and speaks all things in us."[119] Second, the right hand is "exalted," which means it "soars high, overcomes, and always gains the victory."[120] Believers not only have this consolation from God, that they are pure and righteous as Christ is, but also they receive help from him, by which they finally overcome death, hell, and every evil. Such great and exalted works of reconciliation and consolation are attributed to the great and glorious hand of God. "And if we die, His hand will really lead us to a life that has no end. God's right hand is so exalted that neither tribulation nor distress, neither sword nor famine, neither angels nor princes can pull it down (Rom. 8:35-39)."[121] If we cling to the right hand of God with a firm faith, we are just as exalted, and nothing on earth or in heaven can subdue us. Whoever relies on the arm of people or the hand of princes will plunge into the abyss of hell, with no hope of salvation. Victory belongs to the righteous, who live not in themselves but solely in God. Hence, third, the psalmist restates his first point: "The right hand of the Lord does valiantly." This means the psalmist cannot sing it often enough, as he is so

118. LW 14.82 (WA 31, I.142).
119. LW 14.82 (WA 31, I.142).
120. LW 14.82 (WA 31, I.143).
121. LW 14.82 (WA 31, I.144).

jubilant over the miracles God does for him. Out of sheer joy, he sings the song over and over again, that "God is our power," and nothing but the right hand of God can sustain us in trials.

Luther applied the right hand of God to the threefold work of Christ: Christ redeems us from the law, sin, and death. The threefold redemption includes both the crucifixion and resurrection of Christ as part of Luther's gospel of reconciliation.[122] The right hand of God is Christ freeing us from law, the gate of sin, leading us to the gospel, the gate of righteousness, and vanquishing death and death's chief, the devil and his skills, if only we believe. The main point to realize is that "these words are wholly spiritual"[123] and can only be sung and understood by faith, not to be apprehended by reason and natural eyes. Faith clings to God, whose children we are in Christ and whose right hand is our salvation. For the holy and the blessed ones, the right hand of God works mightily and is victorious and exalted. The world might reject them, but they alone are the children of God, purely on account of Christ's work on Calvary and Easter. And that indeed is worth singing and speaking about repeatedly, as this Psalm praises God "especially" for his greatest benefit, "Christ and his kingdom of grace—first promised and now revealed."[124]

---

122. LW 14.83 (WA 31, I.145). See n. 46.
123. LW 14.83 (WA 31, I.146).
124. LW 14.47 (WA 31, I.67).

Christ, the Rejected and Chief Cornerstone

Luther considers verse 22, "The stone which the builders rejected has become the chief cornerstone," as a reference to the cross and resurrection of Jesus Christ. The word "rejected" refers to the suffering, death, and humiliation to which Christ was subjected; the "the chief cornerstone" indicates his resurrection, life, and eternal reign.[125] The psalmist illustrates this by use of the parable of a building. When a stone is unfit and useless for a building, it must be rejected, or else it disfigures the whole building. Another builder appears and knows well not only how to use the stone to make it fit into the wall without disfiguring the building but also as a cornerstone in the foundation. Likewise Christ would not match the way and holiness of the Pharisees or the whole world itself. Not knowing how to use him, they condemned and rejected him. But God, the real Builder, chose him and made him the cornerstone of the foundation on which the whole Christian church, made up of Jews and Gentiles, rests. With the unbelieving world, Christ remains rejected; with the believing righteous, Christ remains precious, noble, and valuable (1 Pet. 2:7).

Those who find this stone offensive and reject it are the noblest, wisest, holiest, most learned, and greatest. The poor, miserable sinners, the outcast, the despised, and the unlearned accept Christ gladly. Both are builders. The simple folk, the rejected, and the unlearned are "the most necessary, most useful and best people on earth," who edify and govern for

125. LW 14.96 (WA 31, I.171).

the good of the people by the word of God.[126] However the wise, the prudent, the rich and the learned cannot tolerate the word of God and those who declare it, for they do not fit their building. As builders, they do it "*ex officio*; for they must see to it that their building has no crack, rent or disfiguration."[127] The two buildings stand in opposition to each other; the one rejects the other. The rejected building, however, possesses a "mighty Builder, who on one Stone" bears two strong and everlasting walls.[128] Nevertheless, the other building and the builders that delight in condemning and rejecting are reduced to nothing before this mighty Builder, who is the Lord himself, as evident in verse 23, "This is the Lord's doing; it is marvelous in our eyes." In his July 3 letter to Melanchthon, 1530, the reformer, after having reread the Augsburg Confession and applauded Melanchthon for it, cited this verse to exhort him to trust in God alone, marvel at God's wondrous work in the cause of the reformation, and not let doubt reign over him. Luther wrote:

> You [Melanchthon] are wrong and commit sin, however, in this one point in that you go against the Scripture, where Christ says of himself: "We do not want this one [doubt] to rule over us, and you strike out against that "cornerstone, which the builders have rejected". Where there is such great blindness and obstinacy of the demons what would you expect except rejection? For they [papists] will not concede to us the title "builders," which they appropriate for themselves, and this is just. We, however, have to be glorified with the title [s] "destroyers," "scatterers," "confusers," so that we might be

126. LW 14.97 (WA 31, I.172).
127. LW 14.97 (WA 31, I.172).
128. LW 14.95 (WA 31, I.172).

counted among the evildoers, since even the stone itself has been rejected, counted among the robbers, and condemned [as one of them]. Therefore we have no other hope for salvation than in the Lord alone, he has to do the wondrous deeds, and he will not desert this stone, for it follows: 'This [stone] has been made the cornerstone. This has been done by the Lord, however, not by us; therefore it is marvellous before our eyes.'[129]

God chooses and exalts those whom the world rejects, as St. Paul said in 1 Cor. 1:27: "God chose what is foolish in the world to shame the wise." Luther cited Hab. 1:5, "Look among the nations, and see; wonder and be astounded. For I am doing a work in your days that you would not believe it if told," to speak of the amazing work God does that often contradicts human reason. "This is a particularly great work in which He makes the rejected Stone the selected Cornerstone."[130] This work that God performs must continue to amaze us, as the psalmist declares: "It is marvelous in our eyes." The righteous must occupy themselves with it, grasp it, and hold this cornerstone. Otherwise they might fantasize and conjure up a god according to their image, as a theologian of glory does.

The Cross as the Locus: God's Hiddenness in His Opposites

No matter how hard it is, Luther advised, contemplate the "rejected Cornerstone, the crucified God,"[131] in order to let

---

129. LW 49.343–44.
130. LW 14.98 (WA 31, I.174).
131. LW 14.105 (WA 31, I.181). See note 70 where it is stated that the phrase "the

him be effective in us. This underscores Luther's theology of
the cross, in which God hides himself in his opposites, not in
power but in suffering, not in strength but in weakness, not
in majesty but in shame, not in wisdom but in folly. True
theology must be concerned with God as he has chosen to
reveal himself, not with some preconceived notions of God.
Because the theologian of glory expects God to be revealed
in glory, majesty, and strength, he deduces that God cannot
be present in the cross of Christ. He rejects the scene of
dereliction on the cross as the self-revelation of God. He
refuses to accept the reality as it is and thus becomes an enemy
of the cross. As Luther puts it: "The theologian of glory calls
evil good and good evil. The theologian of the cross calls
the thing what it actually is."[132] The true theologian accepts
the reality as it is, that it is God incarnate who suffers death,
even death on the cross, for the sake of our salvation. This is
contrary to human expectation, that "God must suffer himself
to be made, corrected, and formed, from the beginning of
the world to its end."[133] The true saving knowledge of God
is to be sought in the crucified Christ. In Luther's words:
"true theology and recognition of God are in the crucified
Christ."[134] The greatest marvel lies in the fact that God hides
himself in the cross of Christ in order to form a people no

crucified God" appears often in Luther's homiletical and devotional writings. In his
theological writings, Luther distinguishes between their proper and improper usage.
See my "Chalcedonian Christology and Beyond: Luther's Doctrine of *Communicatio
Idiomatum*," *The Heythrop Journal* 45, no. 1 (January 2004): 54–68.
132. See "Thesis 21, Heidelberg Disputation, 1518," in LW 31. 53. Forde, *On Being a
Theologian of the Cross*, 81.
133. LW 14.99 (WA 31, I.175).
134. LW 31.53.

longer under his wrath but under his mercy. The cross is the
locus of God's hiddenness in his opposites. Only in the shame
and humility of the cross, the opposite of majesty and glory,
could one find the true and gracious God. Victory over sin,
death, and Satan is made possible through the humiliation of
the cross in which God determines himself. God's work of
salvation confounds the world but causes his people to marvel
at it and praise God as the outcome. Should the flesh gain the
upper hand, the image of the crucified God would no longer
seize us with awe and wonder. There would be nothing
amazing if the carnal-minded ones were to take offense at
God's paradoxical work and prescribe for God alternative
ways in which they think God ought to act.

The saints' great comfort is found in the structure, "first
rejected and then elected,"[135] Christ, the only cornerstone in
whom the world's reject becomes God's elect. We must seek
to be found in nothing but Christ, the crucified God, through
whom the saints abide forever, beyond rejection, while the
persecutors perish, beyond recognition. Christ is "the King
of Grace,"[136] before whom no righteousness, no works, or no
holiness will endure. All our labors are chaff in the wind and
cannot be the cornerstone. "It can never be otherwise. We
read (I Cor. 3:11) that this rejected Stone is the Cornerstone
or Foundation."[137] There is cause for praise for those who
are built on Christ, not on human works or the might of

135. LW 14.98 (WA 31, I.174).
136. LW 14.102 (WA 31, I.178).
137. LW 14.97 (WA 31, I.174).

the princes. Thus verse 26: "Blessed be He who enters in the name of the Lord! We bless you from the house of the Lord."

The Person and Work of Christ:
Blessing Triumphs over Curse

Here the psalmist identifies "the child"[138] who comes in the name of the Lord. This is evident in verse 27: "The Lord is God, and He has given us light. Bind the festival with branches, up to the horns of the altar!" Though a rejected stone, the Lord is still God, who has appeared and enlightened us through the gospel and the light we feel in our hearts. Abiding here is the dual nature of Christ, the rejected cornerstone: "If He were not a man, He could not be the rejected Cornerstone; for God cannot be rejected. And yet He is not only a man but also God Himself."[139] Here the psalmist faces the offenses of the Jews and of those to whom it is idolatry to say that "a man is God." Against such, Luther wrote: "This is the true God Himself, for no one else can grant release from sin or death or enlighten hearts except God. His work proves that He is God."[140]

The incarnation, the unity of the two natures in the person of Jesus Christ, is conceived in terms of the central fact of salvation, the passion and death of Christ. As Congar rightly said, "For Luther, the Incarnation is not only inseparable from the redemptive act; the metaphysical mystery of the hypostatic union is considered solely in the act of salvation

---

138. LW 14.103 (WA 31, I.180).
139. LW 14.103 (WA 31, I.180).
140. LW 14.103–04 (WA 31, I.180).

of which it forms the very reality."[141] Luther's theology of the cross has to do with the definitive revelation of God in Jesus Christ and his salvific way with us. Hence Luther focuses on the "for us" (*pro nobis*) aspects of Christ's person.[142] Soteriology is at the heart of Luther's Christology.[143] The fundamental issue in Luther's atonement theology, says Forde, is "not whether there is a blood precious enough to pay God or even to the devil, but whether God has acted decisively to win us."[144] The indivisible person of Christ, fully God and fully man, interposed himself in the path of the law and suffered the alien work of condemnation in order to bestow upon us the proper work of the gospel of reconciliation. This is borne out in Luther's commentary on Galatians (1535), where he taught that Christ became a curse for us (*pro nobis*) to set us free from the curse of the law.[145] Luther elaborates:

> Thus the curse, which is divine wrath against the whole world, has the same conflict with the blessing, that is, with eternal grace and mercy of God in Christ. Therefore the curse clashes with the blessing and wants to damn and annihilate it. But it cannot. For the blessing is divine and eternal, and therefore the curse must yield to it. For if the blessing in Christ could be conquered, then God himself would be conquered. But

141. Yves Congar, "Considerations and Reflections on the Christology of Luther," in *Dialogue Between Christians* (London: Geoffrey Chapman, 1966), 377.
142. Kolb, *Martin Luther*, 112–13.
143. See "Small Catechism," in *The Book of Concord*, 345, where Luther understood Christology by way of soteriology, conceiving the person of Jesus Christ in terms of his work of redemption.
144. Gerhard O. Forde, "Luther's Theology of the Cross," in *Christian Dogmatics*, 2 volumes, ed. Carl Braaten & Robert Jenson (Philadelphia: Fortress Press, 1984), I.51.
145. LW 26.278 (WA 40, I.434–35).

this is impossible. Therefore Christ, who is divine power, Righteousness, Blessing, Grace and Life, conquers and destroys these monsters—sin, death, and the curse—without weapons or battle, in His own body and in Himself as Paul enjoys saying.[146]

This is the secret of the victory: blessing is locked in mortal combat with curse in "this one person" (Christ) but triumphs over curse.

The cross is the self-manifestation of God's love in its opposite, in the suffering of the righteous One which is to be interpreted according to the joyous change of place between the sinner and Christ. Christ is first a pure and innocent person, both as God and man, so that he could "assume upon himself our sinful person and grant us his innocent and victorious person."[147] By a joyous exchange, Christ, "inside our mask,"[148] carried our sin, suffered, and died; and for us he became a curse so that he might conquer it and bestow upon us his eternal blessings. "But because He was a divine and eternal Person, it was impossible for death to hold him. Therefore he arose from death on the third day, and now He lives eternally; nor sin, death, and our mask be found in Him any longer; but there is sheer righteousness, life, and eternal blessings."[149]

God let himself be overtaken by death in the suffering and dying of Christ, and yet he remained the victor over death. To be found in Christ is to behold our sin resting on Christ, but as overcome by his resurrection. Our sins are

146. LW 26.261–62 (WA 40, I.440–41).
147. LW 26.278 (WA 40, I.434–35).
148. LW 26.278 (WA 40, I.434–35).
149. LW 26.284 (WA 40, I.443–45).

resting on Christ, and His victory is resting on us, if only we believe. The link between law and gospel corresponds to that between Christ's cross and resurrection. Just as the effects of the law are most manifest in Christ's passion and death, so too our sin and God's wrath by which our consciences are terrified is revealed through the cross. In contrast, Christ's resurrection communicates to us the efficacy of the cross, that Christ assumed our sins, died for them, and then triumphed over them.

The gospel has appeared, and a new day has dawned. Christ, fully God and fully human, has abolished the old custom. The feast of the tabernacles that Jews used to celebrate now gives way to the new festival, in which the Lord himself is worshiped as the new king, who rides in with grace and appears to the world in his word. In the name of the Lord, all believers, Jews and Gentiles, are given a participation in the altar, a privilege, not found in the law. Luther intimated: "the glad day of the Gospel dawns and the kingdom of grace begins, in which sin and death end and righteousness lives and rules."[150] Thus as a wish of joy, the psalmist pours out his heart in verse 25, "Save us, we beseech Thee, O Lord! O Lord, we beseech Thee, give us success!" His focus here is not on distress and pain but on the cry for help, the promise of deliverance, and the fulfillment of a joyful wish, which knows no end.

150. LW 14.101 (WA 31, I.178).

The Gate of Sin and the Gate of Righteousness

Verse 18, "Open to me the gates of righteousness, that I may enter through them and give thanks to the Lord," is a heartfelt prayer for the gospel and the kingdom of Christ, already anticipated in the forefathers of the Old Testament.[151] As regards this, Luther quoted Christ's saying to his disciples in Luke 10:23–14: "Blessed are the eyes which see what you see! For I tell you that many prophets and kings desire to see what you see, and did not see it, and to hear what you hear, and did not hear it."[152] The psalmist regards the New Testament as "gates of righteousness" by which the burden of the law of Moses may be lifted. In contradistinction to the Old Testament, where the burden and works of the law of Moses are pressed upon us, the New Testament discloses the gospel, in which there is nothing but forgiveness of sins and God's grace. Quoting Pauline texts, Luther warns against confusing law and gospel. The law is not grace and therefore has no power to justify. Paul called the Law of Moses "the dispensation of condemnation" (2 Cor. 3:9) and "an agent of sin" (Gal. 2:17). He wrote, "the sting of death is sin, and the power of sin is death" (1 Cor. 15:56). "The Law, in its administration and treatment, aims at works, creates sinners, and multiplies sin and wrath."[153] It cannot create or contribute to righteousness, and therefore it may be called "gates of sin or unrighteousness."[154] However grace alone

---

151. Preus, *From Shadow to Promise*, 183, where he recognized that the grace of God, though was not yet apparent to the ancients, was being prophesied.
152. LW 14.90 (WA 31, I.162).
153. LW 14.91 (WA 31, I.163).

justifies and is called "the gate of righteousness." The psalmist identifies this gate not as "gates" but "the gate of the Lord," through which only the righteous can enter. Thus verse 20: "This is the gate of the Lord: the righteous shall enter through it."

Hypocrites, scoundrels, and sinners may enter the gate of the holy temple in Jerusalem. But only the righteous can enter the gate of the Lord. He who takes pride in being a Christian must also take pride in being holy and righteous. This is articulated, says Luther, in the third article of the Creed: "I believe in the Holy Christian Church." Since Christendom is holy, a Christian must also be righteous and holy, or he is not one. Unless he is holy and righteous, he cannot enter this gate, pray, offer praise, or serve God. He does not know God, even though he dwells among Christians and may even occupy an office, serving outwardly as pastor or bishop or partaking of the sacrament. As persons in Adam, we all are damned sinners, devoid of righteousness or holiness of our own. But as persons in Christ and with Christ, we are holy and righteous. Christ has removed and vanquished our sin and clothed and adorned us with his holiness. Thus, the whole Christian church is holy, not by itself but purely by the imputation of Christ's holiness. "This is not boastfulness; it is a necessary confession and an article of faith."[155] This article was condemned at the Council of Constance, together with this verse and all Holy Scriptures. John Hus confessed that there is one holy Christian church,

154. LW 14.91 (WA 31, I.163).
155. LW 14.93 (WA 31, I.166).

and if the pope did not want to be called holy, he disqualified himself as a member of it, much less its head. For this Hus was burned as a heretic. Against such, Luther said it is "false and blasphemous humility" not to glory in one's imputed status in Christ.[156] Whoever hesitates about his declared status, holy and righteous in and through Christ's holiness, denies Christ's own word and the testimony of Scripture, of which it is said: "He has cleansed her by the washing of water with the Word" (Eph. 5:26). Whoever believes and is righteous in Christ enters the gate, with no respect of persons. Christ's kingdom does not consist of external ways or behavior (Luke 17:20); it is found in the heart, cleansed by Christ's own word and embraced as his beloved.

Victory over Death's Chief, the Devil: The Art of Forgetting Self

Verse 17 of this Psalm ("I shall not die, but I shall live") touches death out of which God's hand delivers. Death always appears alongside sin and the law, forming a tripartite. The righteous surely feel and taste the power of death. They are really martyrs, for they must live under the constant specter of death posed not only by the tyrants and the ungodly but also by the devil. The devil invokes sin, death, and hell, a triumvirate of evils.[157] "This is his trade,"[158] at which he is

---

156. LW 14.93 (WA 31, I.166).
157. LW 14.84 (WA 31, I.149). See also "A Sermon on Preparing to Die, 1519," in LW 42, where Luther spoke of three evil images (death, sin, and hell) that afflict Christians and three counter images (life, grace, and heaven) that overcome these evil images. Austra Reinis, *Reforming the Art of Dying. The ars moriendi in the German Reformation 1519–1528* (Aldershot: Ashgate, 2007), 54–62.

a past master. He has been the prince of death, who has practiced thoroughly how to offer a poor conscience the foretaste of death. The devil tolerates neither the word of God nor those who uphold, sing, and speak it. He besets the saints in life and death and incites in their hearts fear, doubt, and despair, so that they eventually forget and forfeit God. Especially in death or at one's deathbed, when the heart is faint, the devil is skillful at magnifying the horror of sin and terror of divine wrath in order to foment fear and conjure up hell in us. However no one ever "sees his real sins, namely, unbelief, contempt of God's Word, the failure to fear, love, and trust as he should"; nor would it profit him to see them as they are, for he cannot endure them without falling into despair. For this reason God permits the devil to operate with the "sins of commission,"[159] rather than those of omission. What is worse, the devil takes our best works and drives them into our conscience as worthless and condemned, causing us to wish we had done nothing but great sins instead of these works. At the end, the conscience becomes so wretched that sins no longer frighten it. "He [devil] easily creates hell and damnation for you because you take one drink too many or sleep too long, and soon you become sick with conscience scruples and despondency and practically die of grief."[160] The devil tempts us to disown our best works as having been done by God and thus to blaspheme God, in which case death and hell are not far away.

158. LW 14.84 (WA 31, I.149).
159. LW 14.84 (WA 31, I.148).
160. LW 14.84 (WA 31, I.148).

To effectively wrestle with the devil and battle with death, the saints must develop "an art to forget self": "Nothing is better and more vital for victory than learning to sing this song of the saints, that is, to look away from self and to cling to the hand of God."[161] This phrase "forget self" means not judging ourselves from our own perspective, which sees our sins, and which the devil encourages, but looking to God's judgment on us: innocent! Here Luther vividly dramatizes the concept of imputation in a monologue: What does God think of me? How does he regard me? His regard is imputation. Luther writes:

> It works like this: I am nothing. The Lord is all my strength… I am stripped of everything, of myself, and all that is mine. I can say: "Devil, what are you fighting? If you try to denounce my good works and my holiness before God, why, I have none? My strength is not my own: the Lord is my Strength. You can't squeeze blood out of a turnip! If you try to prosecute my sins, I have none of those either. Here is God's strength—prosecute it until you have had enough. I know absolutely nothing about either sins or holiness in me. I know nothing whatever except God's power in me."[162]

Luther advised that the righteous must learn to mock the devil with an empty pocket as a poor householder mocks a thief who finds nothing in the house to steal, whether at night or noon.[163] This is parallel to Luther's use of the concept of the burial of our sinful identity in Christ's tomb through baptism in Rom. 6 and Col. 2.[164] The devil could not do

---

161. LW 14.85 (WA 31, I.149).
162. LW 14.85 (WA 31, I.150).
163. LW 14.85 (WA 31, I.150).

anything to a soul so naked that it can respond neither to sin nor to holiness, except to relinquish puffing up our sin and decrying good works. We must refer him to the right hand of God, so that he must by all means give up all his tricks. But if we forget this "prescription"[165] and allow him to seize us in our sins and good works, and we become preoccupied with him, then he will shape us according to his evil intent. The outcome is we will depart from God, his right hand, and all his mighty works and blessings.

The art of forgetting oneself is an age-old discipline for all the saints, past, present, and future. Just as we must fight, as do all the saints, to rid ourselves of sin and to cling to God's right hand as his word instructs us, so also we must battle with the chief of death, the devil, until we are free. When the devil presses in our lives with death, we should learn to turn away our gaze from self to God, and "recount the deeds of the Lord," not of humans. Emptying ourselves, we cling to God's hand and say:

> Devil and tyrant, I shall not die, as you pretend. You lie! I shall live, for I will not speak of my own works or those of any man. I know nothing about myself or my own holiness. I have before me only the works of the Lord. Of them I shall speak; them I will glorify; on them I will rely. He it is who delivers from sin and death. If you can overthrow His works, you have overthrown me too.[166]

---

164. Kolb, *Luther and the Stories of God*, 16.
165. LW 14.85 (WA 31, I.150).
166. LW 14.86 (WA 31, I.151).

Luther's Personal Motto: "A Masterpiece" of Comfort and Help

On the wall of the room where Luther worked hung his personal motto: "I shall not die, but live, and recount the deeds of the Lord" (v. 17).[167] This is the central message of the Psalm. It is christocentric, as it applies to Jesus and through him, to all believers. Of all people, Luther had much to fear what mortals might do to him. And yet verse 17 so inspired Luther's faith that he declared with audacity and certainty: "the dying live; the suffering rejoice; the fallen rise; the disgraced are honored. It is as Christ says, 'He who believes in me, though he dies, yet shall he live'."[168] Luther further declared that whenever the scriptures "deal with God concerning comfort and help in their need, eternal life and the resurrection of the dead are involved."[169] God's right hand mightily lifts the heart and soothes it in the midst of death, so that it can say: "Though I die, I die not. Though I suffer, I suffer not. That I fall, I am not down. Though I am disgraced, I am not dishonoured."[170] After receiving divine comfort, the psalmist speaks of the amazing help: "I shall live." Just as God delivered the psalmist, so now Christ liberates us from the domain of death. "When Christians deplore the fact that they suffer and die in this life, they comfort themselves with another life than this, namely, that of God Himself, who is

---

167. See LW 14.45 (WA 31, I.66), preface, n. 4. Cited in James Limburg, *Psalms* (Louisville: Westminster John Knox, 2000), 402.
168. LW14.86 (WA 31, I.152). See Scott H. Hendrix, edited and translated, *Early Protestant Spirituality* (New York: Paulist Press, 2009), 57.
169. LW 14.87 (WA 31, I.154).
170. LW 14.86 (WA 31, I.152).

above and beyond this life."[171] As alluded in verse 24 of this Psalm, Easter is the day the Lord has made; let us rejoice and be glad in it! This explains why Luther esteems this verse as "a masterpiece," because it deals with the death of death:

> How mightily the psalmist banishes death out of sight! He will know nothing of dying and sin. At the same time he visualizes life most vividly and will hear nothing but life. But whoever will not see death, lives forever, as Christ says: "If anyone keeps My Word, he will never see death" (John 8:51). He also immerses himself in life that death is swallowed up by life (I Cor. 15:55) and disappears completely, because he clings with a firm faith to the right hand of God. Thus all the saints have sung this verse and will continue to sing it to the end. We note this especially in the case of the martyrs. So far as the world is concerned, they die. Yet their hearts say with a firm faith: "I shall not die, but live."[172]

Everlasting life begins where faith begins. It begins now but extends beyond this life. Thus the departed saints, whom the tyrants believed they had silenced and suppressed, still live and speak, for they never cease or desist. They remain fully alive and proclaim forever the works of the Lord, that for which they were killed. While this text offers the saints most consolation and help, it is the worst and most depressing one for the persecutors of the saints, for their plan to silence and suppress the saints fails in the end. Though the saints are dead, their blood and spirits still preach, just as the departed Abel still speaks through his faith (Heb. 11:4). With sarcasm, Luther wrote of the pope who burned John Hus: "He must

171. LW 14.87 (WA 31, I.154).
172. LW 14.87 (WA 31, I.153).

concede that John Hus is his master."[173] For the killing of Hus teaches that no human powers, that of princes or popes, could thwart the proclamation of the works of the Lord. The blood of the martyrs still rises against the pope and nullifies his power. The reality here is that Abel spoke more after his death than before, as did Hus and the other martyrs. The works of God advance further and more after death than before. The singer, the song, and the doctrine survive the persecution, and nothing can undo the right hand of God.

With the help of Aristotle's rhetorical devices of confutation, understatement, and interpretation,[174] Luther fastened the theme of comfort in verse 18, "The Lord has chastened me sorely, but He has not given me over to death." This, to him, is "also a masterpiece,"[175] which enables the saints to face death with courage and hope. The psalmist and the world think very differently of death. The psalmist has boasted that he will not die, but live, but the flesh, world, men, and princes regard death as death, and nothing else, and seek in every possible way to weaken him. The psalmist comforts himself with this: "On the contrary, this dying is nothing. It is only a fatherly rod, not wrath. It is only a foxtail, nothing serious. God is only chastising me as a dear father chastises his dear child."[176] "This surely is," says Luther, "a good interpretation and an effective confutation, to make a

173. LW 14.88 (WA 31, I.157).
174. Aristotle, *Problems. 11, Books XX11–XXXV111. Rhetorica ad Alexandrum*, trans. Walter S. Hett and Harris Rackham (Cambridge, Mass.: Harvard, 1957). Book 36 was cited in LW 14.88 (WA 31, I.157). For a recent study of Luther's use of rhetoric in preaching, see Neil R. Leroux, *Luther's Rhetoric* (St. Louis: Concordia, 2002).
175. LW 14.88 (WA 31, I.157).
176. LW 14.89 (WA 31, I.158).

benevolent rod out of the word 'death'."[177] No human reason or wisdom could teach this art, except the Holy Spirit and the right hand of God. Flesh and blood would readily turn a benevolent rod into death and hell and lead one to give up and despair. God's right hand teaches that death may "hurt a little, and it is not sugar; it is a rod. However, it does not kill, but rather helps me live."[178]

It is a "much greater art"[179] to be able to sing this verse at the hour of death, when the devil's skill is most hostile. The devil impresses "a most forceful picture of death" in a helpless heart that death becomes totally unbearable and unendurable. "He magnifies what a horrible, abominable, eternal thing death is and raps out the wrath of God."[180] He mediates the image of death by showing forth God's wrath against sinners so as to cast the dying down into abject terror. Here what is needed is "a good interpreter," one who can outdo the devil and overcome him by saying:

This is still not death, nor is it wrath. It is gracious chastisement and fatherly punishment. I still know that He will not turn me over to death. I will not believe it is wrath, even though all the devils of hell were to affirm it in chorus. Were an angel from heaven to say this, let him be accursed (Gal.1:8). Were God himself to say it, I would still believe that He was trying me as He tried Abraham, merely feigning wrath, and not in earnest. For He does not take back His promise. Here is the truth: "He chastises me, but He will not kill me. I insist on this and will not

177. LW 14.89 (WA 31, I.158).
178. LW 14.89 (WA 31, I.158).
179. LW 14.89 (WA 31, I.158).
180. LW 14.89 (WA 31, I.160). Reinis, *Reforming the Art of Dying*, 55.

let anyone take it from me or explain, interpret, or expound it differently."[181]

Not that the psalmist does not feel death but he refuses to feel it or call it death and clings unwaveringly to the gracious right hand of God. Not that he denies that God sends him death but that he and God share the same understanding: death is nothing but a father's rod and a child's chastisement. These lofty words do not proceed from the lips of men and princes; neither can they enter their hearts, as St. Paul says: "We impart a secret and hidden wisdom of God.... None of the rulers of this age understood this" (1 Cor. 2:7–8).

When afflicted by death, the theologian of the cross should not attune his ears to the voice of the devil, whose sole purpose is to bring destruction and death, like a highway robber.[182] Instead he hears both the voice of the law, that death comes as God's fatherly chastisement, and the voice of the gospel, that death has been swallowed up by life. Hidden in God's gracious chastisement is "a blessed comfort."[183] Inherent here is Luther's view of dying understood in the light of the distinction between law and gospel, the twin but apparently contradictory acts of the one and same God. The annihilating voice of death as in law is useful, that is, causally useful, if it drives us into the arms of Christ, who himself is sheer life, and we have life in him. The voice of the law that incites sin, death, and God's wrath is replaced by the voice of the gospel, which removes these deadly images. To

181. LW 14.89 (WA 31, I.160).
182. Althaus, *The Theology of Martin Luther*, 259.
183. LW 14.142 (WA 18.481).

banish death out of sight, "the true interpreter" allows God's word to reign above all; he does not allow reason, flesh, and the devil to assume the role of interpreting reality. As the true interpreter, the theologian of the cross is radical in his declaration of the reality *in se*, that though we are in death, we are in life. Wrath is not the final word; mercy is. That too is God's promise, through which the terror of death is mitigated, and it makes dying much easier. Were anyone from heaven to teach otherwise, let him be accursed (Gal. 1:8).

Rejoice in God's Work of Humbling: Alien Work and Proper Work

The psalmist sings out of pure joy verse 21, "I thank thee that Thou hast humbled me and become my Salvation." He willingly submits himself to the paradoxical work of God in his life, an essential aspect of Luther's theology of the cross. God has performed an alien work of humbling him as in law in order that he might achieve a proper work of saving him as in gospel; the former serves the latter. God reproves us through his Word and reduces our wisdom, strength, and holiness to naught, so that we appear before him as totally guilty sinners. The word of God evinces "impressive power,"[184] which terrorizes our consciences and afflicts us with troubles, so that our old Adam is crucified and our self-confidence is dead. The work of humbling, alien to God's nature, is God's gracious will that works for our good. It

184. LW 14.94 (WA 31, I.170).

is not the devil's work, for the psalmist does not say: "The devil humbles me."[185] If it were, the outcome would certainly be destruction. Whoever can suffer and endure God's alien work and at the same time thank and praise God for his gracious will in it can sincerely sing this verse: "I thank thee that Thou dost humble us." The twofold sacrifices—humility and thanksgiving—are juxtaposed and are found acceptable to God.

Furthermore the psalmist speaks of the comfort and help, "an ever greater and richer gift"[186] bestowed by God to those whom he has humbled. Just as he afflicts, so also he comforts, the former leads to the latter. God makes us strong when he causes us to suffer; he exalts us when he humbles us. This behooves the afflicted to come upon God in the day of trouble and offer up an unending, great, and daily sacrifice of praise in the gate of the Lord: "I thank thee that Thou art my Salvation, my Helper and Savior." Hidden in this verse are the innumerable wonders of God, which cause all Christendom to sing in unison: "I thank thee that Thou hast humbled me, and hast helped me again." In Luther's paraphrase:

> Art Thou not a wonderful and delightful God, to govern us so amazingly and so kindly? Thou exaltest us when Thou humblest us. Thou makest us righteous when Thou makest us sinners. Thou leadest us to heaven when Thou castest us into hell. Thou grantest us the victory when Thou causest us to be defeated. Thou givest us life when Thou permittest us to be killed. Thou comfortest us when Thou causest us to mourn. Thou makest us to rejoice when Thou permitted us to weep.

185. LW 14.95 (WA 31, I.170).
186. LW 14.95 (WA 31, I.170).

Thou makest us to sing when Thou causest us to cry. Thou makest us strong when we suffer.[187]

Conclusion: Declaration and Denouncement

The psalmist begins on a note of thanksgiving and ends with the same. Thus verses 28–29: "Thou art my God, and I will give thanks to Thee; Thou art my God; I will extol Thee. O give thanks to the Lord, for He is good; for His steadfast love endures forever." The psalmist concludes with a firm declaration, that he will not cease preaching and praising his God.[188] He certainly knows who God is and how God regards him, rejected by the world but elected of God. This is the psalmist's resolution, that he remains undisputed about the steadfast love of God despite contrary appearances, unshaken by all manner of disgrace and danger and undismayed when his kindness is not met with gratitude.

Added to his declaration is the psalmist's solemn denunciation of all offenses. The good deeds we do to people do not last forever. They often meet with ingratitude, which is part of human nature. "Human nature cannot stand ingratitude."[189] Ingratitude has driven many people insane. Hence we might turn vindictive or vengeful when people return our good with evil. We might become indifferent as a block of wood and unmoved like a balky horse, thus leaving the good undone, especially when there arises again need for it for those who once provoke us with ingratitude. It is self-

187. LW 14.95 (WA 31, I.171).
188. LW 14.105 (WA 31, I.181).
189. LW 14.103 (WA 31, I.181).

preoccupied kindness, when kindness is done with a hope of return or reward; it is selfish kindness, when it is done not for God's sake or for the sake of virtue but only for one's own sake. When we seek thanks and honor from those to whom we do good, we are actually seeking mastery over them. We may be tempted to boast of our good works. All of the offenses are contrary to the spirit of Christ.

No amount of human misdeed could detract from the sheer goodness of God. "Therefore He does not stop doing good because of the wickedness of men. Thus He proves that He is good by nature, and that His goodness does not stand or fall by the vice or virtue of another, as human goodness stand on the virtue of one and fall by the vice of another and even become worse than he is."[190] The righteous in Christ should feel the compunctions of conscience when they fail to do good to people as they should. Grace should have awakened them to the point where they would think: "Well, I did not do that good deed for him because of his wickedness, nor shall I stop on this account. God bestows much good on me, daily, though all my life I have done nothing but grieve Him."[191] Such thoughts do not come from the example of the ungrateful neighbor but from that of Christ, which causes the righteous to consider their own ingratitude so that they might live not for themselves but for the interests of others, not in themselves but in Christ.

Christ is not only the cause of our salvation but also our model of imitation.[192] The cross of Christ has a double

190. LW 14.106 (WA 31, I.182).
191. LW 14.106 (WA 31, I.182).

function: an expiatory function, that sin and wrath are averted, and an exemplary function, that we imitate Christ as an act of conformity to his image. Both functions constitute the one reality of Christ: the crucified God. To embrace Christ as our Savior is to embrace him as our model; the former necessarily leads to the latter. "Human kindness is brief and temporary, it is done only to those who adore and honor them. But God and His children do good without returns."[193] Just as God gladly wastes his mercy upon the undeserved, so also the Christian gladly wastes his kindness upon the ungrateful (Prov. 16:4). The true Christian, as a response to Christ's sacramental efficacy, moves from a conviction of sin under law to joy in overflowing love under gospel, from Christ the sacrament to Christ the model. Like Christ, he must follow the path to glory and life through misery and death, as is borne out in Gal. 6:7, "I bear on my body the marks of Jesus." Thus no amount of human weakness should deter him from loving, as Christ does, for "the servant is not better than his Master" (Matt. 10:25).[194] Since Christ was humbled and exalted as much as and more

192. Norman Nagel, "'Sacramentum et Exemplum' in Luther's Understanding of Christ," in Luther for an Ecumenical Age, ed. Carl S. Meyer (St. Louis: Concordia, 1967), 175, where he discusses the medieval pairing of sacramentum et exemplum. The former describes Christ's saving work and the latter his exemplary work. Nagel argues that the example motif diminishes in Luther in the 1520s, but this Psalm shows that he certainly did not totally abandon it. Gustav Wingren, The Christian's Calling: Luther on Vocation, trans. Carl C. Rasmussen (Philadelphia: Mühlenberg, 1957), 172, wrote of Luther that "Christ is not to be imitated by us, but to be accepted by faith."
193. LW 14.106 (WA 31, I.182).
194. Tuomo Mannermaa, Two Kinds of Love. Martin Luther's Religious World (Minneapolis: Fortress Press, 2010), 67–75, where he analyzes how Christians are "Christs" to their neighbors.

than all the faithful, we should not be surprised if we also suffer such tribulation and affliction. Just as Christ was appointed to the vocation of the cross, so also his followers, in a joyous exchange, assume the cross as their vocation.

Conclusion

This volume is an exercise of the theology of the cross, in which Luther follows the wonderful road God prescribes for him (and us) to travel, namely, God's way hidden in Christ and his opposites. The theology of the cross brings suffering into focus for what it really is, unmasking banality and superficiality. True knowledge of God and a proper perspective of who we are is to be determined by the cross of Christ. The shadow of the cross stamps upon the godly ones a cruciform existence. Just as Christ went through humiliation to exaltation, so also believers are not exempted from hardship. They suffer temptation, loss, despair, and pain just as the psalmist and Christ himself did. The cross is laid upon God's very own so that they are not relieved of it, unless by death or apostasy. The assaults or afflictions include both the private burden that an individual carries and external oppositions of heresies and fanaticism against the church, strife within churches, and the prolonged enmity of the pope and those under his command. The ongoing struggles—internal and external—are a characteristic condition of a godly person and a true church. Where it is absent, there is cause for concern, for there is no church without cross and assaults.

Luther's exposition of the Psalms of lament highlights the major constituents of his theology of the cross: the experience of temptation (*tentatio*), law and gospel, alien and proper work, wrath and mercy, the paradoxical work of God under the appearance of contraries, the distinction between the hidden and the revealed God, Christ's atoning efficacy for sin, faith in God's Word, and despair of reason. Though assaults might come from various sources, the devil, the world, or the flesh, Luther did not hesitate to attribute them to the work of God in his life. He regarded them as part of God's alien work, his instruments he uses to nourish faith. They cast us down and so serve the interests of God's proper work, which is God's preoccupation (salvation). This is God's ordained way, on which we must walk: we must despair of everything in us and in the world in order to cling wholeheartedly to Christ and what he has achieved for us.

The godly ones live in the broken and fragmentary world that needs the hearing and healing of the gospel; the former is the basis for the latter. Struggle is a place in which God's work and human brokenness or hostility of the world intersect. "Struggle," as Thompson writes accurately, "is a sign of life,"[1] for its opposites lay hidden in it: God's marvelous works and his insurmountable comfort. With this,

---

1. Mark D. Thompson, "Luther on Despair," in *The consolations of Theology*, edited by Brian S. Rosner (Grand Rapids: Wm. B. Eerdmans, 2008), 64. Also quoted in Parsons, *Martin Luther's Interpretation of the Royal Psalms*, 174.

Luther came to realize that real theology is done not in the balcony of an academic library but in the highway of life, often colored by darkness, despair, hopelessness, and grief. These assaults are perennial but salutary, as they provide the contexts in which the godly person learns to do true theology, even as he learns to lay hold of God's efficacious promise, his word, and from that word derives innumerable consolations. Thus at table in 1532, Luther asserted: "Experience alone makes a theologian."[2] Based on Ps. 119, he fleshes out this proposition in his *Preface to the Wittenberg Edition of Luther's German Writings*, in which he wrote of "three rules" that make a true theologian: prayer (*oratio*), meditation (*meditatio*), and trials (*tentatio*).[3] As this book shows, his accent is on the last:

> Thirdly there is *tentatio*, *Anfechtung* (trials). This is the touchstone which teaches you not only to know and understand, but also experience how right and true, how sweet and lovely, how mighty, and how comforting God's word is, wisdom above all wisdom.[4]

Not idle speculation, but genuine theology, forged in the furnace of struggle and despair, and under the assault of the devil, makes "a real doctor" of Luther, as he said: "For as soon as God's Word takes root and grows in you, the devil will

2. LW 54.7 (WA TR 1.16).
3. LW 34.286–87 (WA 1.660).
4. LW 34.286–87 (WA 1.660). For a discussion of Luther's three rules that make a theologian: *oratio*, *meditatio*, and *tentatio*, see Bayer, *Martin Luther's Theology*, 32–36; his *Theology the Lutheran Way*, 42–65; Pless, *Martin Luther*, 17–22; Westhelle, *The Scandalous Cross*, 35–8; John Kleinig, "Oratio, Meditatio, Tentatio: What Makes a Theologian?" *Concordia Theological Quarterly* 66, no. 3 (2002): 255–67.

harry you, and will make a real doctor of you, and by his assaults will teach you to seek and love God's Word."[5] Luther said the same in his table talk with his students:

> I did not learn my theology all at once, but had to search constantly deeper and deeper for it. My temptations did that for me, for no one can understand Holy Scripture without practice and temptations. This is what the enthusiasts and sects lack. They don't have the right critic, the devil, who is the best teacher of theology.... If we don't have that kind of devil, then we become nothing but speculative theologians, who do nothing but walk around in our own thoughts and speculate with our reason alone as to whether things should be like this, or like that.[6]

Luther, by virtue of his call as professor of exegesis, felt a duty to teach and preach the Scripture, even if that meant entering into controversial arguments with the church officials and the heretics. His encounter with the Psalter shaped the development of his way of thinking. He soon discovered that what he learned from the university did not concur with what he obtained from the Bible. Reality, for the reformer, is not defined by Aristotle or by any creaturely means but solely by Christ and his work, as attested in the Scripture. Luther's exposition of the Scripture (including the Psalter) centers on "what the words do, not merely in what they mean,"[7] for to him, the word is inherently causative and thus re-creative,

5. LW 34.287 (WA I.660).
6. LW 54.50 (WA TR I.147). Translation is Kleinig's. See his "Oratio, Meditatio, Tentatio," 356–57.
7. Gerhard O. Forde, "The Word That Kills and Makes Alive," in *The Marks of the Body of Christ*, ed. Carl E. Braaten and R. W. Jenson (Grand Rapids: Wm. B. Eerdmans, 1999), 8.

fashioning the new creature in Christ. Luther submits to the authority of the Scripture and holds fast to its virtues. This is particularly evident in his own words in his commentary on Ps. 68:

> The strength of Scripture is this, that it is not changed into him who studies, but that it transforms its lover into itself and its strengths.... Because you will not change me into what you are ... but you will be changed into what I am.[8]

Thus Luther was appalled by an "insidious plague of boredom" toward the word of God in God's people. As a corrective, Luther exhorted his own to constantly meditate on Scripture for comfort and guidance, just as he himself did in his commentary on Psalms. In his *Preface to the Large Catechism*, he offered further reasons why preoccupation with the word is important:

> I implore them not to imagine that they have learned these parts of the Catechism [10 Commandments, Apostles' Creed, Lord's Prayer] perfectly . . . Even if their knowledge of the Catechism were perfect (though that is impossible in this life), yet it is highly profitable and fruitful daily to read it and make it the subject of meditation and conversation. In such reading, conversation, and meditation the Holy Spirit is present and bestows ever new and greater light and fervor . . . . Nothing is more effectual against the devil, the world, the flesh, and all evil thoughts than to occupy oneself with the Word of God, talk about it and meditate on it . . . For this reason alone you should eagerly read, recite, ponder and practice the Catechism, even if the only blessing and benefit you obtain from it is to rout the devil and evil thoughts. For he cannot bear to hear God's

---

8. LW 10.332–33 (WA 3.297).

Word. God's Word is not like some empty tale, such as the one about Dietrich of Bern, but as St. Paul says in Rom. 1:16, it is "the power of God," indeed, the power of God which burns the devil and gives us immeasurable strength, comfort, and help.[9]

This study has also demonstrated that Luther was no impassive, cold, stoic, and mere intellectual person, espousing a piety of detachment from the cares of his people. Just as the personal nature of a living and loving God shines in his exposition, so also Luther's own personal character shines through his writings, proving that he is truly a theologian involved in the care of the soul.

The genius of Luther is his commitment to the biblical text as a means of pastoral encouragement, and as such, his theology is essentially practical. With the biblical and theological substance he gained from the Holy Scripture, he sought to inculcate the good news of justification by faith in his people, leading them to experience it within the dialectic of law and gospel. The reformer shows no ambivalence in naming things as they really are—sin, wrath, death, judgment, and hell—while at the same time naming the cure for each: sin cured by grace, wrath by mercy, death by life, judgment by redemption, hell by heaven. However, only the godly person truly feels the tension between the contraries, this paradox that stands at the heart of his self-perception: "A godly man feels sin more than grace, wrath more than favour, judgment more than redemption. An ungodly man feels almost no wrath, but is smug as though there were no wrath anywhere, as though there were no God anywhere

9. "*Large Catechism*," in *The Book of Concord*, 9–11.

who vindicates His righteousness. This happens mostly in those who strive for some appearance of religion."[10] He counsels how troubled conscience may find relief; teaches believers to put to death sinful desires that disrupt the good, so that the new person in Christ may rise to serve God and to shun evil; teaches us to meditate on the works of God with profit; exhorts us on how to pray for and deal with the enemies; and teaches believers to embrace the paradox of God's hiddenness in the contrary appearances, mercy in wrath, consolations in affliction, joy in pain, hope in despair. All of these show that for Luther the care of the soul is indeed a theological task, one that impresses the heavenly gospel upon the soul as the balm, not a psychological one that seeks creaturely ways to alleviate the brokenness. Contrary to Hughes's assertion that lament is negative and blasphemous,[11] this study shows that lament occupies a significant place in the saintly person as it leads him to the God of mercy. Luther's pastoral sensitivity shines as he allows the powerful passions of impatience, complaints, hate, anger, protest, and blasphemous thoughts against God to be part of the Christian life. He advises moderation in our lamenting and warns against an excessive kind that edifies and permits the old Adam to reign above the new person in Christ, ultimately leading to sheer despair. The new person laments, struggling with God in the context of faith. Godly and genuine lament is trust's wrestling with God, the God who has promised to meet us, even when our physical eyes fail to apprehend it.

10. LW 12.358 (WA 50, II.395).
11. Hughes, *Lament, Death and Destiny*, 104.

As "a care-taker of souls" (*Seelsorger*),[12] Luther also shows considerable freedom in speaking of times when there is no relief, unless or until God acts mercifully. However, Luther's theology of the cross also addresses those extreme situations when the afflicted finds no relief but remains in grief, as in Ps. 88 where the psalmist's lament does not end in doxology but ends with this: "Darkness is my closest friend" (v. 18). The afflicted soul finds no resolution to his misery, none on earth until the end when all miseries will end in the resurrection of Jesus Christ.[13] In those situations where darkness abides as the closest ally, where perpetual complaints occur, where everything appears black, bleak, and burdensome, where God's presence seems eclipsed, one must learn the art of discerning theological or spiritual reality beneath temporal appearances and grasping the true characteristics of God's kingdom hidden under the opposites. For Luther, a person of faith can discern the difference between the concrete life in which struggles occur and the hidden, spiritual reality beneath them. Faith enables the sufferer to face the painful realities of life, not in his strength but God's. Only those who are in Christ could confront the horrible appearances and triumph and reign over them. So when facing the crisis of belief and the assaults of the world, a theologian of the cross discerns in that context its opposites. He discerns not as the world does, not through physical but spiritual eyes. Thus he learns to embrace the invisible things and refuses

---

12. Spitz, "Luther's Ecclesiast. A Historian's Angle," in *Seven-Headed Luther*, 117.
13. LW 11.187–88 (WA 4.360). Luther had only two pages, commenting on Ps. 88:10: "Wilt Thou work wonders for the dead?"

to be overcome by the visible, atrocious circumstances. This requires faith on the part of the afflicted souls as well as the skill and grace to discern, so that in their affliction they might behold God and ascend to the Lord through his opposite, Christ's lowly humanity and the cross.

The cross is the locus of God's love hidden in suffering. Contemplate the wounds of Christ, and the afflicted one will know for sure that he belongs to him, even amid contrary appearances. Hence in those whose lives are nothing but a series of disconnected fragments of laments, faith assures that they remain connected with God and are profoundly embraced by God, though they feel profoundly forsaken. For those whose lives reflect everything except a sensible story with progressive development and futuristic hope, they are still in hope, even amid despair; for those whose lives comprise nothing but anguished complaint with no beginning and no clear end, God's purpose to redeem remains intact. Where there is no promise of either better times or restitution of better health, the promise of God's comfort is a surety that causes the afflicted heart to lament to God with sighs, not with words. The promise of God's comfort encompasses not just the promise of heaven but also God's presence and power (foolish and weak as it might appear) right here and now today: the new creation has begun, the new life already bestowed. God keeps hope alive and does so in the context of our lamenting and sighing. Even when God is silent and seems aloof and indifferent, the Holy Spirit comforts the wounded "with sighs too deep for words" (Rom. 8:26), which pierce through the clouds and touch heaven. That is where divine comfort lies, in an unutterable manner that when the afflicted soul cannot utter cries to God, Christ intercedes for him from his ascended throne, and the Spirit within him does the same. Abundant consolation flows from above into the wounded hearts, soothing and spurring them to trust in God and to hope against hope. This spiritual reality is hidden, not perceived by the senses, except by faith. The afflicted soul shuns speculating on the naked or absolute God, inquiring what God might do or might not do. Instead he flees from the inscrutable will of the naked God and clings to the promises and mercy of God in the revealed God, the one with whom he has to do. He thus forgoes abstract speculation on why evils befall him, for it suffices to know that God is on his side and that God's grace will ultimately triumph over all contradictions of life.

The Psalms display the posture of the justified sinner, *simul iustus et peccator* (simultaneously saint and sinner), as one of waiting, defined in active terms: "hoping, trusting, and believing in God." "My soul," Luther speaks in the psalmist's voice, "always has its face straight toward God and confidently awaits His coming, no matter how it may be delayed."[14] The very essence of the Christian life under the cross is nothing but "one of trusting and hoping in God and a relying on, and waiting for, Him."[15] Just as "direct opposites" by nature—that we are saint and sinner at the same time—are in one person, so also hope and despair, the opposites, are

14. LW 14.192 (WA 18.518).
15. LW 14.201 (WA 18.526).

in one person at the same time "because in us two natures are opposed to each other, the old man and the new man."[16] Just as hope and despair coincide as opposites in us, so also do joy and sorrow and praise and lament. However, the godly person laments in hope, and hope sets him on the way to recovery. Commenting on Ps. 130:7: "My soul waits for the Lord, from the one morning watch to the next," Luther exhorted us not to give up, even in distressful situations:

> Once you have begun to trust in God, then do not stop. Let the evening and the night pass, just remain watchful until morning comes again. For the new man, whose occupation is nothing but waiting for the Lord and tarrying for Him, should not give up, as the outer man does and must do.... [T]herefore, the whole life, work, and activity of the inner man is masterfully described. It is nothing else than relying on God and letting His will stand in every respect.[17]

Fruitful study of the holy things (grace and sin, etc.) in the Psalms foments Luther's fundamental conviction that the God with whom we have to do is one who is for us (*pro nobis*), despite the contrary appearance of the circumstances, and who showers his boundless grace to those who cry to him, for "with him there is nothing but kindness and mercy."[18] And Christ is the definitive and concrete embodiment of the grace of God: "Christ is God's grace, mercy, righteousness, truth, wisdom, power, comfort, and salvation given to us by God without any merit on our part."[19] In response to the

16. LW 14.191 (WA 18.518).
17. LW 14.193 (WA 18.520).
18. LW 14.194 (WA 18.520).
19. LW 14.204 (WA 18.529).

grace of God that has appeared in Christ, Luther confessed: "Whenever I found less in the Scriptures [the Psalter included] than Christ, I was never satisfied; but whenever I found more than Christ, I never became poorer."[20] The Psalter, says Luther in his *Preface to the Psalter*, "gives off such a fine and precious fragrance that all pious hearts felt the devotion and power in the unknown words and for this reason loved the book."[21] And that "fine and precious fragrance" is Christ, on whom all eyes are fixed, and from whom derives eternal joy and fulfillment, even when lament is necessary, when we are driven to prayer.

20. LW 14.204 (WA 18.529).
21. LW 35.253.

Bibliography

Primary Sources: Martin Luther

Luther, Martin. D. *Martin Luthers Werke: Kritische Gesamtausgabe*. 100 volumes. Weimar: Hermann Böhlau Nachfolger, 1883–.

———. D. *Martin Luthers Werke. Kristische Gesamtausgabe*. *Briefwechsel* 11 volumes. Weimar: Hermann Böhlau Nachfolger, 1901–61.

———. D. *Martin Luthers Werke. Kristische Gesamtausgabe. Tischreden*. Weimar: Hermann Böhlau Nachfolger, 1912–21.

———. *Luther's Works*. American Editions. 55 volumes. Edited by Jaroslav Pelikan and H. T. Lehman. St. Louis: Concordia; Philadelphia: Fortress Press, 1955–1967.

Martin Luther's Basic Theological Writings. Edited by Timothy Lull. Minneapolis; Fortress Press, 1989.

Early Theological Writings. The Library of Christian Classics. Volume 16. Translated and edited by James Atkinson. Philadelphia: Westminster Press, 1962.

Luther's Letters of Spiritual Counsel. Edited by Theodore Tappert. Philadelphia: Westminster Press, 1955.

Secondary Sources

Althaus, Paul. *The Theology of Martin Luther*. Translated by Robert C. Schultz. Philadelphia: Fortress Press, 1966.

Anderson, Bernhard W. *Out of the Depths: The Psalms Speak For Us Today*. Louisville: Westminster/John Knox, 2000.

Anderson, H. George, J. Francis Stafford, and Joseph A. Burgess, eds. *The One Mediator, The Saints, and Mary. Lutherans and Catholics in Dialogue VIII*. Minneapolis: Augsburg Publishing House, 1992.

Aristotle, *Problems. 11, Books XX11–XXXV111. Rhetorica ad Alexandrum*. Translated by Walter S. Hett and Harris Rackham. Cambridge, MA: Harvard University Press, 1957.

Asheim, Ivar, ed. *The Church, Mysticism, Sanctification, and the Natural in Luther's Thought*. Minneapolis: Fortress Press, 1967.

Aurelius, Carl Axel. "*Quo verbum dei vel cantu inter populos maneat*: The Hymns of Martin Luther." In *The Arts and the Cultural Heritage of Martin Luther*, edited by Eyolf Østrem et al., 19–34. Copenhagen: Museum Tusculanum Press, 2003.

Barth, Hans-Martin. *The Theology of Martin Luther. A Critical Assessment*. Translated by Linda M. Maloney. Minneapolis: Fortress Press, 2013.

Bautch, Richard J. "May Your Eyes Be Open and Your Ears Attentive: A Study of Penance and Penitence in the Writings." In *Repentance in Christian Theology*, edited by Mark J. Boda and Gordon T. Smith, 67–85. Collegeville: Liturgical Press, 2006.

Bayer, Oswald. *Living by Faith: Justification and Sanctification*. Translated by G. W. Bromiley. Grand Rapids: William B. Eerdmans, 2003.

———. "Luther as an Interpreter of Holy Scripture." In *The Cambridge Companion to Martin Luther*, edited by Donald McKim, 73–85. Cambridge: Cambridge University Press, 2003.

———. *Martin Luther's Theology: A Contemporary Interpretation.* Translated by Thomas Trapp. Grand Rapids: William B. Eerdmans, 2008.

———. "Theology as *Askesis:* On Struggling Faith." In *Festkrift für Peter Widmann: Gudstankens aktualitet,* edited by M.W. Petersen, B.K. Holm, and A. Jacobsen, 35–54. Copenhagen: Forlaget ANIS, 2010.

———. *Theology the Lutheran Way.* Edited and Translated by Jeffrey G. Silcock and Mark C. Mattes. Grand Rapids: William B. Eerdmans, 2007.

———. "Toward a Theology of Lament." In *Caritas Et Reformatio: Essays on Church and Society in Honor of Carter Lindberg*, edited by David Whitford, 211–20. St. Louis: Concordia Publishing House, 2002.

Biel, Gabriel. *Collectorium circa quattuor libros sententiarum.* 4 volumes. Edited by H. Rückert, M. Elze, R. Steiger, W. Werbeck, and U. Hofmann. Tübingen: J.C.B. Mohr, 1973–92.

Billman, Kathleen D & Daniel L. Migliore. *Rachel's Cry: Prayer of Lament and Rebirth of Hope.* Cleveland: United Church Press, 1999.

Bonhoeffer, Dietrich. "Meditation on Psalm 119." In *Dietrich Bonhoeffer Works,* Volume 15, edited by Dirk Schulz, 496–527. Minneapolis: Fortress Press, 2011.

Bornkamm, Heinrich. *Luther and the Old Testament.* Translated by Eric and Ruth Gritsch. Philadelphia: Fortress Press, 1969.

———. *Luther's World of Thought*. Translated by Martin H. Bertram. St. Louis: Concordia Publishing House, 1958.

Braaten, Carl E. "The Problem of God-language Today." In *Our Naming of God. Problems and Prospects of God-Talk Today*, edited by Carl E. Braaten, 11–33. Minneapolis: Fortress Press, 1989.

Bradshaw, Paul. *Daily Prayer in the Early Church*. New York: Oxford University Press, 1982.

Braun, John, ed. *Sermon Studies on Selected Psalms*. Milwaukee: Northwestern Publishing House, 2002.

Brecht, Martin. *Martin Luther: Shaping and Defining the Reformation 1521–1532*. Translated by J. L. Shaff. Minneapolis: Fortress, 1990.

Brock, Brian. *Singing the Ethics of God: On the Place of Christian Ethics in Scripture*. Grand Rapids: William B. Eerdmans, 2007.

Brown, Sally & Patrick D. Miller, eds. *Lament. Reclaiming Practices in Pulpit, Pew and Public Square*. Louisville: Westminster John Knox Press, 2004.

Brueggemann, Walter. *Israel's Praise: Doxology against Idolatry and Ideology*. Minneapolis: Fortress Press, 1988.

———. *Praying the Psalms*. Winona: St. Mary's Press, 1982.

———. *Spirituality of the Psalms*. Minneapolis: Fortress Press, 2001.

———. *The Message of the Psalms: A Theological Commentary*. Augsburg Publishing House, 1984.

———. *The Psalms and the Life of Faith*. Minneapolis: Fortress Press, 1995.

Bullock, C. Hassell. *Encountering the Book of Psalms: A Literary and Theological Introduction*. Grand Rapids: Baker Academic Press, 2001.

Burnaby, John, trans. "The Spirit and the Letter." In *Augustine: Later Works,* Library of Christian Classics. Vol. 8. Philadelphia: Westminster Press, 1955.

Chadwick, Henry, ed. and trans. Saint Augustine, *Confessions.* Oxford: Oxford University Press, 1991.

Countryman, L. William. *Conversations with Scripture: The Psalms.* New York: Morehouse Publishing, 2012.

Ebeling, Gerhard. *Luther: An Introduction to His Thought.* Translated by R. A. Wilson. Philadelphia: Fortress Press, 1970.

Elert, Werner. *The Structure of Lutheranism.* Translated by Walter Hansen. St. Louis: Concordia Publishing House, 1962.

Estes, James M. *Peace, Order and the Glory of God. Secular Authority and the Church in the Thought of Luther and Melanchthon, 1518–1559.* Leiden: E. J. Brill, 2005.

Floysvik, Ingvar. *When God Becomes My Enemy.* St. Louis: Concordia Publishing House, 1997.

Forde, Gerhard O. "Breaking the Conspiracy of Silence—A Sermon on Psalm 51:15." In *The Preached God: Proclamation in Word and Sacrament,* edited by Mark C. Mattes and Steven D. Paulson, 291–97. Grand Rapids: William B. Eerdmans, 2007.

———. *"Exsurge Domine!* A Sermon on Psalm 74:22–23." In *A More Radical Gospel: Essays on Eschatology, Authority, Atonement, and Ecumenism,* edited by Mark C. Mattes and Steven D. Paulson, 206–10. Grand Rapids: William B. Eerdmans, 2004.

———. "Moses' Baccalaureate- A Sermon on Exodus 4:21–26, Psalm 90, and 2 Corinthians 5:14–15." In *The Preached God: Proclamation in Word and Sacrament,* edited by Mark C. Mattes and

Steven D. Paulson, 286–90. Grand Rapids: William B. Eerdmans, 2007.

———. *On Being a Theologian of the Cross: Reflections on Luther's Heidelberg Disputation, 1518.* Grand Rapids: William B. Eerdmans, 1997.

———. *Theology is for Proclamation.* Minneapolis: Fortress Press, 1990.

———. *Where God Meet Man. Luther's Down-to-Earth Approach to the Gospel.* Minneapolis: Augsburg Publishing House, 1972.

Gaebler, Mary. *The Courage of Faith. Martin Luther and the Theonomous Self.* Minneapolis: Fortress Press, 2013.

Gaiser, Frederick J. *Healing in the Bible: Theological Insight for Christian Ministry.* Baker Academic Press, 2010.

George, Timothy. *Reading Scripture with the Reformers.* Downers Grove: IVP, 2011.

Gerrish, Brian. *Grace and Reason: A Study in the Theology of Luther.* Oxford: Clarendon, 1962.

Gilbertson, Carol & Greg Muilenburg, eds. *Translucence: Religion, the Arts and Imagination.* Minneapolis: Fortress Press, 2004.

Goldingay, John. *Praying the Psalms: Grove Spirituality Series.* Bramcote: Grove Books, 1993.

Gritisch, Eric W. *Martin Luther's Anti-Semitism: Against His Better Judgment.* Grand Rapids: William. B. Eerdmans, 2012.

Gritisch, Eric W., and Robert W. Jenson, *Lutheranism: The Theological Movement and Its Confessional Writings.* Philadelphia: Fortress Press, 1976.

Hagen, Kenneth. *A Theology of Testament in the Young Luther: The Lectures on Hebrews.* Leiden: E. J. Brill, 1974.

————. "*Omnis homo mendax:* Luther on Psalm 116." In *Biblical Interpretation in the Era of the Reformation: Essays Presented to David C. Steinmetz in Honor of His Sixtieth Birthday,* edited by R.A. Muller and J. L. Thompson, 85–102. Grand Rapids: William B. Eerdmans, 1996.

Hägglund, Bent. *The Background of Luther's Doctrine of Justification in Late Medieval Theology.* Philadelphia: Fortress Press, 1971.

Hamm, Berndt. *The Early Luther. Stages in Reformation Reorientation.* Translated by Martin J. Lohrmann. Grand Rapids: William B. Eerdmans, 2014.

Heckel, Johannes. *Lex Charitatis: A Juristic Disquisition on Law in the Theology of Martin Luther.* Translated and edited by Gottfried G. Krodel. Grand Rapids: William B. Eerdmans, 2010.

Helmer, Christine, ed. *The Global Luther. A Theologian for Modern Times.* Minneapolis: Fortress Press, 2009.

Hendrix, Scott. *Ecclesia in Via: Ecclesiological Developments in the Medieval Psalms Exegesis and the Dictata Super Psalterium (1513–1515) of Martin Luther.* Leiden: E.J. Brill, 1974.

Hendrix, Scott, ed. *Early Protestant Spirituality.* New York: Paulist Press, 2009.

Hillerbrand, Hans J., ed. *The Oxford Encyclopedia of the Reformation.* 4 volumes. Oxford: Oxford University Press, 1996.

Hinlicky, Paul R. *A Path for Christian Theology after Christendom.* Grand Rapids: William B. Eerdmans, 2010.

Holl, Karl. *What did Luther Understand by Religion?* Philadelphia: Fortress Press, 1977.

Holladay, William L. *The Psalms Through Three Thousand Years:*

Prayerbook of a Cloud of Witnesses. Minneapolis: Fortress Press, 1996.

Isaac, Gordon. *In Public Defense of the Ministry of Moses: Luther's Enarratio on Psalm 90*. PhD Dissertation. Milwaukee: Marquette University, 1996.

Jacobson, Rolf and Karl Jacobson. *Invitation to the Psalms*. Grand Rapids: Baker Academic, 2013.

Jacobson, Rolf, ed. *Soundings in the Theology of the Psalms: Perspectives and Methods in Contemporary Scholarship*. Minneapolis: Fortress Press, 2011.

Janowski, Bernd. *Arguing with God. Theological Anthropology of the Psalms*. Translated by Armin Siedlecki. Lousville: Westminister John Knox Press, 2013.

Jüngel, Eberhard. *God as the Mystery of the World. On the Foundation of the Theology of the Crucified God in between Theism and Atheism*, translated by Darrell L.Gruder. Grand Rapids: Wm. B. Eerdmans, 1983.

Kolb, Robert. *Bound Choice, Election, and Wittenberg Theological Method: From Martin Luther to the Formula of Concord*. Grand Rapids: William B. Eerdmans, 2005.

———. "The Doctrine of Christ in Nikolaus Selnecker's Interpretation of Psalm 8, 22, and 110." In *Biblical Interpretation of the Era of the Reformation: Essays Presented to David Steinmetz in Honour of his Sixtieth Birthday*, edited by David Curtis, Richard A. Muller, and John Lee Thompson, 313–32. Grand Rapids: William B. Eerdmans, 1996.

———. *Luther and the Stories of God. Biblical Narratives as a Foundation for Christian Living*. Grand Rapids: Baker Academic, 2012.

————. *Martin Luther. Confessor of the Faith.* Oxford: Oxford University Press, 2009.

————. *Martin Luther as Prophet, Teacher, and Hero: Images of the Reformer 1520–1620.* Grand Rapids: Baker Books, 1999.

Kolb, Robert, and Timothy J. Wengert, eds. *The Book of Concord: The Confessions of the Evangelical Lutheran Church.* Minneapolis: Fortress Press, 2000.

Kolb, Robert and Charles P. Arand. *The Genius of Luther's Theology. A Wittenberg Way of Thinking.* Grand Rapids: Baker Academic, 2008.

Kolb, Robert, Irene Dingel & Lubomir Batka, eds. *The Oxford Handbook of Martin Luther's Theology.* Oxford: Oxford University Press, 2014.

Kraeling, E. G. *The Old Testament Since the Reformation.* New York: Harper & Rows, 1955.

Lefèvre, Jacques d'Etaples. *Quincuplex Psalterium.* Paris: Henri Estienne, 1509.

Leroux, Neil. *Luther's Rhetoric.* St. Louis: Concordia Publishing House, 2002.

————. *Martin Luther as Comforter: Writings on Death.* Leiden: J. J. Brill, 2007.

Lienhard, Marc. *Luther: Witness to Jesus Christ.* Translated by Edwin H. Robertson. Minneapolis: Augsburg Publishing House, 1982.

Limburg, James. *Psalms.* Louisville: Westminster/John Knox, 2000.

Lohse, Bernhard. *Martin Luther's Theology.* Translated by Roy Harrisville. Minneapolis: Fortress Press, 1999.

Lubac, Henri de. *Medieval Exegesis: Four Senses of Scripture.* 4 volumes. Grand Rapids: William B. Eerdmans, 1998–2000.

Maas, Korey. "The Place of Repentance in Luther's Theological Development." In *Theologia et Apologia: Essays in Reformation Theology and its Defense Presented to Rod Rosenbladt*, edited by Adam Francisco, Korey Maas, and Steven P. Mueller, 137–54. Eugene, Oregon: Wipf & Stock, 2007.

Maas, Robin. "A Simple Way to Pray: Luther's Instructions on the Devotional Use of the Catechism." In *Spiritual Traditions for the Contemporary Church*, edited by Robin Maas and Gabriel O' Donnell, 162–69. Nashville: Abingdon, 1990.

Mannermaa, Tuomo. *Two Kinds of Love. Martin Luther's Religious World*. Minneapolis: Fortress Press, 2010.

Matheson, Peter. *The Imaginative World of the Reformation*. Edinburgh: T. & T. Clark, 2000.

Mays, James Luther. "The Self in the Psalms and the Image of God." In *God and Human Dignity*, edited by R. Kendall Soulen and Linda Woodhead, 27–43. Grand Rapids: William B. Eerdmans, 2006.

McGrath, Alister E. *The Intellectual Origins of the European Reformation*. Oxford: Basil Blackwell Inc., 1987.

———. *Iustitia Dei. A History of the Christian Doctrine of Justification*. Cambridge: Cambridge University Press, 1998.

———. *Luther's Theology of the Cross*. Oxford: Basil Blackwell Inc., 1985.

Meyer, Carl S, ed. *Luther for an Ecumenical Age*. St. Louis: Concordia Publishing House, 1967.

Migne, J.-P. *Patrologia*, Series Latina. 221 volumes. Paris: Garnier Fratres, 1978ff.

Miller, Patrick. *Interpreting the Psalms.* Philadelphia: Fortress Press, 1986.

———. *They Cried to the Lord: The Form and Theology of Biblical Prayer.* Minneapolis: Fortress Press, 1994.

Moltmann, Jürgen. *The Source of Life. The Holy Spirit in the Theology of Life.* London: SCM, 1997.

———. *The Trinity and the Kingdom.* Translated by Margaret Kohl. New York: Harper & Row, 1981.

Muhlhan, Brett. Being *Shaped by Freedom. An Examination of Luther's Development of Christian Liberty, 1520–1525.* Eugene, Oregon: Pickwick Publications, 2012.

Ngien, Dennis. *Gifted Response: The Triune God as the Causative Agency of our Responsive Worship.* Milton Keynes, UK: Paternoster Press, 2008.

———. *Luther as Spiritual Advisor: The Interface of Theology and Piety in Luther's Devotional Writings.* Milton Keynes, UK: Paternoster Press, 2007.

———. *The Suffering of God according to Martin Luther's 'Theologia Crucis'.* New York: Peter Lang, 1995.

Oberman, Heiko. "Gemitus et Raptus: Luther und die Mystik." In *The Church, Mysticism, Sanctification, and the Natural in Luther's Thought,* edited by Ivar Asheim. 24–59. Minneapolis: Fortress Press, 1967.

Oberman, Heiko A. *Forerunners of the Reformation: The Shape of Late Medieval Thought.* Philadelphia: Holt, Rinehart and Winston, 1966.

———. *Harvest of Medieval Theology: Gabriel Biel and Late Medieval Nominalism.* Durham: Labyrinth, 1983.

Ozment, Steven, ed. *The Reformation in Medieval Perspective* Chicago: Quadrangle Books, 1971.

———. *Homo Spiritualis: A Comparative Study of the Anthropology of Johannes Tauler, Jean Gerson and Martin Luther (1509–1516) in the Context of Their Theological Thought.* Leiden: E. J. Brill, 1969.

Parsons, Michael. *Luther and Calvin on Grief and Lament.* Lewiston, New York: Edwin Mellen Press, 2013.

———. *Martin Luther's Interpretation of the Royal Psalms: The Spiritual Kingdom in a Pastoral Context.* Lewiston, New York: Mellen Press, 2009.

———. *Text and Task: Scripture and Mission.* Milton Keynes, UK: Paternoster Press, 2005.

Paulson, Steven. *Lutheran Theology.* New York: T & T Clark, 2011.

Placher, William C. *The Domestication of Transcendence. How Modern Theology about God Went Wrong.* Louisville: Westminster John Knox, 1996.

Pless, John T. "The Triangular Shape of the Pastor's Devotional Life." In *Lord Jesus Christ, Will You Not Stay: Essays in Honor of Ronald Feuerhahn on the Occasion of His Sixty-Fifth Birthday*, edited by J. Bart Day et al, 317–31. Houston: Feuerhahn Festschrift Committee, 2002.

———. *Martin Luther: Preacher of the Cross.* St. Louis: Concordia Publishing House, 2013.

Posset, Franz. Pater *Bernhardus: Martin Luther and Bernard of Clairvaux.* Kalamazoo: Cistercian Publications, 1999.

Preus, James S. *From Shadow to Promise: Old Testament Interpretation from Augustine to the Young Luther.* Cambridge: Harvard University Press, 1969.

Pseudo-Dionysius. *Pseudo-Dionysius: The Complete Works.* The Classics of Western Spirituality. Translated by Paul Rorem. New York: Paulist Press, 1987.

Reardon, Patrick Henry. *Christ in the Psalms.* Ben Lomand, CA: Conciliar Press, 2000.

Reid, Stephen, ed. *Psalms and Practice: Worship, Virtue and Authority.* Collegeville: Liturgical Press, 2001.

Reinis, Austra. *Reforming the Art of Dying. The ars moriendi in the German Reformation 1519–1528.* Aldershot: Ashgate, 2007.

Ringgren, Helmer. *The Faith of the Psalmists.* Philadelphia: Fortress Press, 1963.

Rittgers, Ronald K. *The Reformation of Suffering: Pastoral Theology and Lay Piety in Late Medieval and Early Modern Germany.* Oxford: Oxford University Press, 2012.

Robertson, Edwin. *Dietrich Bonhoeffer's Meditations on Psalms.* Grand Rapids: Zondervan, 2002.

Rosner, Brian S., ed. *The Consolations of Theology.* Grand Rapids: William B. Eerdmans, 2008.

Schaff, Philip, ed. *Augustine: Anti-Pelagian Writings.* In *Nicene and Post-Nicene Fathers.* Volume 5. Grand Rapids: William B. Eerdmans, 1956.

———, ed. *Augustine: Expositions on the Book of Psalms.* In *Nicene and Post-Nicene Fathers.* Volume 8. Grand Rapids: William B. Eerdmans, 1956.

Selderhuis, Herman J. *Calvin's Theology of the Psalms.* Grand Rapids: Baker Academic, 2007.

Senn, Frank, ed. *Protestant Spiritual Traditions.* New York: Paulist Press, 1986.

Seybold, Klaus and Mueller, Ulrich B. *Sickness & Healing: Biblical Encounter Series.* Nashville: Abingdon Press, 1981.

Shepherd, Victor. *Interpreting Martin Luther. An Introduction to His Life and Thought.* Vancouver: Regent College Publishing, 2008.

Steinmetz, David C. *Reformers in the Wings.* Philadelphia: Fortress Press, 1981.

Tappert, Theodore G, trans. and ed. *The Book of Concord: The Confessions of the Evangelical Lutheran Church.* Philadelphia: Fortress Press, 1959.

Tsai, Lee-Chen A. *"The Development of Luther's Hermeneutics in His Commentaries on the Psalms."* PhD thesis, Aberdeen: University of Aberdeen, 1989.

Vainio, Olli-Pekka, ed. *Engaging Luther: A (New) Theological Assessment.* Eugene: Cascade Books, 2010.

Vogelsang, Erich. *Die anfänge von Luthers Christologie: nach der ersten Psalmenvorlesung, insbesondere in ihren exegetischen und systematischen zusammenhängen mit Augustin und der scholastik dargestellt.* Berlin: W. de Gruyter, 1929.

Wallace, Howard Neil. *Words to God, Word from God: The Psalms in the Prayer and Preaching of the Church.* Burlington, VT: Ashgate Publishing Company, 2005.

Waltke, Bruce K and Houston, James M. *The Psalms as Christian Worship: A Historical Commentary.* Grand Rapids: William B. Eerdmans, 2010.

Webster, John B. *Barth's Moral Theology: Human Action in Barth's Thought.* Edinburgh: T & T Clark, 1998.

Wengert, Timothy J., ed. *Harvesting Martin Luther's Reflection on Theology, Ethics, and the Church.* Grand Rapids: Eerdmans, 2004.

————. *Martin Luther's Catechisms: Forming the Faith*. Minneapolis: Fortress Press, 2009.

————, ed. *The Pastoral Luther. Essays in Honor of Martin Luther's Practical Theology*. Grand Rapids: William B. Eerdmans, 2009.

————. *Reading the Bible with Martin Luther*. Grand Rapids: Baker Academic, 2013.

Weiser, Arthur. *The Psalms: A Commentary*. Philadelphia: The Westminster Press, 1962.

Wesselschmidt, Quentin F., ed. *Ancient Christian Commentary on Scripture: Psalms 51–150*. Downers Grove, Illinois: IVP, 2007.

Westermann, Claus. *The Living Psalms*. Grand Rapids: William B. Eerdmans, 1989.

————. *Praise and Lament in the Psalms*. Atlanta: John Knox Press, 1981.

————. *The Psalms: Structure, Content & Message*. Minneapolis: Augsburg Publishing House, 1980.

Westhelle, Vitor. *The Scandalous God. The Use and Abuse of the Cross*. Minneapolis: Fortress Press, 2006.

Whitford, David M, ed. *T & T Clark Companion to Reformation Theology*. London: T & T Clark, 2012.

Wicks, Jared. *Man Yearning for Grace: Luther's Early Spiritual Teaching*. Cleveland: Corpus Books, 1973.

Wingren, Gustaf. *The Christian's Calling: Luther on Vocation*. Translated by Carl C. Rasmussen. Philadelphia: Mühlenberg, 1957.

Witvliet, John D. *The Biblical Psalms in Christian Worship*. Grand Rapids: William B. Eerdmans, 2007.

Wolff, Hans Walter. *Anthropology of the Old Testament.* Philadelphia: Fortress Press, 1981.

Zachman, Randall C. *The Assurance of Faith: Conscience in the Theology of Martin Luther and John Calvin.* Minneapolis: Fortress Press, 1993.

Zenger, Erich. *A God of Vengenance? Understanding the Psalms of Divine Wrath.* Translated by L. M. Maloney. Louisville: Westminster John Knox, 1996.

Journal Articles

Anderson, Gary A. "King David and the Psalms of Imprecation." *Pro Ecclesia* XV (Summer 2006): 267–80.

Arand, Charles. "The Battle Cry for Faith. The Catechisms' Exposition of the Lord's Prayer." *Concordia Journal* 21 (1995): 42–65.

Aurelius, Carl Axel. "Luther on the Psalter." *Lutheran Quarterly* 14 (Summer 2000): 193–205.

Bayer, Oswald. "The Modern Narcissus." *Lutheran Quarterly* 9 (Autumn 1995): 301–13.

———. "Does Evil Persist?" *Lutheran Quarterly* 11 (Summer 1997): 143–50.

———. "The Plurality of the One God and the Plurality of the Gods." *Pro Ecclesia* XV (Summer 2006): 338–54.

Bence, Barry. "The Psalms in Ministry." *Word & World* 5, no. 2 (Spring 1985): 188–91.

Bielfeldt, Dennis. "Deification as a Motif in Luther's *Dictata super psalterium.*" *The Sixteenth Century Journal* 28 (Summer 1997): 401–20.

Black II, C. Clifton. "Unity and Diversity in Luther's Biblical Exegesis: Psalm 51 as a Test-Case." *Scottish Journal of Theology* 38, no. 3 (1985): 325–45.

Blaufuss, Dietrich. "Löhe Preaches the Psalms." *Logia* (Holy Trinity 2008): 7–12.

Boulton, Matthew L. "'We Pray for His Mouth': Karl Barth, Erving Goffman, and a Theology of Invocation." *Modern Theology* 17, no. 1 (2001): 67–83.

Braaten, Carl E. "Let's Talk about the 'Death of God'," *Dialog* 26, no. 3 (Spring 1987): 209–14.

Brock, Brian. "Bonhoeffer and the Bible in Christian Ethics: Psalm 119, the Mandates, and Ethics as a 'Way.'" *Studies in Christian Ethics* 18, no. 3 (2005): 7–29.

Brueggemann, Walter. "The Shape for Old Testament Theology: 2, Embrace of Pain." *Catholic Biblical Quarterly* 47, no. 1 (1985): 28–46.

Dockey, David S. "Martin Luther's Christological Hermeneutics." *Grace Theological Journal* 4 (1983): 189–203.

Ebeling, Gerhard. "The 'New' Hermeneutics and the Early Luther." *Theology Today* 21, n. 1 (Apr., 1964): 34–46.

Gaiser, Frederick J. "The David of Psalm 51: Reading Psalm 51 in light of Psalm 50." *Word & World* 23, no. 4 (2003): 382–94.

———. "I Come with Thanks Most Grateful: Paul Gerhardt and Psalm 111 on Studying God's Work." *Word & World* 27, no. 3 (Summer 2007): 325–30.

———. "I Sing to Praise You (Psalm 30): Paul Gerhardt and the Psalms." *Word & World* 27, no. 2 (Spring 2007): 195–205.

———. "It Shall Not Reach You: Tailsman or Vocation? Reading

Psalm 91 in Time of War." *Word & World* 25 (Spring 2005): 191–202.

———. "Your Sins are Forgiven. Stand up and Walk: A Theological Reading of Mark 2:1–12 in Light of Psalm 103." *Ex Auditu* 21 (2005): 71–87.

Gerrish, Brian A. "'To the Unknown God': Luther and Calvin on the Hiddenness of God." *Journal of Religion* 53, no. 3 (July 1973): 263–92.

Gleason, Randall C. "The 'Spirit' and 'Letter' in Luther's Hermeneutics." *Bibliotheca Sacra* 157, n. 628 (Oct.–Dec. 2000): 466–85.

Hägglund, Bengt. "The Background of Luther's Doctrine of Justification in Late Medieval Theology." *Lutheran World* 8 (1961): 24–46.

Harrisville, Roy. "Paul and the Psalms: A Formal Study." *Lutheran Forum* 5 (Spring 1985): 168–79.

Helmer, Christine. "Luther's Trinitarian Hermeneutic and the Old Testament." *Modern Theology* 18, no. 1 (January 2002): 49–73.

Hendrix, Scott. "Luther against the Background of Biblical Interpretation." *Interpretation* 37 (July 1983): 229–39.

Hinlicky, Paul R. "Luther's Theology of the Cross—Part One." *Lutheran Forum* 32, no. 2 (Summer 1998): 46–49.

———. "Luther's Theology of the Cross—Part Two." *Lutheran Forum* 32, no. 3 (Fall 1998): 58–61.

Jens, Walter. "Psalm 90, On Transience." *Lutheran Quarterly* 9 (Summer 1995): 177–89.

Jenson, Matt. "Suffering the Promise of God: Engaging Oswald

Bayer." *International Journal of Systematic Theology* 13, no. 2 (April 2011): 134–53.

Jenson, Robert W. "Psalm 32." *Interpretation* 33, no. 2 (1979): 172–76.

Kadai, Heino O. "Luther's Theology of the Cross." *Concordia Theological Quarterly* 63, no. 3 (1999): 169–204.

Kärkkäinen, Veli-Matti. "The Christian as Christ to the Neighbor: Luther's Theology of Love," *International Journal of Systematic Theology* 6, no. 2 (2004): 101–17.

Kelly, Robert. "The Suffering Church: A Study of Luther's *Theologia Crucis*." *Concordia Theological Quarterly* 50 (1986): 3–17.

Kiecker, James G. "Luther's Preface to His First Lectures on the Psalms (1513): The Historical Background to Luther's Biblical Hermeneutic." *Wisconsin Lutheran Quarterly* 85 (Fall, 1988): 287–95.

Kolb, Robert. "God's Gift of Martyrdom: The Early Reformation Understanding of Dying for the Faith." *Church History* 64, no, 3 (September 1995): 399–411.

———. "Luther on the Theology of the Cross." *Lutheran Quarterly* 16, no. 4 (2002): 443–66.

———. "Luther's Theology of the Cross Fifteen Years after Heidelberg: Luther's Lectures on the Psalms of Ascent." *Journal of Ecclesiastical History* 61, no. 1 (2010): 69–85.

Limburg, James. "Psalm 121: A Psalm for Sojourners." *Word & World* 5, no. 2 (Spring 1985): 180–87.

———. "The Autumn Leaves: Pages for the Psalter for Late Pentecost." *Word & World* 12, no. 3 (1992): 272–77.

McConville, J. G. "Statement of Assurance in Psalms of Lament." *Irish Biblical Studies* 8 (April 1986): 64–75.

Meyer, Lester. "A Lack of Lament in the Church's Use of the Psalter." *Lutheran Quarterly* 7 (Spring 1993): 67–78.

Miller, Patrick. "Dietrich Bonhoeffer and the Psalms." *Princeton Theological Seminary Bulletin* Volume 15 (1994): 274–82.

Neary, Michael. "The Importance of Lament in the God/Man Relationship." *Irish Theological Quarterly* 52 (1986): 180–92.

Ngien, Dennis. "Chalcedonian Christology and Beyond: Luther's Doctrine of *Communicatio Idiomatium*." *The Heythrop Journal* 45, no. 1 (January 2004): 54–68.

Oberman, Heiko O. "Notes on the Theology of Nominalism." *Harvard Theological Review* 53 (1976): 47–76.

Pannenberg, Wolfhart. "A Theology of the Cross." *Word & World* 8, no. 2 (1988): 162–72.

Paulson, Steven D. "Luther on the Hidden God." *Word & World* 19, no. 4 (1999): 363–71.

———. "The Wrath of God." *Dialog* 33, no. 4 (1994): 245–51.

Pilch, John J. "Luther's Hermeneutical 'Shift.'" *The Harvard Theological Review* 63 (1970): 445–48.

Pless, John T. "Bonhoeffer the Preacher." *Concordia Pulpit Resources* 16 (September 17, 2006–November 26, 2006): 7–10.

Preus, James S. "Old Testament *Promissio* and Luther's New Hermeneutic." *The Harvard Theological Review* 60 (1976): 145–61.

Reinke, Darrell R. "From Allegory to Metaphor: More Notes on Luther's Hermeneutical Shift." *The Harvard Theological Review* 66, no. 3 (1973): 386–95.

Slenczka, Reinhard. "Luther's Care of Souls for our Time." *Concordia Theological Quarterly* 67 (January 2003): 33–64.

Strelan, John. "*Theologia Crucis, Theologia Gloriae*: A Study in Opposing Theologies." *Lutheran Theological Journal* 23 (December 1989): 89–100.

Throntveit, Mark. "The Penitential Psalms and the Lenten Discipline." *Lutheran Quarterly* 1 (Winter 1987): 495–512.

Tostengard, Shelton. "Psalm 22." *Interpretation* 46 (April 1992): 167–70.

Tracy, David. "The Hidden God: The Divine Other of Liberation." *Cross Currents* 46, no. 1 (Spring 1996): 5–16.

Velema, W. H. "Preaching on the Psalms." *Evangelical Review of Theology* 21, no. 3 (1997): 258–67.

Vercruysse, Joseph E. "Luther's Theology of the Cross at the time of Heidelberg Disputation." *Gregorianum* 57 (1976): 523–48.

Wengert, Timothy. "'Peace, Peace … Cross, Cross'." *Theology Today* 59, no. 2 (July 2001): 190–205.

Westermann, Claus. "The Role of Lament in the Theology of the Old Testament." *Interpretation* 28 (January 1974): 20–38.

Wolterstorff, Nicholas. "The Wounds of God. Calvin's Theology and Social Injustice." *Reformed Journal* 37, no. 6 (1987): 14–22.

Wright, David. "The Ethical Use of the Old Testament in Luther and Calvin: A Comparison." *Scottish Journal of Theology* 36 (1983): 463–85.

Index of Names

Index of Subjects

Repentance, 1–2, 29, 41,
    47–48, 57, 86
Resurrection, xiii, xv, 149,
    159–60, 179–80, 185–87,
    271–72, 287–88, 306
Righteousness, of God, 28, 32,
    42, 61, 64–65, 80, 103,
    124–25, 134, 281–82

Salvation, 88, 113, 145, 227,
    231, 266–67, 269, 295, 300
Sanctification, 61–65, 78
Scholastic theology, 154
Sigh, 179–96
Simul iustus et peccator, 308
Spirit and letter, the, 126–28,
Synteresis, 90, 117–18, 147,
    152–55

Tentatio, temptation, xxiv–xxv,
    11, 300–301

*Theology of cross, Theologia
    crucis,* xii, xxiv, xxvii, 3,
    101, 130, 133, 181–85,
    222–23, 246, 291–93, 301,
    308
*Theology of glory, Theologia
    Gloria,* xii, 130
Tropological sense of
    scripture, 89, 96, 124–25,
    131, 140, 151–53

Work of God, alien and
    proper, xxv, 5, 7–8, 11, 13,
    17, 21–22, 122–23, 203,
    223–24, 292–93
Worship, 135–37
Wrath or anger, God's, xxii,
    xxxiv, 4–5, 8–9, 17, 30, 37,
    40–41, 57, 67, 70, 74–75,
    78, 81–82, 129, 167–72,
    180, 188, 204–6, 239